EMPOWERING WOMEN FOR EQUITY:

A Counseling Approach

CHERYL BLALOCK ASPY, PhD

DAYA SINGH SANDHU, EdD

EMPOWERING WOMEN FOR EQUITY

10 9 8 7 6 5 4 3 2 1

American Counseling Association
5999 Stevenson Avenue
Alexandria, VA 22304

Director of Publications
Carolyn Baker

Publishing Consultant
Michael Comlish

Copyeditor
Elaine Dunn

Cover design by BonoTom Studio

Library of Congress Cataloging–in–Publication Data

Aspy, Cheryl B.
   Empowering women for equity : a counseling approach / by Cheryl
Blalock Aspy and Daya Singh Sandhu.
     p.   cm.
   Includes bibliographical references.
   ISBN 1-55620-214-8 (alk. paper)
   1. Women — Counseling of — United States. 2. Women — United States —
Social conditions. 3. Sexism — United States — Prevention. 4. Sex
discrimination against women — United States — Prevention.
5. Equality — United States. I. Sandhu, Daya Singh, 1943 –
II. Title.
HV1445.A85   1999
362.83′86′0973 — dc21
                                                  98-54165
                                                     CIP

This book is dedicated to my daughter, Christine Aspy, the joy of my life, and to women who have influenced me profoundly:

My mother, Amelia Blalock

And my five sisters:

Sandra Grider

Annette Simpkins

Barbara Wallace

Beth Kea

Pam Hall

—Cheryl Blalock Aspy, February 1999

This book is dedicated to the most important women in my life,

Ushi, my wife

Gurbachan Kaur, my mother, and

Jaswinder Kaur, my daughter.

—Daya Singh Sandhu, February 1999

Contents

Foreword

I expect this book to become one of the classics of the counseling literature. This expectation arises from my thoughts about the kinds of books that will be important for counselors as we enter the new millennium. I am convinced that the most relevant and widely read works of the future will be connected by some common strands, including an orientation toward client empowerment, a recognition of the importance of context, and a willingness to address political action along with direct service. The work of Cheryl Aspy and Daya Sandhu exemplifies these values.

As Aspy and Sandhu know, a focus on empowerment is especially important when counselors work with women. To me, empowerment counseling from a gender-sensitive perspective recognizes the impact of stereotyping and discrimination, builds on clients' strengths rather than emphasizing deficits, and helps clients overcome gender-based impediments to healthy functioning. Some counselors believe that they can be helpful to women if they, themselves, behave in "unbiased" and "nonsexist" ways. In fact, however, counselors who want to be truly effective need to be proactive in addressing the impact of social, political, economic, and cultural factors on their clients' lives.

Moreover, they need to help their clients begin to focus on these issues as well. Women who have been mired in self-blame often find themselves able to move ahead once they become aware of injustice and develop skills for overcoming the barriers that unequal treatment has placed in their paths.

This book has as its basis a very positive and conceptually sound empowerment model that complements the authors' previous work on prejudice prevention and reduction. Readers will be glad to see how successful Aspy and Sandhu have been in designing practical counseling methods based on their theoretical framework. For instance, an extended case study in Section II follows a client as she moves from exploring her personal issues to developing insight into the social and cultural environment within which she has been operating to acquiring skills for political action. I found it inspiring to see how counseling helped this client, Helen, make a transition from a situation in which she felt disempowered to one in which she could see the potential for positive action, both on her own behalf and on behalf of other women. The authors of this book make a clear statement that women are not at fault for conditions in which they have fewer opportunities, lower pay, and higher poverty levels in comparison with men. Counselors must help all their female clients reach the highest possible levels of physical, emotional, intellectual, and spiritual functioning. To avoid simply "blaming the victim," however, counselors must also join with others in taking responsibility for addressing the power differentials within society. Aspy and Sandhu shed light on a host of factors that influence the context within which development takes place. In a very complete literature review, they investigate the social construction of gender, trace the history of inequity, and explore the impact of the women's movement. Their approach is unusually interdisciplinary for a counseling text, especially when they spell out the economic, political, legal, and historical components of the current gender gap.

The authors also demonstrate their understanding of the complexities of multiple oppressions and cultural identities, weaving cogent discussions of race, ethnicity, age, sexual orientation, and disability into their narrative. I have noticed over the years that, as counselors become more aware of the context of their clients' lives, they also become more committed to participating in political action. When they see recurrent themes among their clients, they begin to consider ways in which they can prevent some of the problems that they constantly see before them. On any given day, a counselor may see a woman who is a victim of violence or abuse, a woman whose career goals have been stifled by unequal treatment, a woman who is trying to deal with the stress of responsibility for both child care and elder care, and a woman whose self-esteem has been shattered by internalized oppression. The context within which these individual events take place is one in which victimization has been allowed to flourish. In Chapter 3 of this book, the authors describe some of the negative trends that are likely to affect the future of women, including "(a) perpetuation of bias through inequitable legal decisions from the bench, (b) unequal political representation, (c) thickening of the glass ceiling, (d) increased domestic violence, and (e) increased child-care shortage." Given this context, how can we help individual clients without monitoring carefully the plight of the Violence Against Women Act, the elimination of affirmative action programs, the dismantling of the welfare system, and the low wages paid to child-care workers?

Aspy and Sandhu help their readers to understand that helping individual clients and addressing environmental factors are two sides of the same coin. They suggest that working with women on individual skill development and trying to remove some of the barriers that prevent them from meeting their potential are complementary efforts. I believe they are correct in this assessment. In recent years, counselors have become quite effective in dealing with legislative efforts that relate to our status as a profession. We should also put these advocacy skills to work more directly on behalf of broader social issues.

The classic counseling texts of the future will help us overcome many of the dichotomies that have limited our creativity in the past. Following the lead of Aspy and Sandhu, the authors we read will teach us that we do not have to choose between direct service and political action, between intrapsychic and interpersonal levels of intervention, or between the theoretical and the practical. Each one complements the other.

—Judith A. Lewis
Governors State University

Prologue

At the dawn of a new millennium, this book, *Empowering Women for Equity: A Counseling Approach*, brings together a wealth of important information. Furthermore, this book comes along at a critical time not only in the history of the United States but also in the world.

The landscape has shifted and continues to shift for women. Old boundaries that defined and controlled women for centuries are being challenged. But challenge is not enough; these boundaries must be removed. Today's and tomorrow's counselors must be ready to meet the challenge and, through the process of empowerment, help women achieve equity.

While reviewing, this book, I was impressed by the positive way that Cheryl Aspy and Daya Sandhu expressed the thesis that equity is possible. As we approach a new century, counselors must not only believe that equity is possible but, in addition, must believe it will be achieved. Counselors must look to the future and plan for a new century—a century that addresses rather than ignores equity. To achieve this goal at the turn of the century, counselors must become brazen advocates. This means that counselors must become bold challengers of the traditional order and above all fearless in advocating for the principles on which the counseling profession was founded. This book, through theory and practice, not only helps the reader have an understanding of the roots of the problem but in addition provides solutions.

It is with pleasure that I recommend this book to you the reader. Through this book, you will find stimulating ideas and new ways to improve on that which you already know. Truly, counselors, students, and other mental health professionals will reap benefits from this book.

—Loretta J. Bradley
Texas Tech University

Preface

E very project has its own life span. In the beginning, we think we are the artificers only to discover later that we are just the tool. So it was with this book. We can trace the beginning back a decade ago to a first reading of *In a Different Voice* by Carol Gilligan (1982) and then her visit to our campus (The University of Louisville), where she reminded us again of the need to help young women not only find their voices but also treasure them amid society's pressure to mute them in return for acceptance.

This is one of the most distressing problems of the 20th century, and it has resulted in the inability of women to achieve equity in opportunities and remuneration. Even programs such as Affirmative Action that were devised to address the problem are under attack and may not survive this century. Sexism and gender inequity are manifestations of a complex individual, social, and political problem requiring solutions that incorporate targeted actions in each area. For women, these inequities may lead to a sense of powerlessness that has been negatively related to mental health and self-efficacy. Carol Gilligan documented the problem as occurring in middle school when young girls "lose their voices" and begin to reflect cultural expectations rather than the embodiment of their innate talents and abilities. High teenage pregnancy rates and the increasing number of women and children in poverty do not bode well for the next century.

Ellen McWhirter (1994) defined empowerment in counseling in her book, *Counseling for Empowerment*:

> Empowerment is the process by which people, organizations, or groups who are powerless or marginalized (a) become aware of the power dynamics at work in their life context, (b) develop the skills and capacity for gaining some reasonable control over their lives, (c) which they exercise, (d) without infringing on the rights of others, and (e) which coincides with actively supporting the empowerment of others in their community. (p. 12)

This definition is consonant with the one used in this book and further defined by the Multidimensional Model of Prejudice Prevention and Reduction (MMPPR) that we described in our last book, *Counseling for Prejudice Prevention and Reduction* (Sandhu & Aspy, 1997). This model operationalizes the empowerment process and thus makes it available for counselors to apply to multiple problems of disempowerment.

However, we recognize the difficulty of applying any model or construct across a broad range of individuals. We agree with Jordan, Kaplan, Miller, Stiver, and Surrey (1991), who said, "We do not want to repeat the error of other theoreticians: speaking as if there is one voice, one reality for humans, for women, when in fact we recognize the exquisite contextuality of human life" (p. 7).

The purpose of this book is to describe the process of empowerment through which women (really female persons of all ages) can achieve equity and to delineate the skills by which counselors can assist them. This is a phenomenal task for any book, especially given the constraints of late 20th-century culture in the United States. However, our approach begins with the belief that women can achieve equity and that it will occur through a process of individual skill development coupled with efforts to remove the social and political barriers that have prevented women from achieving their true potential. Much like the early immigrants of the last century, women will realize their opportunities through hard work and determination *as well as* through a change in society that recognizes women as equal with men. Women must also view the world through the lens of hope—the belief that equity is possible. To the degree that women recognize the source of the barriers to equity and work collectively to remove them, they will create opportunities for all women and perhaps give some women the confidence to step out on faith and try what might have been unthinkable earlier.

We have organized the book to provide a developmental look at the problem, its manifestations, its remedies, and the processes through which the problem can be vanquished. We also provide case studies of four women who have achieved success in areas previously dominated by men. Finally, we provide a collection of instruments for determining attitudes and behaviors regarding gender.

Section I of the book provides a window into the realities of the status of women in our time. In Chapter 1, we trace the evolution of the gender gap and describe it in terms of its economic, political, and professional impact. *Some* women have always been able to climb to the highest levels of success, and knowing that such success is possible is part of the hope-building process that must occur even as our society is being remolded into a more hospitable environment for women. Certainly, we may celebrate one woman's success, but we desire to explicate and facilitate a practicable path for all.

xvi *Empowering Women for Equity: A Counseling Approach*

Chapter 2 addresses the specific problems of women related to their race/ethnicity, age, sexual orientation, and health. Each of these descriptors changes the playing field for women and for most of them, not in a positive direction. Despite its ideals, the United States is still a prejudiced nation. Individuals hold on to worn-out ideas and refuse to disavow them even though there is no evidence to support them.

At work even now are factors that will influence gender equity in the 21st century. In Chapter 3, we have attempted to discern them from current literature, and we have explored their implications for gender equity in the future. We recognize the difficulty of extrapolating current data beyond their time; however, we also know that change is most often slow and the result of continual vigilance and dedicated effort.

Section II details and demonstrates the application of the MMPR to gender inequity. This model explicates the individual, social, and political contributions to prejudice or inequity. In Chapter 4, we describe five predisposing factors toward prejudice for an individual either as a victim or perpetrator. These include (a) unresolved personality conflicts, (b) negative racial/ethnic (or gender) self-identity, (c) negative self-concept or self-efficacy, (d) low-order interpersonal skills, and (e) low-order cognitive skills. Each of the five factors is defined and explained, examples are described, and useful counselor techniques are suggested. Unfortunately, in U.S. culture the process of engenderment of women may actually contribute to negative self-identity and low self-esteem.

Problems such as prejudice and gender inequity arise in a social context, and understanding the dynamics of these social structures is critical for defining workable solutions. Chapter 5 elucidates the predisposing factors that support and sanction gender inequity within a social context. These include traditions of group inferiority or superiority, negative child-rearing practices, group isolation, and group paranoia. We conclude this chapter by describing counseling techniques for working with clients who seek to achieve equity.

In Chapter 6, we detail political strategies to address the use of power for problem solving. Gender inequity has arisen because women have been denied access to power and the decision-making processes it confers. In this chapter, specific types of power and their application to the problem of gender inequity are explicated. Applications of power in U.S. culture revolve around military power, financial power, legal power, information control, and disease control. For women to achieve equity, they must learn to acquire and exercise power in these areas. We present specific suggestions for helping women and girls to increase their access in these areas.

If we have learned anything through the years of our study, we know that every woman approaches and experiences the world through physical, emotional, intellectual, and spiritual dimensions. Just as the body must work as a whole, so must any one individual find balance and fulfillment through high-level functioning in all four areas. In Section III of the book, we describe the practical competencies and processes for achieving prerequisite levels of functioning in each of the four areas.

We recognize that development is not tidy and linear and that, at any one time, a person may be able to focus on only one area and, in so doing, lose gains made in other areas. Such is the human condition—wonderfully diverse, never perfect, but always magnificent when life finds new expression. It is, after all, in the struggles of life that people find meaning and material for future growth, for it is in those times that people put their beliefs and skills to the test. These skills are not unique to women but are essential for all highly functioning individuals. Our inclusion of them is important because women must not settle for less than their optimum even though societal messages suggest otherwise.

Chapters 7 through 10 are devoted to designating specific competencies in the physical, emotional, intellectual, and spiritual dimensions. These chapters contain specific, necessary abilities that every woman must cultivate if she is to prepare herself to accept equity when it is offered. The Biblical story of Esther and her opportunity to change the fate of her people was instructive for us. Who knows, perhaps all skill development is but preparation for an opportunity of a lifetime. Shakespeare described opportunity in this way in *Julius Caesar*:

"There is a tide in the lives of (wo)men which taken at the flood leads on to fortune." We believe that women should have equal opportunity to the tide because it is their right and because beyond opportunity lies "fortune." Women (as well as men) must be personally prepared to take advantage of opportunities to achieve this reward.

We must also interject a word of caution. There is nothing within the pages of this book to support the notion that victims are somehow at fault for their conditions, that is, "blaming the victim." Women do not choose and have not caused fewer opportunities, less pay for equal work, higher poverty levels, or the "glass ceiling." Society in the United States has for too long accepted inequality as the norm. It is the collective responsibility (of both men and women) to create a world in which girls may dream of careers that interest them just as boys do. However, women who have achieved access to power must take leadership in extending power to other women, because it is important for all women to achieve an equal voice in making the decisions that will determine the future of women.

Section IV is devoted to describing the process by which individual women have achieved equity. We have selected four women whose journeys to success have taken them to the highest levels in their fields. We probe their lives for beacons for other women to follow and find them in many forms—candles and floodlights. Ultimately, we learn that every female (regardless of age) must be encouraged to find within herself the belief in her own worth and ability so that she can begin the journey and find the joy of the process. For these women in quite different fields—Sandra Day O'Connor, Maya Angelou, Sally Ride, and Betty Lentz Siegel—the journeys have also differed greatly, and yet the confidence they have found within themselves along with opportunities are factors they share in common.

The final section contains instruments for assessing the various attitudinal components related to gender equity. We have also included appendixes that provide information to help counselors access organizations and resources to assist women in achieving equity. For those who would use this book for teaching, we have included a curriculum complete with goals, objectives, reading assignments, and study questions.

It has been our intent to address all topics from both a theoretical and practical point of view. We believe that this allows the reader to both integrate and test theory while taking advantage of our evaluation, synthesis, and analysis of this material. We have translated the results of our analyses into specific applications that can be implemented within the counselor's professional world.

Each chapter concludes with suggested activities for skill development. Where appropriate, case vignettes and counseling transcripts have been provided to demonstrate specific techniques. We envision this book as suitable for classroom instruction as well as personal growth and development.

Our hope is that counselors will use this book as a part of their own skill development (in whatever context) and then teach these skills to their female clients. In so doing, we believe that, in some measure, we will have advanced the cause of gender equity in our time.

Acknowledgments

There are so many individuals who have helped make this project a reality through their meaningful contributions. Sometimes their help was the visible kind, such as editing or reading, and sometimes their help was indirect, when they supported us through encouragement and by removing barriers that lay before us. These individuals are too numerous to name, but they are our friends, families, and colleagues who kept us on task and whole as we worked. We are greatly indebted to them and hope that we have let them know just how important they are to us.

Additionally, there are a few individuals whose contributions are evidenced within the book and to whom we owe a special debt of gratitude beyond measure. Our heartfelt thanks go to LaVonne Wolfe Glover for her careful collection of references and citations; Craig Ziegler, doctoral student, for his help with statistical analysis in the development of the Gender Equity Perception Scale; Dr. Loretta Bradley for reading the manuscript and encouraging us by her comments; our colleagues in our respective departments for their understanding and encouragement; our families for their love, patience, and support; our publisher, the American Counseling Association, personified in Carolyn Baker and Elaine Dunn, the copyeditor, both of whose recommendations led immeasurably to the improvement of the manuscript; Dr. Judith A. Lewis for her willingness to write the Foreword; our reviewers, Dr. Patricia Arredondo and Dr. Ellen Piel Cook, for their immediate understanding of the message in our mission and for helping us refine and shape it through their perceptive suggestions; and Dr. David N. Aspy, our colleague, friend, and husband whose creativity, caring, and enthusiasm continually inspired this work.

About the Authors

Cheryl Blalock Aspy, PhD, MEd, BS, received her BS and MEd degrees from Texas Woman's University and a PhD in Measurement, Statistics, and Evaluation from the University of Maryland in 1981. She is a fourth-generation native of Quitman, Texas, and was recently named a 1999 Outstanding Alumna of Texas Woman's University.

During the 1980s, she and her husband David Aspy were codirectors of the Carkhuff Institute of Human Technology in Amherst, Massachusetts, where they studied and encouraged the development of effective teaching and counseling models to increase thinking and productivity in classrooms, counseling settings, and organizations.

In 1987, she became the research director at the Department of Family and Community Medicine at the University of Louisville and later accepted a similar position at the University of Oklahoma Health Sciences Center. During her academic medicine career, she has authored or coauthored proposals that were awarded over $2.5 million in funding. Her research addresses the components of an effective doctor–patient relationship, influences on adherence to medication prescriptions, treatment of incontinence, evaluation of teen pregnancy prevention programs, and the effect of intercessory prayer. She also participated in the development of a fellowship for physicians in humanism in medicine, the only one of its kind in the United States.

Currently, Dr. Aspy teaches behavioral medicine to second-year family medicine residents at the University of Oklahoma College of Medicine, where she serves on the admissions Board. She is the author or coauthor of four books, over 35 articles, and numerous book chapters and monographs and serves on the editorial boards of *Family Medicine* and *The Journal of Invitational Theory and Practice*. She has presented over 50 national and international workshops and seminars on a variety of skill development topics and is an advanced trauma life support educator.

She and her husband have one child, Mary Christine, who is a sophomore in high school.

Daya Singh Sandhu, EdD, NCC, NCCC, NCSC, is chairperson and professor in the Department of Educational and Counseling Psychology at the University of Louisville. He received his BA, BT, and MA (English) degrees from Punjab University, India. After moving to the United States in 1969, he received his MEd from Delta State University, Specialist in English degree from the University of Mississippi, and Doctor of Counselor Education from Mississippi State University. He has more than 30 years experience in education, both at the secondary and the university levels. He taught English, mathematics, physics, and chemistry in India. In the United States, he taught English for 11 years in public schools and also served as a high school guidance counselor and agency testing coordinator for 7 years with the Choctaw Agency, Bureau of Indian Affairs Schools, in Philadelphia, Mississippi. Since 1989, he has taught graduate courses in counselor education and counseling psychology at Nicholls State University and the University of Louisville.

Dr. Sandhu has a special interest in school counseling, multicultural counseling, neurolinguistic programming, and the role of spirituality in counseling and psychotherapy. Previously, he has published two books, *Numerical Problems in Physics* (1967) and *A Practical Guide for Classroom Observations: A Multidimensional Approach* (1991). In 1997, he co-authored *Counseling for Prejudice Prevention and Reduction.* Recently, Dr. Sandhu has edited another book, *Asian and Pacific Islander Americans: Issues and Concerns for Counseling and Psychotherapy* published in 1999 by Nova Science Publishers. He has also published more than 50 articles in state, national, and international journals. His first book was of Punjabi poetry, *Satranghi Pingh.* Dr. Sandhu is also an experienced presenter and professional workshops trainer. He has made more than 100 presentations at the international, state, and local levels. His presentations have focused on a wide variety of subjects that can be broadly classified under school counseling and multicultural counseling.

Dr. Sandhu has served on various committees of the American Counseling Association, such as the Human Rights Committee, the Interprofessional and International Collaboration Committee, and the Association for Multicultural Counseling and Development Award Committee. Currently, he is a member of the executive board of the Council for the Accreditation of Counseling and Related Educational Programs.

He has also served as a member of several editorial boards, including the *Journal of Multicultural Counseling and Development, Journal of Humanistic Education and Development, The School Counselor, Journal of Accelerative Learning and Teaching,* and *The Journal of Counseling Development.*

Section I

The Current and Future Status of Women in the United States

When I (Cheryl Aspy) was young, I fully expected that we would have personal flying craft, colonies on the moon, exploration trips to Mars, and computers that would control all aspects of our homes with voice commands. I think I even believed that I would be able to travel to those moon colonies on vacation. Such is the problem with trying to speculate on the future.

However, capturing the present can be equally troubling because the descriptions people provide are at best snapshots of a particular location or object at a specific time. For many women, the present may be closer to the future than we have portrayed, and for some, the realities that we describe are but hoped-for dreams.

What we know is that women have made progress; however, any one individual's progress varies somewhat depending on her race/ethnicity, age, sexual orientation, and disabilities. If women are to embrace empowerment, we must not only assume responsibility for our own growth, but must also find ways to facilitate the women around us.

In the following three chapters, we address the power differential that is at the heart of gender inequity, the personalogical variables (characteristics of the person) that inhibit access to both power and the opportunity it provides for equity, and, finally, the future and the factors that are at work even now in making gender equity what it will become. From this diagnosis, we realize there is much to be done if gender equity is to be realized. The remainder of the book is dedicated to illuminating that trail.

1

Power and Gender:
The Power Differential

At the 1998 graduation ceremony for physicians completing their residency in family medicine at the University of Oklahoma, each graduate was introduced to the audience by a faculty member. The introductions varied with the personalities of the faculty members, but common to each was a story about how each resident had performed in some crucial part of his or her training. One woman who had previously completed a residency in family medicine was honored for completing a fellowship in sports medicine. She was introduced with the following story:

As part of Stephanie's training, she accepted the position as team physician for a private high school's football team. This was the

3

first experience with a woman physician in this role at this high school, and they were somewhat uncertain of how things would progress. In the first game of the season, the star quarterback received a concussion very early in the game. Recognizing the potential seriousness of his injury, Stephanie told the coach the young man would not be able to continue in the game. The coach was visibly upset and demanded that the young man be allowed to play. Towering above her, he said, "What do you know about football anyway, you've never played the game!" She stood her ground, looked directly into his eyes, and said, "What do you know about medicine, you've never been a doctor!" The coach acquiesced, and the young star did not play that evening.

This is a new story that would not have been possible even 15 years ago. But what it tells us is that there is new hope for women based on the competency they can achieve given the opportunity for study and training. Because it is a new story in the struggle for equity, it is still a rare one. Most women do not have the same opportunities as men simply because they are women, and as we discuss in this chapter, gender is a socially constructed reality against which all women (and men) are evaluated. Sarachi (1995) reported that around the world, "girl children receive less education, less food, and less health care than boys" (p. 7). Christ (1980) summed up a sad spectacle of human history when she stated:

Most of history has been told from the perspective of men's power. Research on biological differences between the sexes has been geared toward explaining men's dominance in society. And divinities of both Eastern and Western religions have been used to justify male superiority in family, society, and religion. (p. 11)

After all, it has been *his story* that made *history*. Daly's (1985) epigram "If God is male, then the male is God" (p. 19) reflected the dominance achieved by males through the centuries. In contrast, women's *herstory* became a story of political, economic, social, and spiritual subservience.

Gender as Social Construction

To understand the need for gender equity, we must first explore the meaning of gender and how the genders came to have different values within U.S. culture. Lorber (1994) proposed that gender is:

> an institution that establishes patterns of expectations for individuals, orders the social processes of everyday life, is built into the major social organizations of society, such as the economy, ideology, the family, and politics, and is also an entity in and of itself. (p. 1)

This pervasive notion of gender is difficult to study apart from the social institutions that have constructed it. Lorber (1994) continued:

> Because gender is ubiquitous in human society, the belief has been that it must be genetic or physiological and that gender inequality is ultimately based on procreative differences. But a close examination of females' and males' relationship to procreation reveals that it is females who are at an advantage, not males. (p. 6)

The concept of gender is more than the psychological construct of sex roles. Sex-role identity is developed within the individual and, as such, is not the responsibility of the society. Gender, on the other hand, is defined and reinforced within every facet of society, and it is this social assignment and expectation of compliance with gender that makes it so pervasive. Rivers (1991) captured the essence of female gender role expectations:

> By the time I had reached adolescence, I was aware that society had carved out a niche for me, now that I was about to become a woman. I was offered one ticket, good for a lifetime, to the bleachers. . . . It was assumed that the right order of the universe was for men to do, and women to admire. (p. 22)

The concept that "biology is destiny" has played a dominant role in the social order and, thus, the lives of women. Fortunately, there are new, bold, and encouraging views to challenge this concept (Lauer, 1998). Beall and Sternberg (1993) contended that cognitive factors, role models, and social factors can override any biologically predisposed male and female behaviors, if such exist.

Feminists have developed theories to explain the phenomenon of gendered inequity. Radical feminists, Marxist feminists, and psychoanalytic feminists all use patriarchy to explain what has oppressed women (Lorber, 1994), but each of them uses a different definition of patriarchy. For radical feminists, patriarchy is domination of women by men through control of their sexuality and childbearing. For Marxist feminists, patriarchal domination of women is a continuation of their husbands' exploitation as workers in the capitalistic marketplace. And for psychoanalytic feminists, patriarchy is "the symbolic rule of the father through gendered sexuality and the unconscious" (Lorber, 1994, p. 3).

Racial/ethnic feminists and cultural feminists challenge gender categories as oppositional (Butler, 1990; Collins, 1989; Flax, 1990; Garber, 1992). For racial/ethnic feminists, there is a stratification based on class, race, and gender that produces domination by the overclass, including both men and women, and subordination of the underclass, also including both men and women. Cultural feminists view sexuality and gender as shifting, dynamic categories, and, thus, a feminist politics based solely on women as subordinated is not truly representative (Lorber, 1994).

Kimball (1995) proposed that all feminist theories could be categorized into two classifications: the similarities tradition or the differences tradition. She suggested that in the similarities tradition gender differences either in social competencies or intellectual skills "are either nonexistent or far too small to explain existing gender differences in power, prestige, and income in public and private life" (p. 3). Thus, although biological differences are recognized, what they mean as well as how important they are is a creation of society.

An example of this phenomenon is the differences in mathematics performance between girls and boys (Fennema, Carpenter, Jacobs, Franke, & Levi, 1998). Fennema et al. found that after completing third grade, girls used more standard algorithms than did boys in solving mathematical problems and that using self-generated algorithms was associated with successful solution of extension problems. In hypothesizing about the meaning of this finding, Noddings (1998) said:

> And finally, are the socialization pressures that encourage boys to be independent and girls to follow the rules so strong that encouragement to change only in math class can't overcome the pervasive pressures? If I were to bet on one of the standard possibilities mentioned here, I'd bet on this last one. (p. 17)

Bohan (1993) and Lott (1990) suggested that individuals do not *have* gender, but that they *do* gender as a part of socially constructed expectations. West and Zimmerman (1987) implied that gender was like culture, in that it required everyone to participate in order to perpetuate it. The implication of the similarities traditions is that behavior has no gender (Lott, 1990) and that the characterization of behavior as masculine or feminine perpetuates stereotypes and further separates work along gender lines (Desjardins, 1989).

Difference theorists do not want women to settle for equality with men in a man's world. Cohn (1993) stated, "gender discourse becomes a 'preemptive deterrent' to certain kinds of thought" (p. 232). Harding (1986) addressed the problem of human characteristics being dichotomized, gender associated, and differentially valued. The aggression of males is valued, whereas the peace and disarmament that are associated with females are devalued (Cohn, 1993).

Feminist theories of differences recognize and promote gender roles and characteristics with the view that the traditional feminine attributes have been undervalued. Thus the primary goal for these traditions is not equity but the "creation of a different, more humane world that incorporates traditional feminine values as a central human focus" (Kimball, 1995, p. 10).

Simone de Beauvoir (1949/1953), the champion of second-wave feminism, believed that male dominance was a result of a system of power relations that sentenced women to a secondary role in society. She further contended that the personal is political. Willis (1992) positioned the struggle as one "between [women's] sense of entitlement to freedom and men's stubborn assumption of dominance" (p. 160). She said:

> Since the denial of personal autonomy defines women's oppression—and since patriarchal ideology holds that allowing women autonomy would destroy civilization if not the human species itself—a moral defense of freedom is necessarily at the heart of feminism. (p. 160)

However, Amiel (1997) suggested that gender politics threatens freedom when a particular gender (women) receives "status" (rights of birth) before the law. She cited the expenditure for breast cancer research ($550 million) compared with the amount spent on prostate cancer research ($80 million) as evidence that statism is growing because it thrives on status rather than contract. She said, "One can only imagine what would have happened to Mr. Bobbitt if he had cut off his wife's breasts while she slept" (p. 9)[1]. She further recommended that freedom could only be achieved in a society

> that stops thinking of citizens in terms of their status according to skin pigmentation, gender, sexual orientation or victimology, and remembers the value of individual liberty. (p. 9)

---

[1] On June 23, 1993, Lorena Bobbitt severed her husband's penis after he allegedly raped and beat her. In November 1993, John Wayne Bobbitt was acquitted of sexual assault and in January 1994, Lorena was declared not guilty of assault by reason of insanity.

Whatever theory one uses to explain the phenomenon of gender inequity, the results are personal, social, and political. In the following section, we describe the gender gap in the United States in the latter 20th century. Although progress has been made in many ways, the gap remains—economically, politically, and professionally. Women today remain the second sex.

Gender Equity and Inequity

Gender equity is difficult to define without also limiting the concept one is trying to explicate. Wirth's (1945) definition of *minority* included a description of the negative connotation of minority status, which included gender inequity:

> A group of people who, because of physical or cultural characteristics, are singled out from others in society in which they live for differential and unequal treatment, and who therefore regard themselves as objects of collective discrimination. . . . Minority status carries with it the exclusion from full participation in the life of the society. (p. 347)

Ponterotto and Pedersen (1993) supported the use of this definition in regard to females even though women constitute over 50% of the population. They stated: "by our definition, they are also a minority group in the sense of the economic and political power they hold" (p. 8).

We believe that gender equity is the realization of complete equality in all aspects of the social order regardless of gender and that inequity is the domination, subordination, and oppression of the female gender—the devaluing of the feminine. Kimball (1995) described the goal of gender equity in her statement:

> The essential focus of feminism is on the commitment to eliminate domination and privilege, subordination and oppression. . . . The goal is a world where all women and men can be both equal and different, a world free of privilege and hierarchy. (p. 176)

Flax (1992) also made recommendations regarding gender equity. She stated, "feminists should seek to end domination— not gender, not differences, and certainly not the feminine" (p. 194).

Gender is both a cause and an effect in today's society when equity is considered. Even though there are laws forbidding the use of gender in decisions for jobs, educational opportunity, health care coverage, and housing, the sad fact remains that women are still second-class citizens who earn less for equal work and have less access to the highest levels of their professions. A much larger proportion of women live in poverty than do men, primarily because they must care for children alone.

Myrdal (1944) suggested that many citizens in the United States experience a moral conflict between their stated ideals and actual behavior. On one hand, they espouse the general egalitarian principles of the "American creed," but on the other hand they engage in prejudiced practices. It is interesting to note that, for women, denial of their right to vote was one of the most blatant contradiction of American ideals. Carol Gilligan (1982) pointed out:

> psychological theorists. . . implicitly adopting the male life as the norm, have tried to fashion women out of a masculine cloth. It all goes back, of course, to Adam and Eve—a story which shows, among other things, that if you make a woman out of a man, you are bound to get into trouble. In the life cycle, as in the Garden of Eden, the woman has been the deviant. (p. 6)

In this chapter, we trace the cause of gender inequity to its roots in gender stratification and the gender division of labor. We explore power, its interpretation as a gendered phenomenon, and how it mediates gender inequity. Finally, we also explore the effects of gender inequity on the economic, political, and professional lives of women today. But we do not end there. A new story is possible, and we believe that this book can be instrumental in helping women write it. We are optimistic that gender inequity is not forever. Our hope is that women can seize their destinies through a careful analysis of the problem and, from that analysis, determine the actions that must be taken individually, socially, and politically.

Knowledge is power, and never before in history have women had the access to knowledge that is available today. They can restructure society not to become equals in a man's world, but to change society to value more highly those dimensions that are associated with the feminine. Markus (1987) said:

> some of the specific ways of experiencing the world, together with some associated personality traits, while functioning in the present as part of the mechanism of oppression, in virtue of being ascribed exclusively to women. . . ought not to be lost, but be re-evaluated as possible components. . . of the restructuration of the dominant culture. (p. 97)

Background

Women's struggle for equity is certainly not a new phenomenon. Mary Wollstonecraft wrote *Vindication of the Rights of Women* in 1792, and hers was not the first statement on the subject. However, Castro (1990) suggested that the current wave of American feminism can be traced to a power struggle in four acts. She described the first act as the official struggle in Congress for an equal rights amendment that began officially in 1946 when this legislation came before Congress for the first time.

The second act was characterized by a backlash from a depiction of the "housewife's syndrome." This syndrome essentially described the housewife as dissatisfied and neurotic. Practical feminists emerged to suggest that this dissatisfaction was perhaps not neurotic and could be cured if women could have both a career and a family. At this time, Betty Friedan (1963) published *The Feminine Mystique* and restored the housewife to her dignity, making her dissatisfaction a problem for society rather than an individual neurosis.

The third act was the process of transitioning from the official governmental studies of the equity problem to a fully organized feminist agenda. The fourth act was the development of an ideology and an action program through consciousness raising. The national strike conducted by American women on August 26, 1970, ushered in the new feminist movement (Castro, 1990). The goal of this statement and every strategy that followed was to gain the power essential for change. However, women and power had long been separated, and the contest to obtain and manage power has been the story of the struggle for the past 28 years.

The central tenets of the struggle have revolved around two concepts that derive from being deprived of equal power. The first is that women deserve equality because they are not inferior to men and are, therefore, equally capable. The second notion is that women should have the freedom to make choices about how they live their lives (Josselson, 1996).

In a 22-year, longitudinal study of 30 women who were seniors in college at the beginning of the study, Josselson (1996) found that their development paralleled the women's movement without their becoming actively involved in it. These women sought the ideals of the two tenets stated earlier, but their struggles were individual rather than part of a collective. She said:

> As they continued to grow, these women increasingly began to ally themselves, at least intellectually, with the women's movement. They came to understand that a gendered analysis helped explicate some of the problems they were experiencing at work. They began to see that there was something systematic in the way in which men mistreated women in the workplace. (p. 254)

Tannen (1994) identified communication styles that are more typical of women than men and that work to women's disadvantage and unfair treatment in the workplace. She suggested that women are more likely to help others save face and that they recognize the contribution of the team rather than draw attention to themselves and their individual contributions. This style is less understood by men, who are usually in charge and may thus misinterpret women's behavior as less competent than men's.

The women's movement has created a new environment of awareness—of both women's competence and what constitutes discrimination. For women, it has given a name to those practices that socialize women into particular ways of behaving that are not recognized by male supervisors. Tannen (1994) stated:

> If supervisors learn to perceive outstanding performance regardless of the performer's style, it will be less necessary for individuals to learn to display their talents. On that happy day, the glass ceiling will become a looking glass through which a fair percentage of Alices will be able to step. (p. 159)

Some visible gains have been made through legislation such as Title IX of the Education Amendments of 1972. Although this law challenged educational institutions' pervasive notion of women's inferiority, schools remain a breeding place of gender-based stereotypes. The attitudes that determine future choices are generally formed during the early years in school, and because of the stereotypes learned there, children may come to believe that activities and interests are gender specific (Whyte, 1986). Inequality permeated and perpetuated in schools undeniably has a snowball effect on women's postgraduate achievement and later on in their work lives (McCormick, 1990).

Sadker and Sadker (1985) argued that even in contemporary society, schools in the United States serve as a training ground where patterns of sexism are practiced routinely that short-change girls in quality education. As a result, both in the workplace and life, men achieve more dominance and power than women.

Sandhu, Portes, and McPhee (1996) found a positive global trend in equity as a result of multiculturalism. They said, "Many pluralistic societies are becoming multicultural societies in that there is a trend to make provisions for equal economic, political, and social participation" (p. 16). World societies can be divided into two main groups, traditional or egalitarian, on the basis of their concepts of equal participation of women and minorities. Haas (1992) identified two major characteristics of egalitarian societies: (a) equal right to contribute to family resources and (b) equally shared family and household responsibilities. Unfortunately, few egalitarian societies meet these qualifications completely, and there is an even more crucial need to change attitudes toward women and their roles in traditional societies. Worldwide, conflict, pain, and tension are the signs of transformation, and many women have begun to demand change (Daly, 1985).

Evolution of the Gender Gap

There are numerous theories of gender inequality, and many of them suggest that women's subordination is based on their procreative status and is arbitrated through social practices. However, Rich (1977) noted that it was gender inequality that created the unequal conditions of procreation, rather than the other way around. Most theories rely on the process of gender differentiation and engenderment (Chafetz, 1990). Gender differentiation is the degree to which men and women differ on traits, and engenderment is the process by which men and women come to be gender differentiated.

Lorber (1994) maintained that the gender gap has a social function and a social history rather than any cause attributed to "sex, procreation, physiology, anatomy, hormones, or genetic predispotitions" (p. 35). She further described the phenomenon:

> It is produced and maintained by identifiable social processes and built into the general social structure and individual identities deliberately and purposefully. I contend, therefore, that the continuing purpose of gender as a modern social institution is to construct women as a group to be the subordinates of men as a group. (p. 35)

Another example of the gender gap is in the area of wage discrimination. Goldin (1990) described wage discrimination as the residual or difference between male and female wages that cannot be explained by a legitimate factor such as education or experience. Thurow (1975) suggested that early statistical discrimination (treatment of women as a group) appeared because most women left the labor force at the time of marriage and thus employers denied them access to job ladders. In addition, workers and employers did not want to work with or be directed by women. There were multiple reasons for this discrimination. Men feared that having women in a particular job would lower earnings and dilute job skills or that it would lower the prestige or status associated with an occupation (Goldin, 1990).

The Gender Gap

The Economic Partition

Every Congress since 1945 has entertained a comparable work bill of some kind or another (Paul, 1989). Equal pay for equal work has been the law of the land since 1963 when the Equal Pay Act was approved as an amendment to the Fair Labor Standards Act. Since then, it has been illegal to pay women less than men for doing "substantially equal" work. Although this addresses obvious problems, it does leave gaps in that women who work in jobs with no equivalent male jobs for comparison tend to be paid much lower wages (Paul, 1989).

Unfortunately, women today earn only 74 cents for every dollar earned by men (Associated Press, 1998). However, the good news is that this is up from only 59 cents in 1970. This differential is not easily explained given the Equal Pay Act. However, while some explain this phenomenon as a devaluing of the type of work that women do, such as nursing and child care, others would say that women select this type of work because it fits their worldview.

When the salaries of the highest paid women executives are examined, the gap remains (Dogar, 1998). While the highest paid women in Fortune 500 companies made an average of $3 million, the average male Fortune 500 CEO made $5.8 million. Education seems to be helpful in narrowing the gap between men and women in that female engineers make nearly 94% of what men make, female college deans make 96% of the salaries of male deans, and female corporate lawyers make 92% of the salaries of male lawyers (Dogar, 1998).

Two recent studies have provided information about the value of gender equity to the economies of world nations. The United Nations Development Programme's Sixth Annual Human Development Report calculated two indexes for each country. The Human Development Index measured quality of life (income, life expectancy, education, and literacy), and the Gender Development Index modified it on the basis of equitable treatment of women. The conclusion of these studies was that no country treats its women as well as its men and that if the country treats its women well, it is likely to score high on quality-of-life measures such as life expectancy, wealth, and literacy. For example, Sweden was ranked first in gender equity "for spending 1/3 of its GDP on social welfare and for ensuring adequate political representation, thanks to a parliament that's 1/3 female" (Schorr, 1996, p. 18). Schorr reminded us "that gender equity isn't just economically smart but morally right" (p. 18).

The opportunity to exert leadership is a proxy for power, and women and men exercise leadership in different ways (Desjardins, 1996). Bensimon (1993) proposed that leadership was influenced by gender in three ways. First, she suggested that women define themselves in relation to others (Gilligan, 1982; Gilligan, Lyons & Hanmer, 1990). Second, women relate to others from a perspective of care and responsibility (Noddings, 1984), whereas men are governed by independent achievement (K. E. Ferguson, 1984). Third, women's worlds tend to be concrete entities dynamically related through social relationships and events, whereas men see the world as a rational entity governed by laws (K. E. Ferguson, 1984). These differing perspectives may lead women into more cooperative efforts that do not recognize and reward individual achievement and, therefore, pay less.

Although behavior has no gender, it continues to be differentially rewarded by gender. For example, being married and having children tend to depress women's earnings while having the opposite effect for men (Paul, 1989).

The comparable worth debate has been addressed in several states in an attempt to ensure that jobs called by different names and requiring similar qualifications and efforts would have equal salaries. By 1990, 20 states had passed legislation that extended the notion of equal pay for equal work (Goldin, 1990). Pay equity legislation was designed to remove the practice of renaming jobs for men and increasing the pay even though women did almost identical work for less pay.

Minnesota was the first state to implement a pay equity act that covered all state employees in 1982 (Evans & Nelson, 1991). Not surprisingly, in the job evaluation process, they discovered that equivalently evaluated male and female jobs did not have equal pay. For example, nurses and pharmacists were equally paired, but before pay equity, the pharmacists (mostly male) were paid almost $400 more per month than the nurses (mostly female). Another striking finding was that animal caretakers (mostly male) received $184 more per month than human caretakers (mostly female). The success of the program was possible because, "all parties agree that pay equity is a remedy for the historic and structural underevaluation of women's work" (Evans & Nelson, 1991, p. 229).

Paul (1989) proposed that women should recognize their ability to compete in the marketplace without special privilege and have confidence that their abilities will allow them to compete successfully for traditionally male jobs that carry higher wages. She said, "The time has passed for women to plead with men for a fair chance in the marketplace; they have that chance, and they should be encouraged to continue taking advantage of it" (p. 132). The question remains regarding what keeps women from taking advantage of such an opportunity if it does exist. Researchers at Florida State University surveyed 457 students, and they discovered that women more often than men lacked confidence in their financial planning ability and investment knowledge, even though their grade point averages were higher than that of the men (James, 1997).

Fudge and McDermott (1991) recognized that female employees, when compared with their employers, have unequal resources in the fight for pay equity. Despite this reality, Acker (1989) noted that "feminists have made pay equity the most visible answer to one of the most crucial questions asked by activists: What are the best strategies for achieving economic equality between men and women?" (p. 3).

Equal pay for equal work would seem to be a concept beyond question. However, every political system exists because it perpetuates itself, and equal pay for equal work must be decided within a political system that has always been and remains a bastion of male dominance. Unfortunately, the path to power for women has been even more obstructed than the road to economic equality. Daly (1985) suggested that women have to be ready for the fight to "overcome the amnesia, aphasia, and apraxia inflicted by phallocracy" (p. xxv).

The Political Partition

In the United States in 1998 there were 56 women (13%) serving in the House of Representatives and 9 women (9%) serving in the Senate. In a nation of 240 million people, half of whom are women, this representational proportion for women seems to defy the promise on which this nation was based.

While women have also made strides in the national focus on sexual harassment since the Anita Hill–Clarence Thomas hearings (Hill & Jordan, 1995), sexual harassment is

not simply an aberration, nor is it exclusively the province of macho males; on the contrary, harassing behavior is something that many of us men have engaged in at some point, if not on the job, then on the streets or on campus or even in our homes. (Allen, 1995, p. 130)

A look at the trend in sexual harassment complaints filed with the Equal Employment Opportunity Commission showed that in 1991, there were about, 6,000 cases filed, whereas in 1997, there were 15,889 cases filed. Reasonable cause was found in about 250 cases (4%) in 1991 and in 808 cases (5.1%) in 1997. The greatest trend has been in damages awarded. In 1991, total damages awarded was about $5 million. In 1997, a total of $49.5 million in damages were awarded ("Growth of Sexual Harassment Cases," 1998).

Recent court cases have reflected a continuing gender bias. In one case, a woman student who alleged she had been raped by two other students filed suit against her college and the perpetrators under the Violence Against Women Act. A U.S. District judge threw out her case because he said that Congress did not have the power to regulate crimes against women (Jensen, 1997). Jensen also described other decisions that (a) suggested prison facilities for women in the District of Columbia need not be equivalent to those for men; (b) allowed the Navy to violate its "Don't ask, don't tell" guidelines when Amy L. Barnes was discharged after she was coerced into admitting to one incident of sex with another woman (before her enlistment) to stop a massive investigation into rumors that she was a lesbian; (c) gave child custody to a convicted murderer in preference to the child's lesbian mother; and (d) declared that rape does not cause extreme physical pain and thus does not qualify as an enhancement under the federal carjacking law. This case resulted in the Carjacking Correction Act of 1996 that acknowledged rape as causing extreme physical pain. Each of these cases reveals an entrenched gender bias against women by current judges and places at risk a woman's right to a fair trial.

Although some judges' behavior has improved in the reduction of the overt hostility once shown to women attorneys, the greater problem is the prejudice that permeates judges' rulings, particularly when women's issues are at stake ("Judges From the Stone Age," 1995). For example, a judge in New York gave five men fines of $750 after they confessed to raping an unconscious woman in a bar ("Judges From the Stone Age," 1995). The solution to this problem is not silent anger but publicly demanding judges who:

> consider themselves aggressive protectors of justice. Ultimately, it is up to [women] to issue the call for such leaders—by voting for fair-minded judges, supporting the politicians who appoint them and loudly reminding offending members of the judiciary that they are public servants, not rulers of their own little fiefdoms. ("Judges From the Stone Age," 1995, p. 64)

In contrast, the Supreme Court recently ruled on several sexual harassment cases after a 12-year silence (Lavelle, 1998). The result of these decisions was to make it easier for individuals who have been harassed to bring a lawsuit, but at the same time, they defined the means by which companies can enjoy some protection by implementing strong programs designed to prevent and discipline harassment.

The Professional Partition

Today, although there are workers of both genders in most occupations, it has been estimated that 60% to 70% of them would have to change occupations to overcome the current segregation by gender (Reskin & Roos, 1990). Unfortunately, even when men and women do work in occupations that are for them nontraditional, the work assignments tend to reflect gender-role expectations such that policewomen often function as social workers and male nurses tend to focus on the technical or physical aspects of the work (Martin, 1980; C. L. Williams, 1989). The reality remains that if a job is highly valued by workers, it is more likely to be held by a White, highly educated male who has extensive work experience (Jencks, Perman, & Rainwater, 1988).

The problem of blue-collar work for women has been for the most part a struggle for access to the training and organizations such as unions that maintain control of these jobs. Although employers might be interested in hiring women for these jobs because they can pay them less, male competition for jobs at higher pay levels must keep women out to maintain the status quo (Walby, 1990).

Because technology evens the playing field between men and women, it would be expected that the technologizing of an industry would make it more available for women. Unfortunately, that has not happened. Burnell (1993) noted that the gendered nature of technology has adverse implications for women. She attributed this engenderment process to male domination of science and technology. She suggested that "male control over technology has been translated into power over female workers and adverse effects on women's work experience" (p. 165).

The male "ownership" of science has left many women scientists in difficult circumstances. Women researchers in the National Cancer Institute were found to have on average received less than two thirds of the budgets allocated to their male counterparts (Seachrist, 1994). Sonnert (1995/1996) believed that this discrepancy in resources is one reason that women scientists have not been able to achieve equity. Recognizing that the problem is one not likely to be solved by a single policy, Sonnert suggested, "What is called for is diversity and flexibility in policy initiatives" (p. 58).

Teaching is one of the jobs that was male dominated in the 1800s and changed to female domination in the 1990s. Goldin (1990) pointed out that the reasons for the gender change were the assumptions that single, middle-class women could live on low pay, they were more patient and nurturing, and they were more willing to accept these conditions for employment. Once they were married, their husbands had a voice, and, until World War II, women teachers were fired for getting married and even into the 1960s were put on leave if they became pregnant. In many ways, teaching is the ideal "woman's work" in that the pay is low, there is little autonomy, and turnover is high (Spencer, 1988).

Women have perhaps made the greatest gains over the past generation in the legal and medical professions. Currently, about one half of the students in both medical schools and schools of law are women. It remains to be seen what this will mean 20 years from now as these women reach the height of their careers. Unfortunately, women in both these professions are not equally represented at the top posts in their fields at the present time.

In 1998, the Supreme Court has nine justices, two (22%) of whom are women (Sandra Day O'Connor and Ruth Bader Ginsburg). Although this does reflect progress in that two of the last three presidents (Ronald Reagan and Bill Clinton) have each appointed a woman to the Court, it also reflects a lack of commitment to equity, in that other vacancies during this time period were filled with men.

For women in the clergy, particularly Southern Baptist clergy, the recent hiring of a woman as a senior pastor for a church in Waco, Texas, was particularly noteworthy. She is the first woman to become senior pastor of a Southern Baptist church (Jennings, 1998). Although there are 90 women in Southern Baptist senior pastorates around the country, most of the leadership in the Southern Baptist Convention still believes that women ministers are not "in line with God's word" (Jennings, 1998, p. 13A).

One of the greatest controversies in recent times throughout the Christian religions is the publication of gender-neutral Bibles (Grudem, 1997; Osborne, 1997). For some, this change has unnecessarily distorted the meaning of scripture (Grudem, 1997), whereas for others, the inclusive-language Bible is an improvement for "inclusiveness, for clarity and accuracy, in passages that refer to men and women together" (Osborne, 1997, p. 38).

Defining Terms

Power

The concept of power has three main definitional components: ability, strength, and authority. Each of these components may respectively be further broken down into such words as competence, capacity, or capability; energy, vigor, or might; and domination, jurisdiction, or command. J. B. Miller (1991) suggested the following working definition of power as:

> the capacity to produce a change — that is, to move anything from point A or state A to point B or state B. This can even include moving one's own thoughts or emotions. . . . It can also include acting to create movement in an interpersonal field, as well as acting in larger realms such as economic, social, or political arenas. (p. 198)

J. B. Miller (1976) recognized that when one has power, the opportunity exists to use that power not only to advance oneself but also "to control, limit, and if possible destroy the power of others" (p. 116). Allen (1995) supported this view of power as a part of the cultural expectation regarding the traditional power relationship between men and women. He said, "Sexual harassment is both a manifestation and a reinforcement of an exploitative system in which men are socialized collectively and individually to expect to have power over women collectively and individually" (p. 135).

Whatever definition is used, the cultural expectation for women is that they should not have power unless it is used in the facilitation or empowerment of others, most often, children. This is the nutritive power defined by May (1967) but a type of power not as appreciated or respected by the dominant culture as the more assertive types (J. B. Miller, 1991).

Empowerment

In the Preface, we cited MacWhirter's (1994) definition of empowerment as:

> the process by which people, organizations, or groups who are powerless or marginalized (a) become aware of the power dynamics at work in their life context, (b) develop the skills and capacity

for gaining some reasonable control over their lives, (c) which they exercise, (d) without infringing on the rights of others, and (e) which coincides with actively supporting the empowerment of others in their community (p. 12).

This definition describes empowerment as occurring within the woman as a result of her awareness and use of power with a concomitant responsibility to support others who are also in the process of becoming empowered.

Hawxhurst and Morrow (1984) defined empowerment as the process of gaining control over one's own life while supporting and facilitating others' control over their lives. They described the components of empowerment as:

(1) an analysis of power; (2) an understanding of female socialization and sex-role stereotyping; (3) the attainment of power at personal, interpersonal, and social levels; (4) advocacy of ourselves and others. (p. 35)

These two definitions are similar in that they both focus on an initial understanding of power and how it influences decision making at the individual level. Both of these definitions also add the responsibility for helping others become empowered.

J. B. Miller (1982) defined the process by which facilitation through empowerment occurs:

[E]mpowering other people means giving them a chance to make their special contribution. Your contribution may be a particular insight, a particular talent, a particular loving way to be with people. Part of my job is to see to it that I can create the conditions so that you can give. And giving is what makes people powerful, not taking. . . one needs to be able to receive what another offers so that there isn't any violence in giving and receiving. . . . Taking and refusing has a sense of force in it. (p. 82)

This notion was recognized by Irwin (1995) in her case study of Ruth, a school principal. She described Ruth's leadership style as empowerment and that it was built upon a "powerful cycle of giving and receiving" (p. 141). This principal believed that "to empower others is the more powerful way to act" (p. 141).

We propose that gender equity can be defined by three components: (a) access, (b) process, and (c) success. Much of the effort in gender equity has been targeted at the problem of access, and in fact, it is illegal to pay women less than men for the same work or to deny a woman a job because she is a woman, or to fire a woman because she is pregnant. However, these events still occur, but a woman does have a remedy through the courts, should she choose it.

The process of gender equity is the focus of much of this book. We believe that there are skills that a woman can develop that, when implemented, provide the process of gender equity. We have categorized these skills into physical, emotional, intellectual, and spiritual dimensions and they are described in Chapters 10 through 13.

The success dimension is more difficult. There are many who believe that equal success is never possible, and for individuals, we would agree. However, a profound question remains: Should one accept the proposition that there are some groups in the United States who should not be able to claim the American dream? If so, what groups? Women? All minorities? Some minorities, but not others? Despite the claims of Herrnstein and Murray (1994), there is no scientific evidence that achievement or mental capacity differs between groups (W. M. Williams & Ceci, 1997). Therefore, there is no reason to accept unequal success between groups. The cause must lie within the social and political processes used for facilitating or retarding the access or process of equity. Chapters 8 and 9 address these processes and the role of counselors in facilitating and supporting change.

Summary

There remains a gender-related power differential despite laws and social efforts to make a change. Behavior does not have gender, but in today's society, behavior is interpreted through the engendered notion of what is appropriate and what is not.

Gender inequity developed as a socially constructed phenomenon to ensure stability of the social order and to concentrate power within men. For women, the effect has been to decrease opportunity within the workforce and thus disempower women economically.

Gender stratification in the workforce is the means by which women's jobs are labeled and devalued. However, never before have women had the opportunities they have today despite the differences that remain in pay equity and access to the highest positions within occupations. Pay equity acts have been helpful in this process as well as Title VII, which provides legal remedies for discrimination. The gains that have been attained have resulted in greatly increased access to educational opportunities, particularly in the professions of law and medicine.

If we anticipate that the gains of women reflect the path ahead, the question remains—How will women use the power that they gain? Jordan (1995) challenged women to maintain their traditionally person-oriented values in their new, more powerful roles rather than abandoning them as the male corporate elite have done for ages.

Gillespie (1996) cautioned that gains won by women cannot be taken for granted and that political debates and interests change with each election. She said:

> We thought after the 1992 elections that the suits finally were beginning to get it right. Instead it seems that they took the idea of the Year of the Woman literally, i.e., we had our year and now it's back to the boys doing business as usual (p. 1).

Applications for Counselors

Counselors who help women achieve empowerment will incorporate into their methods:

- An understanding of gender as social construction.
- The contribution of gender-role socialization in limiting and defining behavior.

- The power differential and its contribution to the status of women.
- The economic, political, and professional gap that contributes to the "minority" status of women.

The process of incorporating these understandings may include:

- Exercises to help women identify socialized behavior from behavior or choice:
  - Visit a mall and observe how men and women accomplish similar tasks, noting variability within as well as between genders.
  - Personal inventorying and attribution of habits and ways of doing things, such as dressing, cooking, parenting, speaking in groups, running committees, and presenting ideas.
- Personal exploration of the role of gender role socialization on life decisions, such as education, career, marriage, and child rearing.

2

Oppression and Disempowerment

In Chapter 1, we described the current gender gap. However, there are subgroups of women for whom the oppression of the gender gap weighs especially heavy owing to their race/ethnicity, age, sexual orientation, and disabilities. These women fight dual battles: one for the right to equality as women and another for equity that is often denied members of minority groups. The struggle is one for freedom according to Nelson (1995), who said:

> Freedom connotes the process of redressing wrongs, of setting things right. It is based on the premise that each human being is endowed with equal worth. . . . Without freedom, there can be no peace. (p. 363)

Race and ethnicity play a large role in defining the access, process, and success of women today. Because the United States has become an increasingly diverse, multicultural society, people face the stresses of attending to languages and customs they do not understand. Alleviation of the stress is sometimes attempted by enforced acculturation through reduction in programs such as English as a Second Language (ESL) and required education for immigrant children. Therefore, we begin this chapter by addressing the specific contribution of race and ethnicity to disempowerment.

The United States has a youth-oriented, almost youth-worshipping society. The stereotypical value of women as decoration (Wolf, 1992) or sex objects (J. T. Wood, 1997) may no longer apply as women age, and thus older women may simply be ignored. This occurs at a time in their lives when many women are also facing loss of their careers through retirement and loss of their companions to early death. It is difficult to be old in these times, especially if poverty and illness have decreased options. Because women value nurturance and intimacy, social norms may place them in the role of primary caregiver across the life span, first for their children, then aging parents, and finally an ailing spouse (Baines, Evans, & Neysmith, 1991). Although this role may be stressful and burdensome, it does provide meaning and a sense of usefulness that when lost can be traumatic.

Prejudice has long been targeted toward individuals because of their sexual orientation. Lesbians not only have faced the burden of discrimination because of their sexual orientation but also experience an added burden—disempowerment because they are women. Their struggle has at times placed them at odds with various feminist movements, and they have had to face the battle alone. We attempt to describe their current plight.

Living with a chronic disability is difficult for anyone, and women who have disabilities are especially likely to become victims of abuse by their attendants. Women who are disabled and "dependent" may not ever be able to claim any of the choices that the women's movement has defined as its goal. For them, the struggle is how to cope with being dependent when their desire to be productive has been thwarted.

There is a difficulty in addressing each of these disempowering experiences individually because that is not how they are lived. Rothenberg (1992) described this problem as we would. She said, "The most basic challenge continues to be the need to explore each form or aspect of oppression while doing justice to the enormously complex ways in which they overlap and intersect" (p. iii). Our goal is to provide a lens through which these factors of disempowerment may be viewed and reversed so that women, regardless of their special characteristics, will be empowered.

Race and Ethnicity

While women have always been oppressed, minority women, especially African American women, have been doubly oppressed. Barber (1995) described the depth of her experiences growing up as an African American in segregated Charlotte, North Carolina. She said, "During my formative years, I was exposed to a social and political climate which challenged my personal sense of value as a human being" (p. 383).

Yamato (1992) defined oppression as "the systematic, institutionalized mistreatment of one group of people by another for whatever reason" (p. 58). She believed that external oppression caused an internalized oppression for its victims such that they are "emotionally, physically, and spiritually battered to the point that they begin to actually believe that their oppression is deserved, is their lot in life, is natural and right, and that it doesn't even exist" (p. 58).

Rothenberg (1992) noted the likely consequences of being born a woman and a person of color as having (a) less education, (b) inferior health care, (c) a lower standard of living, and (d) lower aspirations than those who are White, wealthy, and male. This is not a projection we would want for any person we value, and yet it is the life expectation for minority women.

The history of the United States is replete with anecdotes and laws that define the processes by which the plight of minorities became today's reality. But minority women were not even deemed worthy of law until the mid-20th century. The Equal Pay Act of 1963 and the Civil Rights Act of 1964 were careful not to mix race with equal pay and gender with civil rights (Blankenship, 1996) such that both of these laws had more impact for White women and African American men than for African American women.

Camille Cosby (1998) indicted the racism that is rampant in the United States as the breeding ground that encouraged her son's killer to hate African Americans. She noted that regardless of their accomplishments or educational achievements, African Americans are at risk simply because of the color of their skin.

Hadnot (1998) also noted the fears associated with being Black in the United States. In discussing her East Texas heritage, she said, "I choose not to live where some people believe they are due deference because of skin color. . . . I now know that it doesn't matter where I am. I will never have the kind of protection my parents intended" (p. J10).

Modern racism (Brown, 1990) is more subtle than the blatant anti-Black codes of previous generations. However, because it is woven into the fabric of society, it is much more pervasive and much more difficult to combat. Although it may not be as intentional as previous forms of racism, it does not pain its victims any less.

Hooks (1981) and Hurtado (1989) believed that the plight of African American women was a product of Black men's sexism, White women's racism, and White men's racial and sexual politics that resulted in rejection. Chow, Wilkinson, and Zinn (1996) acknowledged the role of rule in determining what can be studied regarding social problems. They said:

There is little doubt that race, class, and gender lie at the heart of many current issues, as a quick perusal of any newspaper headlines on a given day will show. Dominant forces, however, are hostile to

such thinking, wishing instead to repress it under the rubric of "re-
turning to the basics" or eliminating "political correctness." (p. xi)

The role of cultural identity was explored in a group of Hispanic students who were enrolled in predominantly Anglo American universities. The results revealed that a previously strong
ethnic identity was more likely to predict involvement with cultural activities in the new environment. Because students with
previously weak links to their cultural heritage perceived even
greater threat in the new environment, they were more likely to
distance themselves from cultural support groups (Ethier &
Deaux, 1994).

Elderly Hispanic women were characterized by Sotomayor
(1994a) as being in multiple jeopardy. In addition to being female, elderly, and a minority, Hispanic women are often caught
in the dislocation that accompanies economic downturns because Hispanic men are more likely to work in areas that have
high employment volatility. Sotomayor (1994b) reported, "Between 1981 and 1985. . . the dislocation rate for Latinas was 39
percent higher than the dislocation rate for White women, and
26 percent higher than the rate for Black women" (p. 2). She
also found that Latinos were three times more likely to live in
poverty than were Whites.

Sotomayor (1994a) suggested that intervention efforts be
focused on young Latinas because they have high fertility rates
and thus their children are more likely to grow up in poverty.
Living in poverty at any time in life is a strong predictor of being poor at another time.

The process for empowering minority women must take into
account their unique history and current plight. However, Willis
(1992) noted that competing oppressions will, in the long range,
result in failure for both. She said, "The logic of competing oppressions does not heal divisions but intensifies them. . . for
every person who has no shoes, there is always someone who
has no feet" (p. 116).

Counseling minority women to aid their empowerment
should address such issues as (a) level of ethnic identity,

(b) acculturation, (c) family influence, (d) gender-role socialization, (e) religious and spiritual influences, and (f) immigration experiences (C. C. Lee, 1991). Espin (1993) suggested that min- ority women will find it helpful to explore the effects of sexism, racism, and elitism on their development to facilitate their understanding of the dynamics between their internal exper- iences and external environments.

Age

Friedan (1993) noted three important images of older women. First, there was a significant lack of older women doing anything in the mass media. Second, there was an increasing obsession with trying to prevent aging. Third, there was an increased attention to trying to find a "final solution" for unproductive elderly people who placed an intolerable burden on their families. She stated:

> In studies over the past 20 years, young people, middle-aged people, doctors, occupational therapists, nurses, institutionalized older persons, and even gerontologists saw older people as child-like, mentally incompetent, unattractive, lonely, dependent, and powerless. (Friedan, 1993, p. 50)

This view of elderly people in negative terms leaves them disempowered in every way by a culture that worships youth. Sandhu and Aspy (1997) described the consequences of such a negative view. They said, "Regardless, the force of prejudice creates an environment that is at best unsupportive and at worst destructive of the life force of elderly persons" (p. 24). Kite, Deaux, and Miele (1991) studied stereotypes of age and gender. They found that older women were more likely to be seen as wrinkled and active in their communities than older men but that gender stereotypes of both men and women were common.

In the preface to *Women and Aging* (Alexander, Berrow, Domitrovich, Donnelly, & McLean, 1986), Donnelly described the problem of aging from a feminist point of view, recognizing that aging women tend to vanish in the eyes of society, even in the eyes of feminists. She said:

> I began to read again in the same way I read when I first became a feminist. I looked for images of older women, began to analyze the literature I have read (and published) and the pattern was very clear. Older women, aging women, women who are past a certain age (which seems to be about 55) are not reflected in our society or are depicted in negative stereotype. They are also absent from the feminist media and literature, and I have been a part of that erasure. (p. 7)

Rossi (1995) contended that a renewed focus on research of elderly persons is due in part to the high financial drain that is associated with an aging society. She suggested also that studies of families and lineages were supported in part to determine the willingness of families to assume part of the costs of their parents' care.

Counselors working with elderly women must help them discover meaning in their lives despite the losses they have experienced in functionality or among family and friends. Frankl (1990) suggested that the question facing individuals given the transitoriness of existence was how to say yes to life in spite of death. Thibault (1993) suggested that this time of life, particularly for women, was an opportunity to deepen their relationships with God and to provide models of effective living for others to follow.

Friedan (1993) proposed life review as a way of saying yes to life. However, she also proposed that developing new roles for older people in society was also an essential part of our collective development. She said:

> It is only now that the *empowerment of women* can be seen in its evolutionary significance—as solution, not just problem, in the crises of family and church, economy and government, threatening the very fabric of our society. (p. 629)

Sexual Orientation

Lesbians have long been a target of ridicule, as have gay men and bisexual people (McWhirter, 1994). Until 1973, homosexuality was classified as a psychiatric disorder with accompanying notions of pathology. Because we live in a society that has declared any sexual orientation other than heterosexism as aberrant, women who define themselves as homosexual are at risk for discrimination and disempowerment. Pharr (1992) described homophobia as a weapon of sexism. She said, "To be a lesbian is to be perceived as someone who has stepped out of line, who has moved out of sexual/economic dependence on a male, who is women-identified" (p. 435).

Because the notion of sexual orientation (other than heterosexism) has been publicized and politicized in recent years, lesbians may continue to "pass," that is, to live as if they are not a member of a threatened minority to avoid the cruel insult of discrimination (Hillyer, 1993). The resultant fear of exposure threatens mental and physical health as well as threatening loss of status.

Pharr (1992) identified eight areas of potential loss for lesbians as a result of societal prejudice: (a) employment, (b) family approval and support, (c) custody of children, (d) heterosexual privilege and protection, (e) safety, (f) mental health, (g) community, and (h) credibility. In addition to these areas of loss, lesbians share the same problems as other women. They are mothers, partners, workers, and friends. The only difference is the hostility of the environment because of a "heterosexist, homophobic, and racist society" (McWhirter, 1994, p. 97).

One area of discrimination that lesbians share in common with other women is the stereotype as a sex object (J. T. Wood, 1997). For hetereosexual women, being treated as a sex object means being the target of flirting, lewd remarks, or sexual harassment (Strine, 1992). To be treated as a sex object for lesbians means to be "perceived almost exclusively in terms of their sexuality, which is hardly the sum of their identities any more than of hetereosexuals' identities" (J. T. Wood, 1997, p. 345). Kite and Deaux (1987) also found that gender stereotypes of lesbians reflect an implicit inversion of gender roles. That is, lesbians are assumed to have highly masculine behaviors, and gay men are assumed to have highly feminine ones. This attitude may lead to gay bashing and failure to recognize lesbians' job competence.

Lesbians are also at risk when it comes to health care. Harrison and Silenzio (1996) reported that 4% to 9% of the population was homosexual but these individuals avoided routine health care because of the poor and sometimes embarrassing treatment they received. Rankow (1995) described such treatment as breach of confidentiality, neglect, patronizing attitudes, unwarranted roughness during physical examinations, and efforts to redirect patients' sexual orientation. Greco and Glusman (1998) recommended that physicians deal openly with sexual orientation and that they treat partners of lesbians the same way they would a heterosexual patient's spouse. Rankow and Tessaro (1998) studied cervical cancer screening in a sample of lesbian and bisexual women and found them to be much less likely to have been screened unless their health care providers were knowledgeable and sensitive to lesbian issues.

Rosetti (1995) used the term *postlesbian* to define "a time when the term 'lesbian,' laden with confusing and often negative associations, will no longer be used to identify and isolate women's bodies. Lesbian identity, visibility, and political struggles are currently and inextricably linked with the same issues of sexism, racism, classism, and homophobia that face all American women" (p. 252). Homophobia, she believed, was a weapon of the dominant culture used against women who challenge the rightfulness of a male-dominant society, especially against the early suffragists as well as 1970s feminists.

Pharr (1992) recommended that the next wave of feminism be multiracial and multi-issued. She said, "We know that we won't get there until everyone gets there; that we must move forward in a great strong line, hand in hand, not just a few at a time" (p. 440).

For counselors to work effectively to empower lesbians, they must first be aware of their own personal biases and how these biases may interfere with their competency (McWhirter, 1994). House and Holloway (1992) suggested that counselor trainers should be role models for their supervisees and make appropriate materials available to them as a part of their training programs.

Lesbians, then, may present for counseling with multiple levels of "dis-ease." They live in the same sexist environment as other women and may also face additional disempowerment from the prejudice against them because of their sexual orientation. Ultimately, prejudice is about power—acquiring it for oneself and one's group at the expense of those who are dissimilar; therefore, empowerment must address the problems in society that prevent minority groups from sharing power. The Multidimensional Model for Prejudice Prevention and Reduction described in Section II of this book provides an approach for the complicated individual as well as social problems of our times.

Disability

The Americans With Disabilities Act was passed on July 26, 1990, with the purpose of protecting individuals with mental and physical impairments. This law prohibits discrimination in employment, public service, public accommodations, and telecommunications. This law, like others addressing discrimination and rights of minorities, does not guarantee that any individual with a disability will not experience discrimination, but it does provide a remedy should discrimination occur.

It is important to distinguish between disability and handicap. Hillyer (1993) described the consensus regarding the meaning of "handicapped" as limitations that arise from societal causes, whereas a disability is a physical condition or sometimes a mental or emotional condition. Other definitions suggest that a disability becomes a handicap when it prevents a person from doing what is expected or it limits one or more of a person's major life activities (Fine & Asch, 1989).

Disempowerment through disability is multifaceted and goes to the heart of a person's fear of loss of control, identity, and ability. Culture in the United States is steeped in the traditions of self-determination through hard work and discipline and of independence as the true expression of freedom (Fowler & Wadsworth, 1991). For women with disabilities, these concepts must be redefined because self-worth cannot be determined by occupation or sometimes even productivity. Independence may never be an option because of a world that handicaps the woman with a disability at every turn. In the following paragraphs, we address three ways women with disabilities are disempowered: (a) overvaluation of independence, (b) the expectation of reversibility, and (c) a world of handicaps. In addition, we propose strategies to change disempowerment to empowerment.

Overvaluation of Independence

The first aspect of disempowerment is the overvaluation of independence in the culture. From the perspective of a culture based on the value of independence, the woman with disabilities faces immediate social failure. When that disability is mental, the likelihood of achieving any independence may be impossible for an individual, and yet the "dominating guide" is to try to achieve it.

Hillyer (1993) recounted an example of this attitude when she facilitated a discussion of disability and dependence. Several participants expressed admiration for a paraplegic woman who was building her own house without assistance from a contractor or other helpers. Hillyer noted that "No one questioned the possibly inappropriate or excessive quality of her 'independence'" (p. 11).

For people with disabilities, the resources to enhance independence are often missing. Despite federal and state dollars being allocated for jobs programs, people with disabilities are often unemployed or underemployed (Lombana, 1989). This inability to participate and retain control may lead to a loss of self-esteem, acute anxiety, fear of loss of love and support, or guilt about the effect of the disability on the family (J. F. Miller, 1992).

The Expectation of Reversibility

The second aspect of disempowerment for women with disabilities is the expectation of reversibility. The women's movement has struggled to make possible the widest range of choices for women and the freedom to choose among them. For women with disabilities, choices are limited at the outset by their disabilities, and the struggle may be for acceptance rather than reversal.

However, in today's hard-driving, fast-paced society, everyone is expected to carry his or her own weight. For the person with disabilities, overcoming the limits is almost the expectation—be a superhero. We seem to believe that with all the technological advances, a person with disabilities should be able to perform as "normal" people do.

This is a heavy burden for a person with a disability that is not likely surmounted. The self-concept may be threatened, and the interpretation of love and support causes these women to rationally ask if one can be loved as she is with a disability and that, if reversibility is not possible, will love continue?

A Handicapping World

The third aspect of disempowerment for women with disabilities is the handicapping world in which they live. At every turn, unfriendly surroundings lack the necessities to allow these women to function as freely as they could without the handicapping environment. These handicapping situations are not always as obvious as a multi-story building without an elevator or a curb without a ramp.

The degree of handicapping differs with the type of disability, and most of us are completely unaware of how to be helpful to a person with a disability. It is likely insensitivity and ignorance rather than perversity that creates a hostile environment. For example, a meeting room in a church building had two double doors at the external entry but the single door was not wide enough to allow a wheelchair to pass through. To open both doors, a bolt at the floor had to be unfastened. No person sitting in a wheelchair could possibly open the bolt without assistance because it was on the inside. Even though the entrance complied with wheelchair specifications, the difficulty presented by the bolt disempowered the person in a wheelchair from being able to pass through the doors at will.

The attitudes of society at large regarding people with disabilities range from fear to disgust. It seems obvious that the people who cross the paths of those who have disabilities have an opportunity to treat them like they would other human beings—as unique and valuable. Duffy (1981) used the term *differently abled* rather than *disabled* because all individuals are abled in different degrees. However, Mairs (1987) believed that this language pretends that differences between the able-bodied and those with disabilities are the ordinary ones that distinguish one person from another.

Counselor Strategies

McWhirter (1994) suggested that people with disabilities could be empowered by

> establishing a positive self-concept and identity; recognition of how society's ignorance of, inattention to, and reluctance to address issues related to disabilities [contribute] to limitations experienced by the individual; recognition of how factors in the more immediate environment (e.g., family and coworker attitudes, accessibility) contribute to limitations experienced by the individual; understanding the nature of one's specific disability; advocacy for oneself and

others in medical, employment, and other arenas; and a positive sense of shared identity, purpose, or experience with other people with disabilities. (p. 126)

These recommendations for empowerment suggest that a woman must work first to understand her disability and the reactions of others to it and then work with others in an advocacy role to change the environment in which she lives.

A healthy self-concept is important for every individual, and the fact of a disability should not change it. Christopher Reeve's (1998) autobiography, written after his much publicized fall and subsequent quadriplegia, was titled *Still Me*. He recognized that no longer being able to move or breathe under his own will had not changed who he was in his innermost being. What was of value before remained so after his accident. He attributed his optimism and hope to the support of his wife and friends whose love did not change after his accident.

Suggestions for Counselors

Counselors working with women with disabilities can begin with the development of a knowledge base about disabilities and community resources to assist them. Almost every major chronic disease has a national office, a Web page, and local chapters. These groups are tremendous sources of information of both theoretical and practical value (Chesler & Chesney, 1988).

Persons with disabilities will differ in their desire for information and their need to participate in decision making (R. E. Gray & Doan, 1990). The counselor should be able to work with the individual with a disability to determine her personal values and then help to develop a reasonable advocacy relationship.

The development of high self-esteem is essential for health and well-being in all individuals. For the person with a disability, this process will differ only in the content discussed. Every woman must come to terms with her talents and abilities, strengths and weaknesses, and find within herself reasons to be valued. The counselor's role can be one of teacher, confidante, therapist, and advocate with the goal of helping the woman with disabilities find and achieve her goals.

Multicultural counseling competencies (Sue, Arredondo, & McDavis, 1992) were devised primarily for four ethnic/racial groups: African American, American Indians, Asian Americans, and Hispanics and Latinos; however, these skills "have had useful relevance to other oppressed groups as well" (p. 477) in which race and gender are interpreted.

Arredondo (1994) argued that multiculturalism is a given condition of existence just as race, gender, and sexual orientation are. She suggested that a multicultural approach should be an individual–collectivist approach such that counselors learn to accept their own (as well as their clients') "uniqueness and differences in the context of relationships to groups that influence her or his worldview" (p. 310). Such an approach is supportive of counselors' acceptance of themselves as cultural beings with biases, assumptions, and values of their own that may interfere with their ability to facilitate clients who are culturally different.

Multicultural counseling skills address attitudes and beliefs, knowledge, and skills in three major areas: (a) counselor awareness of her or his own cultural values and biases, (b) counselor awareness of clients' worldview, and (c) culturally appropriate intervention strategies (Arredondo et al., 1996). Table 2.1 at the end of this chapter contains the competencies as adopted by the Association for Multicultural Counseling and Development. The reader is directed to the operationalization of these competencies in 1996 by Arredondo et al.

Summary

Although women have always been oppressed, there are some groups of women for whom the burden of being a woman is especially difficult because of the nature of U.S. society. We have addressed the problems they experience and provided some suggestions for counselors who will work with them.

There are no easy solutions to the problems these women experience because they are embedded within the structure of society: sexism, racism, ageism, homophobia, and bias against those with disabilities. People fear what they do not understand, and they marginalize those who would aspire to full participation. Hope lies in people's sense of common humanity and in the skills people develop to enable their talents.

Applications for Counselors

Counselors who work effectively with women who differ from the majority culture in race/ethnicity, age, sexual orientation, or disability will incorporate the attitudes, knowledge, and skills of multicultural counseling as defined in Table 2.1.

TABLE 2.1
Multicultural Counseling Competencies

I. Counselor Awareness of Own Cultural Values and Biases
  A. Attitudes and Beliefs
     Culturally skilled counselors:
     1. Have moved from being culturally unaware to being aware and sensitive to their own cultural heritage and to valuing and respecting differences.
     2. Are aware of how their own cultural backgrounds and experiences as well as their attitudes, values, and biases influence psychological processes.
     3. Are able to recognize the limits of their competencies and expertise.
     4. Are comfortable with differences that exist between themselves and clients in terms of race, ethnicity, culture, and beliefs.
  B. Knowledge
     Culturally skilled counselors:
     1. Have specific knowledge about their own racial and cultural heritage and how it personally and professionally affects their definitions of normality–abnormality and the process of counseling.
     2. Possess knowledge and understanding about how oppression, racism, discrimination, and stereotyping affect them personally and in their work. This allows them to acknowledge their own racist attitudes, beliefs, and feelings. Although this standard applies to all groups, for White counselors it may mean that they understand how they may have directly or indirectly benefited from individual, institutional, and cultural racism (White identity development models).
     3. Possess knowledge about their social impact on others. They are knowledgeable about communication style differences, how their style may clash or foster the counseling process with minority clients, and how to anticipate the impact it may have on others.

TABLE 2.1 *(cont'd.)*

C. Skills
Culturally skilled counselors:
1. Seek out educational, consultative, and training experiences to improve their understanding and effectiveness in working with culturally different populations. Being able to recognize the limits of their competencies, they:
   a. Seek consultation.
   b. Seek further training or education.
   c. Refer out to more qualified individuals or resource.
   d. Engage in a combination of these.
2. Are constantly seeking to understand themselves as racial and cultural beings and are actively seeking a nonracist identity.

II. Counselor Awareness of Client's Worldview
   A. Attitudes and Beliefs
   Culturally skilled counselors:
   1. Are aware of their negative emotional reactions toward other racial and ethnic groups that may prove detrimental to their clients in counseling. They are willing to contrast their own beliefs and attitudes with those of their culturally different clients in a non-judgmental fashion.
   2. Are aware of their stereotypes and preconceived notions that they may hold toward other racial and ethnic minority groups.

   B. Knowledge
   Culturally skilled counselors:
   1. Possess specific knowledge and information about the particular group they are working with. They are aware of the life experiences, cultural heritage, and historical background of their culturally different clients. This particular competency is strongly linked to the "minority identity development models" available in the literature.
   2. Understand how race, culture, ethnicity, and so forth may affect personality formulation, vocational choices, manifestation of psychological disorders, help-seeking behavior, and the appropriateness or inappropriateness of counseling approaches.
   3. Understand and have knowledge about sociopolitical influences that impinge on the life of racial and ethnic minorities. Immigration issues, poverty, racism, stereotyping, and powerlessness all leave major scars that may influence the counseling process.

   C. Skills
   Culturally skilled counselors:
   1. Should familiarize themselves with relevant research and the latest findings regarding mental health and mental disorders of various ethnic and racial groups. They should actively seek out educational experiences that foster their knowledge, understanding, and cross-cultural skills.
   2. Become actively involved with minority individuals outside of the counseling setting (community events, social and political functions, celebrations, friendships, neighborhood groups, and so forth) so that their perspective of minorities is more than an academic or a helping exercise.

(cont'd.)

TABLE 2.1 (*cont'd.*)

III. Culturally Appropriate Intervention Strategies
  A. Attitudes and Beliefs
  Culturally skilled counselors:
   1. Respect clients' religious or spiritual beliefs and values, including attributions and taboos, because they affect worldview, psychosocial functioning, and expressions of distress.
   2. Respect indigenous helping practices and respect minority community intrinsic help-giving networks.
   3. Value bilingualism and do not view another language as an impediment to counseling (monolingualism may be the culprit).
  B. Knowledge
  Culturally skilled counselors:
   1. Have a clear and explicit knowledge and understanding of the generic characteristics of counseling and therapy (culture bound, class bound, and monolingual) and how they may clash with the cultural values of various minority groups.
   2. Are aware of institutional barriers that prevent minorities from using mental health services.
   3. Have knowledge of the potential bias in assessment instruments and use procedures and interpret findings keeping in mind the cultural and linguistic characteristics of the clients.
   4. Have knowledge of minority family structures, hierarchies, values, and beliefs. They are knowledgeable about the community characteristics and the resources in the community as well as the family.
   5. Should be aware of relevant discriminatory practices at the social and community level that may be affecting the psychological welfare of the population being served.
  C. Skills
  Culturally skilled counselors:
   1. Are able to engage in a variety of verbal and nonverbal helping responses. They are able to send and receive both verbal and nonverbal messages accurately and appropriately. They are not tied down to only one method or approach to helping but recognize that helping styles and approaches may be culture bound. When they sense that their helping style is limited and potentially inappropriate, they can anticipate and ameliorate its negative impact.
   2. Are able to exercise institutional intervention skills on behalf of their clients. They can help clients determine whether a problem stems from racism or bias in others (the concept of healthy paranoia) so that clients do not inappropriately personalize problems.
   3. Are not averse to seeking consultation with traditional healers and religious and spiritual leaders and practitioners in the treatment of culturally different clients when appropriate.
   4. Take responsibility for interacting in the language requested by the client and, if not feasible, make appropriate referral. A serious problem arises when the linguistic skills of a counselor do not match the language of the client. If this is the case, counselors should:

(*cont'd.*)

TABLE 2.1 *(cont'd.)*

---

    a. Seek a translator with cultural knowledge and appropriate professional background.

    b. Refer to a knowledgeable and competent bilingual counselor.

5. Have training and expertise in the use of traditional assessment and testing instruments. They not only understand the technical aspect of the instruments but are also aware of the cultural limitations. This allows them to use test instruments for the welfare of diverse clients.

6. Should attend to as well as work to eliminate biases, prejudices, and discriminatory practices. They should be cognizant of sociopolitical contexts in conducting evaluations and providing interventions and should develop sensitivity to issues of oppression, sexism, elitism, and racism.

7. Take responsibility in educating their clients to the processes of psychological intervention such as goals, expectations, legal rights, and the counselor's orientation.

3

Future Trends

E ven now, there are forces at work that will differentially affect the future of women. Although women have made gains over the past 20 years in earnings and access, there remains a double standard evidenced by the fact that women still earn only 74 cents for every dollar a man earns (Associated Press, 1998).

The general economic trend seems to support slow growth, but whether or not the economy improves or declines, the number of women in the labor force will increase. Whatever the future holds will most likely have a different impact on women than on men, and therefore, women must educate themselves to respond appropriately.

We identified five positive trends and five negative trends that we believe will affect the future of women. The positive trends include (a) a shift in demographics to a collective minority majority, (b) women's increased access to education and employment, (c) increased attention to women's health, (d) increased technology application, and (e) equal protection under the law.

The negative trends include (a) perpetuation of bias through inequitable legal decisions from the bench, (b) unequal political representation, (c) thickening of the glass ceiling, (d) increased domestic violence, and (e) increased child-care shortage. In the following sections, we detail each of these trends and suggest ways that counselors may be involved in facilitating positive change.

Five Positive Trends

A Shift in Demographics to a Collective Minority Majority

It is estimated that by the year 2050, ethnic/racial minorities will collectively outnumber Whites in the United States (DeVita & Pollard, 1996). Although women have a numerical majority in the population today, they live their lives with expectations similar to ethnic/racial minorities in that they do not hold power as White males do. This population change offers women the opportunity to collaborate with ethnic/racial minorities to ensure a more equitable distribution of power.

The changing demographics will affect the nation in multiple ways. With their increasing numbers, ethnic/racial minorities will become the majority in many voting districts and will have access to congressional seats that were previously inaccessible. This access to power by the previously disenfranchised will likely change the focus of political debate to a multicultural emphasis.

Although women have always been a numerical majority, they have never voted as a single group, which reflects the diversity of their opinions. Women do not agree on abortion or gun control or the Equal Rights Amendment. This lack of agreement diminishes their power. However, women who run for political office have been able to build constituencies to support the issues they believe are important. As more women move into the political arena, they will continue to articulate issues around which constituencies will organize, and these constituencies will consist of both men and women.

This dispersion of power across multiple racial and ethnic groups will also renew the pluralism debate. Crevecoeur's (1904) description of the "melting pot" will be replaced by the "salad bowl." This increasing diversity will require more negotiation and a more urgent need for looking at society's problems in a global as well as individual way. Women's notions of justice and fair play will bring a much-needed voice to the political debate.

Women's Increased Access to Education and Employment

Women are moving into professional fields in unprecedented numbers. Today, almost half of the students in professional schools such as law and medicine are women (Cannon, 1996; Franke, 1995). These women will move into the workforce within the next 4 to 8 years and will begin their careers. Their visibility in these professions will greatly increase the number of women in future classes.

Occupations requiring higher levels of education and training are predicted to have the fastest growth rates (Coltrane, 1996). Three occupational categories with the highest anticipated growth rates currently employ predominantly women. These include service (chiefly health and personal service occupations), administrative support, and professional specialty. Growth in these occupations will mean that women will have access to the higher paying, administrative jobs in these fields (Silvestri & Lukasiewicz, 1991).

Increased Attention to Women's Health

Before the late 1980s, almost all clinical research trials were conducted on men (Gore, 1995; Haseltine & Jacobson, 1997). Although women and ethnic/racial minorities were not often used as participants in these studies, the results were applied to them even though there was no evidence that the findings were applicable. The inclusion of women and ethnic/racial minorities occurred because of a change in policy by the National Institutes of Health (NIH Revitalization Act, 1993) that required researchers to include women and ethnic/racial minorities in sufficient numbers so that if the variables studied affect them differently, it could be determined. Guidelines and interpretations by the scientific community have made implementation of this act consistent with the original intent of its design (Anonymous, 1994; Freedman, et al., 1995).

Two examples of this separation of research by gender are noteworthy. In 1982, the Physicians Health Trial (Steering Committee, 1988) was conducted to answer several questions regarding heart disease and stroke after daily aspirin treatment. Because most physicians were men, only men were included in the study. The Nurses trial was started in 1976 to determine the effect of birth control pills on breast cancer and so it included only women (Belanger et al., 1980). Later, when additional funding became available, questions were added to the study to address a broader range of issues.

Because women were not included in the major studies of common diseases such as hypertension, heart disease, and diabetes, it is not surprising that research on diseases that affect only women were also underfunded. Women's diseases have been considered second class for a variety of reasons, and most researchers were men (Haseltine & Jacobson, 1997).

Jensvold, Hamilton, and Mackey (1994) identified a dual dilemma for women scientists. They said, "These two phenomena—not valuing women scientists and not valuing research germane to women—are often but not always found together" (p. 111). For example, breast cancer strikes about one in nine women and yet until very recently, there was very little money available for research in this area (Anonymous, 1997).

Currently women's diseases are being studied because of research dollar availability, and it is likely that in the future, the information regarding women's health will be much more detailed and specific (Haseltine & Jacobson, 1997). This knowledge should translate into more effective treatment methodologies that should ultimately improve the health of women. Improved health also increases the likelihood that women can take advantage of options in the workforce as well as opportunities outside it for a longer period of time.

Increased Application of Technology in All Fields

The growth of technology in the past 30 years has been geometric. Almost every industry is now governed by computer technology. The typewriter has been replaced by the word processor, and although the skills required to operate the two are not that different, technology seems to be masculine rather than feminine (Cockburn, 1985). When women enter a technological field, the jobs tend to be "deskilled" such that the work is structured to be routine, low wage, and highly controlled (Coltrane, 1996).

Despite these negative barriers, technology allows women to overcome the job limits that once labeled work as too dirty or too dangerous for women. Women can indeed manage computers as well as men can, and the struggle for the future will be to ensure that jobs are not gendered but are accessible to those who hold the requisite skills. Part of this effort will include increasing support for pay equity so that jobs cannot be renamed and deskilled for women in order to compensate them at a lower level.

Equity Under the Law

In July 1848, a group of women met at Seneca Falls, New York, to draft the "Declaration of Sentiments" directed toward gaining women's right to vote. They recognized the inherent mistake that the founding fathers had made in denying women full participation in the "grand experiment." In reflecting on the situation that prompted these women to draft such a statement, Eisner (1998) said, "Had I been alive in 1848, I could not have voted, owned a home, controlled when I would bear children, or educated my daughters. My health, my spiritual life, my happiness would have been placed in the hands of men" (p. 9A). However, her advice to women today was to recognize their success and view "themselves as leaders and participants, not outsiders and victims" (p. 9A). Primarily through Title VII of the Civil Rights Act of 1994 (which banned employment discrimination on the basis of gender, race, color, religion, or national origin) and Title IX of the Education Amendments of 1972 (which prohibited discrimination on the basis of gender in educational programs or activities using federal funds), women have made great gains in individual rights, and the next frontier must address inequities that result from the sociological ramifications of being women in modern-day society.

There have been recent trends in such legislation. The Family Leave Act of 1993 provided 12 weeks of unpaid leave to care for a new baby or a seriously ill family member, even though it only applies to companies with more than 50 employees. Although this is a positive trend, European countries and Canada provide much more support for families (Etzioni, 1993; Haas, 1992).

As the demographics of power in the United States shift from White male dominance to increased participation by women and ethnic/racial minorities, we believe that laws will increasingly address those issues that concern women as a community: poverty, domestic violence, child care, moral leadership, and political representation (Eisner, 1998). Eisner stated, "The real threat to us and to our nation lies not in the diminution of individual rights but in the assault on family and community, the canyon between rich and poor, the shame of our cities, the lack of moral national leadership" (p. 9A).

Five Negative Trends

Inequitable Legal Decisions From the Bench

Our system of government was divided into three separate branches to provide checks and balances to prevent any one branch from assuming control. Although the legislative branch has passed laws to help the status of women, the risk comes in the wide latitude granted judges in decision making that ultimately may work to the detriment of women. Remedy of such situations is difficult because superior courts will rarely substitute their judgment for that of a lower court. They may only overturn decisions that are clearly flawed from the point of view of law, not necessarily from the point of view of justice.

In recent years, a number of decisions from the bench have perpetuated the inequities that laws were passed to remove. For example, the Violence Against Women Act (VAWA) was declared unconstitutional by Jackson L. Kiser (chief judge for the United States District Court for the Western District of Virginia), who believed that women could not be given special protection against violence under the law (Jensen, 1997). A woman was raped by two of her college's football players and when the college reversed their suspension, she sued the school and players under VAWA in federal court. The chief judge for the United States District Court of the Western District of Virginia dismissed all charges and declared the VAWA unconstitutional because he believed that Congress did not have the power to regulate crime against women (Jensen, 1997).

In another case, Kenneth Peacock killed his wife after he found her in bed with another man and was sentenced to a mere 18 months in a detention center because Circuit Court Judge Robert E. Cahill of Towson, Maryland, believed that such behavior was understandable given the circumstances of the case ("Judges From the Stone Age," 1995). These examples and others show that a judge may take his or her personal biases into the courtroom and may use them to perpetuate discrimination.

The recourse available in these examples is to remove these judges from the bench by electing more satisfactory individuals. Another possibility is to educate these judges, which has also been shown to be somewhat effective ("Judges From the Stone Age," 1995). What must *not* be done is to allow these individuals to remain in their jobs and to continue their destructive rulings.

Counselors must be attuned to their communities to determine if there are such judges at work in them. Perusing the media for examples of such cases, obtaining information from clients, and soliciting information from groups such as the National Judicial Education Program or the National Organization for Women Legal Defense and Education Fund can be activities that counselors can use to monitor the judicial "health" of their communities. Once identified as perpetuating bias, judges must be educated through programs designed for such purposes ("Judges From the Stone Age," 1995), and counselors can be helpful in bringing the need for a judge's education to the attention of senior judges and the community at large. The role of spokesperson may be intimidating for some counselors, but there is strength in numbers, and local counselors' organizations may adopt this responsibility and develop training programs to assist their members in implementing it.

Unequal Political Representation

Women are currently vastly underrepresented in the political process in the United States, with only 9 women senators and 56 women members of the House of Representatives. The reason for this lack of proportional representation is multidimensional but centers around three basic contributing causes. The first is that the political process favors the incumbent, and the incumbents are mostly male. The second factor is that the election process is very costly and requires support from either a political party or a well-organized political machine that can

solicit contributions, both of which are likely to be male dominated. The third factor is that the political process itself is one
that was created and maintained by men and is much less
hospitable for women. This trend is likely to continue unless
true campaign reform can be accomplished.

Male Incumbents

Every system operates to perpetuate itself, and the male-dominated political system is no exception. Only in recent times
have women been able to run for office on their own records.
Almost all women who served in elected office were widows of
former elected officials who finished out their husband's terms
and were sometimes reelected.

The visibility of incumbents gives candidates the name recognition afforded by having already served in office, which is an
advantage that is difficult for a newcomer to overcome without
vast resources to buy media time. Incumbents usually have
followed a political career path that may have begun with local
office such as mayor, district attorney, or judge followed by state
office. These pathways have also been difficult for women to access because the local power is often held among a small group
of community leaders who are less likely to be women.

Political Party Backing

Because they control entry into primary elections, political parties have long been the access to elected office in the United
States' two-party system. Without the backing of the party, it is
difficult to build a constituency, as evidenced by Ross Perot's
run on a third-party ticket. Despite the personal fortune Perot
made available to finance his candidacy, he received less than
12% of the vote in the 1992 election.

Because women have not been part of the "old boy network," they have not had the general support of the political
parties—they have never been on the pathway. That is not to
say that women have not participated in the political parties,

but that the level of their participation is limited to precinct work and organization rather than as power brokers. If women are to make progress in the political arena, women's organizations must make a commitment to recruit, develop, and support women candidates.

Male-Dominated Political Process

Gilligan (1982) and others have documented that the developmental process is different for women and men. Women tend to value relationship and caring over competition and justice. In U.S. society today, there is a high personal cost in running for office. It is a highly competitive, interpersonally combative process that is much more suited to the preferences of men than of women. To be successful in this arena, women must be more competitive, and for many women, such a distasteful orientation is intolerable.

The role of the media is another aspect that may keep many qualified women (as well as men) from running for public office. The desire for a "story" of any kind may lead to a loss of privacy and tremendous pressure on all family members to act in such a way that they do not call attention to themselves. Living one's life in the eye of the public can be a negative experience and one that many women would be reluctant to ask of their families.

Counselors can be proactive by helping to frame the political debate toward those issues of interest to women as well as organizing women to create a supportive network in which women can work toward full participation in the political process as candidates. The educational needs of women in this area can also be met by the counselors who take this goal as their personal mission.

Thickening of the Glass Ceiling

For years, women who entered traditionally male-dominated fields learned that there was a "glass ceiling" that prevented them from moving into the highest levels of power. Lyness and Thompson (1997) studied financial services executives and found that while men and women had similar compensation and work attitudes, men had more authority, received more stock options, and had more international mobility. The higher in the organization the women rose, the more obstacles they faced, suggesting that there is a second, higher ceiling.

Stroh, Brett, and Reilly (1996) studied turnover rates in male and female managers of 20 Fortune 500 corporations. They found that 26% of the women managers had left their positions after 2 years, compared with 14% of men. Reasons for leaving were not associated with family structure as had been suggested but was related to lack of career opportunity. Thus, the glass ceiling still exists despite the gains that women have made in the workplace, especially during the last 20 years.

Acker (1992) predicted that women's gains in management would level off as many middle-level management positions are eliminated, because of restructuring and male incumbents with seniority retaining the available positions. Unions have long supported a single family wage for men, and if union influence experiences a resurgence, then men's jobs may be protected at the expense of women's, which would replicate the post–World War II pattern (Coltrane, 1996).

Women are expected to occupy about 50% of the labor force by the year 2005 (Kutscher, 1991), and 80% of these jobs will continue to be in only 20 of the 420 occupations listed by the Department of Labor (Miller-Loessi, 1992). Although there will be more women in the workforce, the majority will occupy lower paying, less prestigious positions (Coltrane, 1996). In addition, despite the fact that more women will receive college degrees, the number of openings for jobs requiring college degrees will be less than the number of college graduates through the year 2005.

Women who have broken the glass ceiling were found to possess highly developed political skills (Mainiero, 1994), implying that the workplace requires a kind of gamesmanship. Successful women may "play the game" in a fashion that is acceptable to their male cohorts. Although these skills may be taught, it is likely that women will find the playing field even more competitive if there is an economic downturn.

Lorber (1993) suggested that women physicians would never be true equals in the medical profession in part because of the increasing control of medical decisions by government and other third-party payers. She insinuated that male colleagues use a subtle process to prevent women from replacing senior members of the medical community. This extends to academic medicine in which only 3% of deans are women and only 25%, 20%, and 10% of the faculties are women assistant, associate, and full professors, respectively, despite equal productivity as men (AAMC Project Committee, 1996).

This concept of subtle boycotting that results in women not having access to the higher levels of business, industry, and the professions is a pervasive finding that increases the probability the glass ceiling will thicken. Subtlety is much more difficult to combat than the direct processes that laws can address.

Counselors can be both proactive and reactive in addressing the glass ceiling. Women must be aware of the processes that are at work to prevent them from accomplishing their highest potential, and counselors can participate in this educational process. For women who are victims of this type of discrimination, counselors can use the Multidimensional Model of Prejudice Prevention and Reduction (MMPPR) techniques.

Increased Domestic Violence

In a study of the effects of spouse abuse on pregnancy outcomes, Smilkstein and Aspy (1995) found that about 60% of women admitted to having been a victim of domestic violence at some time in their adult lives. The type of abuse experienced by these women ranged from verbal criticism and hostility to extreme physical violence.

Unfortunately, current estimates of domestic violence suggest that it is on the rise. The cycle of violence is especially deadly for women. From 1 to 4 million women are physically assaulted each year by their partners, according to estimates from a number of sources (Bachman & Saltzman, 1995). Women find it especially difficult to leave these relationships because of lack of alternatives and their hope that each abusive session will be the last. However, it is far more likely that the domestic violence episodes will escalate rather than decline.

Shelters offer an alternative for women, but fear of discovery and reprisal is often enough to keep a woman in the abusive relationship. Legal remedies such as victim protective orders (VPOs) are easily violated, and in many of the cases in which a woman is murdered by her partner, VPOs had been in place.

Smilkstein and Aspy (1995) found that women with a social support network were much less likely to be victims of domestic violence. Women who were isolated from friends and family by their abuser were at much greater risk of injury. Abused women were also more likely to be depressed, to have a poor self-image, and to have an external locus of control.

For counselors, the need to ask about domestic violence is clear. However, these women are not likely to seek counseling unless referred through the courts as part of a domestic violence reduction program. There appears to be a constellation of personality factors for women who are abused, such as depression, external locus of control, low self-esteem, state and trait anxiety, and low family support (Smilkstein & Aspy, 1995). School counselors can be proactive in identifying these characteristics in their student clients and working with them to remediate these predispositions and thus reduce the students' risk for becoming victims of domestic violence.

Prevention is also the best form of treatment, and Smilkstein, Aspy, and Quiggins (1994) suggested that domestic violence may result when one's coping mechanisms are overwhelmed by stress and one's behavioral repertoire for dealing with conflict is limited. These individuals often have seen violence in their families of origin, and they (especially men) have learned to handle stress with aggression. Teaching them effective conflict tactics could prove effective in reducing the cycle of violence. By screening those at risk and teaching them how to handle stress and how to "fight fair," domestic violence can be reduced.

Child-Care Shortage

Recent estimates suggest that about two thirds of children under the age of 18 have mothers who are employed (Phillips, 1989), and over two thirds of these mothers are employed full time. With the increasing departure from the home of working mothers, alternative forms of child care have become critical. Some dual-earner families have adjusted their work schedules so that one parent can be at home with the children. Others use flexible scheduling at the workplace to match children's school schedules.

By far the most common form of nonparental care for preschool-age children is with relatives, although it is declining. The second most common form of care is in child-care centers, which increased 400% between 1965 and 1985. Family day care and in-home sitters, nannies, or au pairs account for the remainder of care options. Family day care has increased slightly, whereas in-home sitters have decreased. When child care is not available, children are left on their own after school hours, and these children have been found to be at greater risk for delinquency and drug use (Alter, Gegan, Kalb, Gwartney, & Maher, 1998; Coltrane, 1996).

There are no emerging solutions to the child-care shortage, because it is estimated that all forms of child care provide care to only a small portion of the children who need it. The problem is multidimensional in that there are more preschool-age children as a result of the cohort of baby-boomers who delayed having children and the large number of adults in the cohort. Furthermore, there is no governmental commitment to child care in the United States as there is in European countries, and that is not likely to change given the current political climate.

In addition, the wages paid to child-care workers are very low, and the turnover is quite high. Licensing is difficult and liability insurance is expensive because of highly publicized cases of child abuse within day-care centers. Because most women who work are in low-paying jobs themselves, the cost of day care can quickly make it prohibitive and send parents looking for new alternatives. This child-care instability is a contributing cause to women leaving the workforce, and it is most often the woman rather than the man because men's wages are usually better and less likely to be sacrificed.

Although greater participation in child care by fathers is a trend, it may not be high enough to ensure a stable environment for children. However, as parents come to view the child-care shortage as a shared problem, it is more likely that solutions will be found. Current factors suggest that parents will continually struggle to find acceptable child care, and it is likely that part of the solution may have to come from the workplace itself. Corporate day-care centers have proved successful and encourage employee loyalty and reduce absenteeism.

Counselors may become advocates for good alternatives for child care. Some schools have implemented after-school programs to ensure that children have safe, constructive places to spend time between the end of the school day and parents' arrival at home, which have been shown to be the most likely hours in the day for juvenile crime (Alter et al., 1998).

Summary

There are both good and bad trends that will affect the status of women in the coming years. As the population of the United States becomes more diversified, women will have more access to power, which will give them the opportunity to address those issues that are of concern to women. We believe that women's access to education and employment will make it possible to ascend to the highest levels of power. Women will also benefit from increased attention to women's health through research and development, and as technology is applied across every field, the jobs available to women should also increase.

Finally, we expect that legislation will be increasingly friendly to women such that remedies for inequities will truly be available.

While these positive trends are unfolding, we also expect that negative trends will tend to impose a retarding effect. The perpetuation of bias through inequitable decisions from the legal bench is of concern beause of the widespread prejudice and stereotypical thinking that still pervade U.S. society. Because women have so little representation in government, it will take a long time to ensure that equal political representation is available. The glass ceiling will remain and will perhaps thicken if the economy takes a downturn. Domestic violence has been increasing and in times of stress—whether a result of the economy or other hardships—is likely to continue to be a source of great suffering for women. Finally, whatever gains women may make in education and employment will be abbreviated by the child-care shortage.

Although there are solutions that can reverse these negative trends, individuals must gather the political will to implement them and change the current reality. This job cannot be accomplished by women alone but must be forged with the help of men who also view the positive development of women as necessary for a healthy society.

Applications for Counselors

Counselors who are aware of the cultural press on their clients will know the trends that are shaping the environment of their communities both positively and negatively. Because these trends will differ across communities, counselors may find the following questions helpful in determining the nature of the trends within their local communities.

Within my community, what changes have occurred or are likely to occur that will affect:
- minority demographics?
- women's access to education and employment?

- women's health?
- the application of technology to women's lives?
- equal protection of women under the law?
- equitable legal decisions from the bench for women?
- political representation of women?
- the glass ceiling?
- domestic violence?
- child-care resources?

Section II

The Multidimensional Model for Prejudice Prevention and Reduction

Prejudice was defined by Allport (1954) as "thinking ill of others without sufficient warrant" (p. 7). Kleg (1993) supported this notion and extended it to include behavior. He said that prejudice is "a readiness to act stemming from a negative feeling, often predicated upon a fixed overgeneralization or totally false belief and directed toward a group or individual members of that group" (p. 14). Although we have introduced a number of feminist theories to explicate gender inequity, we believe that gender inequity is a special case of prejudice toward women and, as such, any individual may be either a perpetrator or a victim. The factors that predispose someone to have a prejudice and then to act on that prejudice (or become a victim of prejudice) are multidimensional, and we believe that prejudice can be modified through the Multidimensional Model for Prejudice Prevention and Reduction (MMPPR; Sandhu & Aspy, 1997): "The basic premise of this model is that prejudice is developed, maintained, and perpetuated by a combination of three major factors: (a) individual personality variables, (b) social mores, and (c) political systems" (p. 151). We believe that counselors must address all three areas simultaneously to be effective. For many counselors, collaboration with others in the social and political arenas may be new ground; however, counselors have a significant role in the process of developing mutual respect and equity among various ethnic, racial, and gender groups.

The MMPPR assumes that the likelihood of an individual or group becoming either a victim or a perpetrator of prejudice is directly related to the sum of the predisposing factors available in the situation. The sum of the individual, social, and political factors operating in a given situation will determine if prejudicial behavior will emerge. For example, if an individual has maladaptive ego defenses and low self-concept and enters into an environment or situation that supports negative identity of his or her group, and the likelihood of punishment is low, then it is highly likely that prejudice will occur. If these factors are internalized, then the individual is likely to be a victim of prejudice, whereas if they are externalized, then the individual is likely to be a perpetrator.

Another aspect of the MMPPR is that it is appropriate for proaction and reaction or for prevention and rehabilitation. By determining predisposition toward prejudicial behavior, counselors may intervene at the individual or group level to ensure that prejudice does not emerge as behavior. Victims and perpetrators may both be rehabilitated after prejudice has been committed.

The MMPPR does not depend on any one counseling method or technique but combines several well-known theories to address varying stages of the counseling process. The model proceeds through five phases. Phase 1 involves trait-and-factor methods to determine the individual's predisposition toward prejudice, either as victim or perpetrator.

The goal of Phase 2 is to determine the individual's awareness of his or her predispositions and the motivation to discuss it. This phase involves application of person-centered counseling techniques.

Person-centered techniques are also used in Phase 3 to help clients become aware of their individual personality predispositions, their native society's interpersonal patterns, and their native society's use of power and political means for addressing inequities. This period of exploration is essential if clients are to understand the dynamics of their prejudicial predispositions.

In Phase 4, the counselor uses psychoanalytic techniques to offer interpretations of the relationships between current coping strategies with their prejudicial predispositions and the way clients would like to behave. From this phase, specific behavioral goals should emerge.

In Phase 5, behavioral counseling techniques are used to develop specific programs to help clients achieve their self-selected behavioral goals. Counselors provide feedback and encouragement to help clients achieve reduction of their prejudicial predispositions or elimination of their prejudicial behaviors.

In the following chapters, we develop in greater detail the individual, social, and political processes counselors may use to address gender inequity targeted toward women. We use the following case in each of the next three chapters to describe the rationale and processes for each component of the MMPPR. The case summarizes the life of a young woman, Helen, who is confronted with an act of discrimination directed toward her by a professor in her graduate program. The frustration, humiliation, and anger she feels is universal and personal. Her challenge is to use this event as both an education for her need for more effective strategies and an application of her skills to intervene on her own behalf.

The Case of Helen

Helen V. grew up in a medium-sized city in the Midwest. She was the middle child of three children born to Paul and Susan V., and she was the only girl. Her brother, Bob, was 14 months older and was two grades ahead in school. He was a sturdy child who used his physical strength to achieve his will. Helen was a particular target, and Bob often coerced her into helping him with his projects. Their brother, Donny, was 5 years younger than Helen, and she was often required to take care of him because both parents worked outside the home to meet the financial demands on the family.

Helen's parents followed traditional gender roles even though her mother worked as a teacher's aide. Susan did all the housework and cooking, and only Helen was required to help her. The boys worked in the yard with their father and did maintenance activities on the house and the cars. Paul was a good mechanic and worked for an automobile dealer as maintenance supervisor and chief mechanic.

The family vacationed every year at a lake in the northern part of the state, where Paul's parents had a cabin. The boys fished with their father while Helen and her mother were left behind to "amuse" themselves with cleaning the cabin and preparing meals. Helen rarely played with her brothers in their games. When she did it was because they desperately needed a player to make even-numbered teams. Of course, the team who had to take her was always considered unlucky.

Helen was a superior student in high school, much more successful than her older brother. When Bob graduated, his parents insisted that he should go to college and he enrolled at the state university about 100 miles away. He was not particularly motivated and managed only mediocre grades. When Helen finished high school, her parents thought college would be too expensive and really a waste of resources because she would probably get married and they really could not afford two children in college at the same time. They suggested that she get secretarial training at the local vocational school, and then she could go to college if that was her desire after Bob earned his degree.

Although disappointed, Helen followed her parents' wishes. She attended secretarial school while working almost full time. She paid rent to her parents and also managed to save money for college. Two years later, her brother earned a business degree and returned to work in their hometown as a store manager. Helen enrolled at the same university her brother had attended with a major in English literature and graduated with honors. Subsequently, she joined the faculty of a large high school in the state's capital city, and following her first year of teaching, she married a high school classmate who had just completed law school. She began work on a master's degree and completed it with distinction in 2 years.

Helen wanted to work full time toward a PhD and a college teaching career. She was offered a teaching assistantship at the university. Her husband adamantly opposed her plans because he wanted to begin a family. His career was going very well, and he believed that Helen should stop work and focus on their home and family. Helen preferred to delay having children until she completed her education, but she finally agreed to try to get pregnant on the condition that she could also continue her studies.

Helen became pregnant during the second semester of that year, but before she revealed her pregnancy, she was nominated, along with another student, to participate in a research project that would ultimately result in a major book project in an area of her interest. The professor in charge of the project planned to interview both students and select the most qualified student. Helen was sure that she would be selected because her master's thesis had involved some of the preliminary work for the project. The other student's course work and experience were less related to the project.

During the interview, the professor asked about Helen's commitments and time available for the project. Helen assured him that she could devote the required 20–30 hours a week. He asked her whether she intended to have children, and although Helen knew this was not a legal question, she believed that the professor's fears could best be allayed by describing her resources and plans for caring for her infant. He thanked her and the next day gave the job to the other student.

Helen was very disappointed and sought her husband's advice. Privately, he was relieved that Helen did not get the job, but he was surprised by the depth of her sadness. He counseled that she could sue if she so desired, but she would have to prove that she lost the job because she was pregnant, not for any other cause. That tactic could be difficult if the other student had any skills that Helen did not have. Helen felt trapped and angry because she believed that pursuing a lawsuit would not be good for her baby. Amid this turmoil, Helen decided to seek counseling.

4

Individual Strategies for Prejudice Prevention and Reduction

P rejudice is a multidimensional problem that requires either individual or group action. Why one individual is prejudiced and another is not is an exceedingly complex problem. Even though we address some predisposing factors in the following sections, we recognize that these factors are not absolutely predictive because they can be mediated by individual, social, or political strategies.

For example, if a young man is reared with traditional gender role expectations, then he may not question why girls and women are supposed to cook, clean, and care for children. This is the expected role for them. However, if someone were to suggest that he perform these tasks, then he is likely to be insulted because such tasks are not associated with his concept of the masculine role.

These gendered roles can be mediated through cognitive processes that may result in a rational, shared approach to household tasks. However, extending these notions from the home to the office may be especially difficult for any individual. In the following sections, we describe both the individual sources of prejudice and the Multidimensional Model for Prejudice Prevention and Reduction (MMPPR) approach in addressing these sources. Also, we use the case of Helen to demonstrate how the model works.

Individual Sources of Prejudice

Unresolved Personality Conflicts

While teaching may be one source of prejudice, unresolved personality conflicts have been posited as another (Katz, 1976; Willie, Kramer, & Brown, 1973). Early developmental experiences influence personality development such that both immature and mature aspects as well as controlling and surrendering dimensions remain. Whenever the dominant aspects are immature and controlling, prejudicial behavior may result (Sandhu & Aspy, 1997).

Maladaptive Ego Defenses
For some individuals, ego development is restricted by an unhealthy environment. The ego is unable to mediate between the wishes of the id and the external constraints of the world. The resulting anxiety may be overwhelming and cause the ego to use protective defense mechanisms (Kaplan, 1993).

While defense mechanisms maintain the ego through difficult times, they may become maladaptive and thus diminish the ability to assess reality. Rationalization, projection, and displacement may be particularly predisposing to the formation of prejudice. The ability to rationalize behavior is one thing that separates humans from animals; however, protecting the ego at the expense of justifying antisocial or prejudicial behavior is an unhealthy personality adjustment.

Presence of Frustration and Aggression

For many individuals and for varying reasons, the lack of goal attainment may become a source of intense frustration. This process creates a cascade of events that may lead to acting out the internal turmoil they experience. The movie *Falling Down* (Kopelson, Weingrad, Harris, & Schumacher, 1993) is an example of this type of frustration leading to a person's acting out aggression. The lead character, played by Michael Douglas, finds himself blocked at every turn. His wife has left him, work is unsatisfying, and finally when his car breaks down in a traffic jam, he leaves his car and encounters a series of frustrating events that tragically end in violence.

Recently, there has been a spate of such behavior among teenagers who act out their frustrations with bullets targeted against family and friends (Lewin, 1998). When these offenders' rooms are searched after the violence, the signs are there, revealing the antisocial thoughts and feelings (Baird, 1998). However, the clues available are not hidden in their private rooms but have often been shared verbally with many individuals. Dr. Alvin Poussaint, Harvard psychiatrist, spoke about these events by saying, "A lot of deaths could be prevented if we responded to the clues people give us in advance" (Terry & Bruni, 1998, p. 14). Although these examples may be extreme, frustration that develops from blocked goal attainment may be an intermediary step toward prejudice that will ultimately be acted out as violence.

Poor Self-Concept

The projection of personal inadequacies is another possible source of individual prejudicial behavior. This projection may emanate from poor self-concept and low self-efficacy. The need to protect the self may allow an individual to project onto another group or individual representing that group the incompetence feared in himself or herself. It is much like the common perversion of the Golden Rule: Do unto others as you would have them do unto you, but do it first.

Low-Order Cognitive Skills

Another source of prejudice in individuals is that of flawed cognitive processes. These consist of simple cognitive structures such as categorizing (Tajfel, 1969), seeking simple solutions (Kleg, 1993), and making extreme judgments on the basis of current circumstances (Katz, 1976). In addition, irrational beliefs may control behavior because these beliefs are not subjected to rigorous intellectual challenge. Each of these may contribute to a kind of emotional learning that is harder to change than the cognitive processes that spawned them (Goleman, 1995).

Categorization

Prejudicial individuals often categorize others into simple groups and attribute to those groups limits of behavior, aptitude, aspiration, and cognition. In the spring of 1998, Reggie White addressed the Wisconsin State Legislature. In this talk targeted toward appreciation of diversity, he classified "Whites" as good businessmen; "Blacks" as talented in music, dancing, and worship; "Hispanics" as good family members; and "Jews" as academically talented. He was surprised at the outrage expressed by many. Yet, this kind of simplistic categorization is the essence of stereotyping that identifies an individual by his or her group membership and attributes to the individual those characteristics associated with the group stereotype.

Seeking Simple Solutions

The need for reductive simplicity in a world of complexity is understandable; however, to disregard facts in order to keep matters simple will result in a great injustice to many. This simplifying process serves as a way of ordering the world into easily defined rules. For example, women do not play sports or lead men. The behavior that follows will serve to implement the rule any time a woman seeks the opportunity to participate at a level outside the defined and accepted category of behavior.

Making Extreme Judgments on the Basis of Current Circumstances

While adolescents are well known for their inability to use perspective—to take the long view of things—this phenomenon may also occur in adults whose development has been thwarted. Bernard Goetz feared that the Black youths in his New York subway car were going to rob him, so he pulled a gun and shot them ("The Quiet Man," 1985). This is an extreme case, but almost any untoward circumstance may be used to justify an extreme position.

There are numerous examples of increases in prejudicial behavior in times of intense job competition caused by an economic downturn. For example, sterilization of Medicaid mothers has been proposed in the past to reduce the number of children on welfare. This ethnic genocide seemed justified in the eyes of a few to protect their economic welfare. The need to protect one's home and family from financial collapse may foster an "us-them" mentality that could result in extreme prejudicial behavior.

Irrational Beliefs

The folklore of every culture is replete with examples of irrational beliefs. These beliefs often serve religious, social, or political purposes and as such have utility for the larger group beyond their factual content. Thus, the social structures at work in the culture serve to maintain and replenish these ideas. For example, at one time scientists of the day believed that disease was caused by an imbalance of humors. Treatment required a balancing intervention that might result in "bleeding" an individual with leeches. The fact that some individuals got better as a result of this treatment serves as an example of the power of belief in the metaphor. Patients believed that their doctors knew what was wrong and how to treat their ailment, and this belief supported and encouraged the desired response. Today, this is called the placebo effect.

Women have been treated differently for centuries because of their "biology," and in recent times, the former Speaker of the House of Representatives Newt Gingrich was quoted widely as supporting the notion that women could not serve in wars in foxholes for extended periods because they would get "infections." Although there is no scientific evidence to support this irrationality, biology is often cited as a reason for supporting a politically popular belief.

Instinctive Fears

Individuals are blessed with a "fight or flight" physiological response phenomenon that prepares one to address danger either by running away or by engaging. What a person recognizes as dangerous is sometimes instinctual and sometimes learned through environmental contact. The list of possible fears is endless, but relevant to this discussion is the fear of those who are different from oneself. People tend to fear those things they do not understand, and being fearful of others who look different in terms of size or color may be included in this category.

Fear, then, becomes a barrier to relationship, and thus the potential for prejudicial behavior is activated. It is instinctive for each individual to strive for self-preservation. Studies of the brain reveal that the earliest and most primitive part, the reptilian, when activated will engage in self-preservation at all costs (Ashbrook & Albright, 1997). In addition, complex learning is inhibited by threat (Caine & Caine, 1997), which may interfere with an individual's ability to learn nonprejudicial ways of being. These negative emotions left unchecked by the rational, reasoning part of the brain may lead to behavior that is clearly prejudiced.

Use of the MMPPR to Address Individual Predispositions Toward Prejudice

Application of the MMPPR in addressing individual predispositions is straightforward, and the techniques will be familiar to most counselors. During Phase 1, an individual is screened for prejudicial predisposition with the Multidimensional Prejudice Predisposition Scale (MPPS; Sandhu & Aspy, 1997; see Section V). The information provided by the scale determines a level of prejudice predisposition and whether or not the prejudice is likely to emerge in a person as either a perpetrator or a victim.

The MPPS contains 15 items, each scored from a possible -5 to a $+5$. Thus, possible scores range from -75 to $+75$. An individual with a positive score directs his or her predispositions outward, whereas a negative score indicates internalization and the likelihood of becoming a victim. Once a score is obtained, the client is given feedback. In the client-centered approach, the counselor explores with the client his or her response to the data and willingness to discuss. As in any form of counseling, the client must be ready and willing to take the next step toward growth, and the length of time devoted to Phase 2 will vary with individual clients.

Phase 3 consists of exploring those dimensions contributing to individual personality conflicts, maladaptive ego defenses, irrational beliefs, poor self-concept, and instinctive fears. By offering the therapeutic conditions of empathy, congruence, and positive regard, the counselor facilitates this exploration process.

In Phase 4, the counselor provides interpretation to facilitate the client's insight into his or her behavior. This process uses techniques of psychodynamic counseling models. The goal is to help clients understand the underlying relationships and contributions to their personality development and to gain insight into how these factors contribute to prejudice predisposition. At the conclusion of this phase, clients should identify some specific behavior changes they are willing to make that are likely to affect prejudicial behavior positively.

In Phase 5, these behaviors are apportioned into tasks that can be implemented and reinforced to ensure behavior change. The counselor assumes a coaching role by providing tasks, giving feedback on performance, and revising the tasks as necessary. Teaching may also become important in this phase as clients learn the skills essential for their new approach to life.

In the following case example, Helen is near the end of Phase 3 and is exploring the dimensions of her personality that are in conflict with her goals. The counselor is using a client-centered approach, which involves responding interchangeably with the client (Carkhuff, 1996). Helen entered counseling because she was angry and frustrated and she felt that there was no real solution for her dilemma. Helen's score on the MPPS was −28, indicating a moderately high predisposition to become a victim of prejudice. The following narratives occurred after several counseling sessions.

The Case of Helen

Counselor: So you're angry and frustrated that your professor refused to give you a chance to show that you could do the work.

Helen: I'm furious both at him and at myself for not being more effective. If I had only worked hard, I could have shown him I was able to do the job regardless of being pregnant. And I'm mad at my husband, too, I guess. He was the one who pushed getting pregnant right now. I wanted to wait. I wouldn't be here now if I had done what I originally wanted to do.

Counselor: Let's sort this out. You're angry at your professor for not seeing your talents.

Helen: I'm not sure if that's it. He did know about my work and he liked it. He used it as part of the preliminary work for the grant application. No, I guess he knew I was talented, but once he had my results, he didn't need me. He was selfish and used me and that's why I'm still angry with him.

Counselor: You resent his putting the project ahead of his responsibility to be your teacher.

Helen: (Pauses.) Well, I guess that is what he did. He wanted the grant to be able to do the study he had planned. My results were just a piece that turned out to be very helpful. He probably would have gotten the grant without them anyway. It's just that I know I am better than the other student, and to have to sit back and watch him do what I know was really perfect for me is so wrong and I can't do anything about it. (Cries and reaches for a tissue.)

Counselor: You're really sad because you've lost something you don't think you can regain.

Helen: (Sniffs, regains control.) Yes, it all seems like such a conspiracy. I was sure that I could continue my studies while I was pregnant. Women do it all the time. But I don't seem to be able to get things together. I really wanted this job. It was my ideal of how graduate school would be and now all that's gone.

Counselor: You're distraught because you'll have to give up your graduate school ideal and you don't want to.

Helen: It's not me giving up! He took it away from me because I'm pregnant and he thought he could push the other student more than me. He doesn't care about anybody—just the project.

Counselor: And you would be satisfied working for a man like that.

Helen: (Drops her head.). When you put it like that, no, I guess I wouldn't have been happy at all. I didn't know he was like this. He has such a great name in the field, I felt lucky to be studying with him. I know what he did was wrong—it really is illegal and I could have sued him for it. It's just that there is such a high price to pay sometimes. He is well known and I'm just a graduate student. Everyone would think badly of me, and how could I go back and finish my degree there?

No, I think I am right in my decision not to sue him.

Counselor: When you first started counseling, you thought you were somewhat at fault because you hadn't proved yourself. Now, you seem convinced that you were not at fault.

Helen: You know, when I was growing up, things were always my fault. I worked hard for my parents' approval, but my brother, Bob, was always their favorite. Nothing I did was ever as important as what he did. I was at fault for answering his [the professor's] question in the first place. He was wrong to ask [about children] and I didn't have to answer. It's just that in that moment, I didn't think I had a choice. I was this little graduate student and he was the great researcher. I wanted him to choose me. I think I was afraid that I would make him mad if I didn't answer. I guess I am a coward.

Counselor: You're disappointed that you haven't gotten past those childhood responses.

Helen: I guess I haven't. I've been a successful teacher and graduate student and I still don't have enough confidence in myself to stand up to a bully. I'd certainly like to though. I want to understand myself so that I can be a better mother to my child than my mother was for me. I know she loved me, but she didn't think that women could ever do things as important as men. That's how she saw the world, and though I've pretended at some level that I don't, I guess I've learned today that I am really no different from my mother. No, that's wrong. I am different. I want to change.

Summary

Prejudice is a complex, multidimensional problem that may result in a predisposition to become either a perpetrator or a victim. Engenderment may be one of the individual sources by which prejudice against women is perpetuated; however, gendered roles may be mediated by cognitive processes that can be supported and facilitated through counseling.

Other individual sources contributing to prejudice formation may include unresolved personality conflicts, low-order cognitive skills, and instinctive fears. Through the MMPPR, counselors work through five phases with their clients. These phases involve several counseling models, including trait-factor, client-centered, psychodynamic, and behavioristic. The process begins with administering the MPPS to determine a client's likelihood of becoming a victim or perpetrator of prejudice. The feedback from this instrument provides the data to begin a discussion of the client's readiness for change. Phase 3 is devoted to exploring the factors that have contributed to development of the problem, whereas Phase 4 and Phase 5 are focused on insight and behavior change, respectively.

In the counseling dialogue involving Helen, the focus was in Phase 3 and was directed to exploring the individual characteristics that had contributed to Helen's current situation. At this point, Helen is ready to move into Phase 4 and work toward understanding more fully the processes that have contributed to her becoming a victim of prejudice. This insight will be useful for identifying specific targets for behavioral change that will occur in Phase 5.

Applications for Counselors

Counselors who help women identify their individual sources of prejudice will facilitate exploration of both emotional and cognitive processes that include:

- Unresolved personality conflicts: maladaptive ego defenses, presence of frustration and aggression, and poor self-concept.

- Low-order cognitive skills: categorization, seeking simple solutions, making extreme judgments on current circumstances, and irrational beliefs.
- Instinctive fears.

The instruments contained in Section V of this book along with the MPPS can be helpful to counselors in determining clients' attitudes toward gender equity, discrimination, sexism in the workplace, gender role, and sex roles. Each of the five instruments makes a unique contribution and can be helpful in the first phase of the MMPPR in identifying clients' needs.

5

Social Strategies
for Prejudice Prevention
and Reduction

I n the musical *South Pacific*, the notion of prejudice was addressed through a song, "You Have to be Carefully Taught."
The song portrays prejudice as the result of careful teaching
that if omitted would result in a much more respectful
world. This notion of prejudice development, while simplistic,
assumes that the dominant culture or parental authorities
convey the belief of racial, ethnic, or gender superiority. These
beliefs become the norm for an individual's behavior, and he
or she may not question the validity of the rights and privileges
so assumed. These beliefs make one an ideal perpetrator of
prejudice.

However, these same phenomena may also allow a person to
become a victim of prejudice. For a woman to believe that she

is inferior because of her gender or that her ethnicity deserves ill treatment because that notion is held by the dominant social order may allow her to expect and perhaps accept victimhood. For the counselor, it is important to understand how these various socially generated conditions influence behavior and to be able to help a client either to prevent the negative impacts from them or to correct the outcomes of previous incidents.

Beyond counseling the individual, a counselor may advocate amelioration of these factors within the culture. The process most often associated with social change is education, which results in subsequent environmental change. Lott (1991) noted that a tenet of social psychology is the "belief in the possibility of personal and social change mediated by environmental factors" (p. 506). She attributed this principle to Lewin's (1951) belief that behavior is a function of the interaction between person and environment. However, changing social and cultural influences is often a slow process. The process begins with a decision about which group to target for educational interventions. For example, one of the most noticeable changes in cultural practices in the United States is the process of recycling. Although there were public service announcements through the media, the largest educational target population was elementary school children, who learned about recycling and brought home the message: What kind of world are you (meaning parents) going to leave me? Parents, faced with such a difficult question, found recycling to be the easier path, and behavior was changed.

The role of the counselor, then, becomes one of teaching — educating the most likely target audience in the skills, knowledge, and attitudes required to effect social change. Christ (1980) summarized the goal for women when she said, "This social quest concerns women's struggle to gain respect, equality, and freedom in society—in work, in politics, and in relationships with women, men, and children" (p. 8).

In the following paragraphs, we outline the various social and cultural factors that contribute to prejudice, and we also recommend ways to change them. In addition, the case of

Helen provides an example of a counseling dialogue regarding these topics and how they related to Helen's dilemma.

Negative Social and Cultural Identity

Hardiman (1982) synthesized racial/ethnic identity models and sex role theories to develop a five-stage generic model of social identity development. The first stage, No Social Consciousness, defines a period in which individuals are unaware of expected social roles or are confused by them. Stage 2 denotes Acceptance, in which group membership causes one to internalize the expected behaviors of the group and to devalue the behaviors that do not fit this group's expectations. In Stage 3, Resistance, the individual begins to question conformity and reconceptualize group membership. Anger and discomfort may emerge. Redefinition and rediscovery characterize Stage 4 as the individual regains pride in group membership while, at the same time, defining specific needs separate from the group. Stage 5, Internalization, is characterized by an integration of identity achieved during the previous levels and concern for others at differing stages of identity development.

The application of this model to gender issues can be seen developmentally. Young children have no gender preferences until about third or fourth grade (Allport, 1954). At that point, there is a clear same-gender preference. For most girls, from fourth grade through adolescence, Stage 2 defines behavior. As girls accept the socially expected gender roles, they may give in to a more limited role than their talents or abilities would indicate. Gilligan (1982) referred to this phenomenon as "losing voice." Some girls may remain at Stage 2 throughout life and never move on to question socially assigned gender roles and to reconstruct them in a less limiting fashion. Girls who do not move on may have a negative social identity—one that limits their opportunities and offers little hope for complete development.

Because society generally prizes male characteristics and behaviors above female ones, the identity formed by girls who do not successfully complete social identity is a negative one and may lead to prejudice directed inward. This internalized inferiority may lead to the likelihood of becoming a victim of prejudice (Sandhu & Aspy, 1997). This negative identity may be latent, in the sense that it will not lead to victimization until a triggering event (Sandhu & Aspy, 1997).

Erikson (1950, 1968) also proposed a theory of identity development. He suggested that an achieved identity was a result of exploration and experimentation, usually in adolescence. Marcia (1966, 1980) elaborated on Erikson's work and proffered a four-stage model of identity development. He suggested that in order to form an adult identity, adolescents must experience an identity crisis that they successfully resolve. His four stages included the following: (a) identity confusion, in which no crisis has been experienced and no commitments have been made; (b) identity foreclosure, in which no crisis has been experienced but the person has made commitments, usually because of parental influence; (c) identity moratorium, in which crisis has been experience, but the person has made no commitments; and (d) identity achievement, in which many crises have been experienced and resolved, and permanent commitments have been made.

For example, an individual in identity confusion is too interested in what others think and is willing to change opinions too readily. During foreclosure, individuals carefully avoid conflict situations, are bound by habits, and are least flexible in their judgments. Individuals in the moratorium phase are the least willing to be influenced by others and are most critical of the establishment. In identity achievement, individuals have a strong ego and are the most stable and mature in their behavior while at the same time are most aware and accepting of their own limits as well as the limits of others.

Identity diffusion is the state prior to a crisis, exploration, or identity commitment. A foreclosed identity results from a commitment made to an identity on the basis of external criteria internalized in childhood. This is not an explored commitment, but rather one that is accepted without question.

When an adolescent has experienced a crisis and is still in the process of exploration and experimentation, he or she is in the third stage, labeled moratorium. When the adolescent makes an identity commitment after undergoing an identity crisis, exploration, and experimentation, then he or she is in Stage 4, or achieved identity.

Schenkel and Marcia (1972) found that for women, commitment to an identity was the contributing factor to mental health functioning in a college population. That is, women who had either a foreclosed identity or an achieved identity also had higher levels of self-esteem and lower anxiety levels. Delworth (1989) proposed that this is a function of women's need to feel anchored.

Whatever the process by which one achieves identity, it is clear that a healthy valuing of the self is essential for healthy relationships with others (Ponterotto & Pedersen, 1993). For women, the anxiety experienced by not having achieved closure on an acceptable gender role may be greater than for men because gender role expectations are much more rigid for women than for men. In addition, society has had a role in denying women equal opportunity because of their gender (Lauer, 1986), and this knowledge presents a greater barrier to success for some women who fear that trying may be useless.

Negative Intergroup Experience

Negative intergroup experiences are those events in which one group is treated by another in ways that are interpreted as harmful. This may occur in an almost unlimited variety of forms, but some of the more common causes are discussed in the following sections and include arrogance, condescension, hostility, ignorance, and insensitivity.

Arrogance

A group of students from a high school in an upper-income community participated in a speech festival held at a high school in a lower-income community. Immediately, the affluent group assumed a superior attitude toward the less affluent group. The members entered the "home" building making wise-cracks about the peculiar smell and warned each other not to go to the restroom. Throughout the day the arrogant attitude continued so that by the conclusion of the event, the host students had come to resent the affluent guests and were making insulting comments to them such as "hotshots," "know-it-alls," and "big-shits."

Arrogance is best prevented by an honest discussion of the universal human condition. For instance, a group of young band recruits was struggling to master the marching rhythm of their team members. They were so bad the band director called them front and center for special instruction. The band members still in formation began to laugh at their cohorts' awkward efforts. The band director stopped the instruction and said, "Listen, these people may one day march you off the field. I know they can play their instruments as well as anybody here. When we are at contests this year, you'll be glad they're playing with us." Thus, he indicated the need for all types of human talents that are distributed throughout the population.

Condescension

One of the most known examples of condescension involved missionaries who went to places such as Africa, Hawaii, South America, and Asia to bring "light" to the resident citizens. One apocryphal story tells of the missionaries who persuaded the natives that it was evil to bare one's breasts in public. Thus, the local women covered themselves, with the result that many of them died of tuberculosis, which had been tempered by the sunlight on their bare skin.

The same condescension is apparent when men assume they know more than women about a professional role just because they are men. A series of investigations have found that the same phenomenon pertains when people assume that certain professional roles are limited to men, for example, school principals, physicians, lawyers, police officers, or chairpersons of all types.

The effect of condescension can be ameliorated by an intentional effort to introduce women professionals to various groups. For example, on career days at schools it is helpful if a profession is represented intentionally by female professionals.

Hostility

Intergroup hostility can generate negative group experiences. An example of this phenomenon could be seen during President Bill Clinton's 1998 visit to Beijing University in Beijing, China. At the conclusion of his 40-minute address, Clinton called for questions and received about five inquiries from Chinese students. All the questions pertained to "touchy" subjects, and to American observers it appeared that the Chinese students were attacking the American way of life by these critical questions. Quite probably, immediately after the question-and-answer session, both groups had a heightened animosity.

The negative aspect of intergroup hostility can be reduced by carefully selecting the active participants and preparing them for their roles. It is certain that President Clinton prepared carefully for the session with the Beijing students and, thus, was better able to respond effectively to the pejorative aspects of the questions. In short, confrontations are better managed by up-front efforts than by on-the-spot interventions, which often reduce to the survival of the fittest and increase intergroup divisions.

Ignorance

A lack of information can cause a negative group experience. In many instances, it is a matter of not having important information about the other group. For instance, a group of White graduate students attended a conference at Hampton Institute, Hampton, Virginia, a primarily Black institution. At a convocation, the pubic address system spontaneously sounded "Lift

Every Voice and Sing," the song that is often referred to as the Black national anthem. The White graduate students continued to talk and remained seated while the African Americans stood in silence. There was a moment of tension until someone nearby said, "Stand up," which the White students did. This could have been prevented by correct information prior to the meeting.

Insensitivity (Nonempathy)

A failure of empathic understanding can be a source of a negative group experience. For instance, some members of a northern Protestant church attended a baptismal service in Louisiana. When the persons being baptized rose from beneath the water, the visitors laughed and giggled loudly. The locals remained silent and quite reverent. The laughter occurred again, and the locals became resentful. When it happened a third time, several of the locals stared menacingly at the visitors who had failed to empathically understand the solemnity of the occasion to the Louisianans. Greater empathy could have prevented the incident.

Dysfunctional Child Rearing

With all the books written about parenting, it seems impossible that any dysfunctional child-rearing practices remain. Unfortunately, they do. Most parents would be able to give a reasonable answer to the question, "What do children need to grow up healthy?" Their responses would probably include something like good food, a safe environment, good schools, and plenty of love and affection. Although these aspects seem straightforward, the data regarding their implementation are not encouraging.

Obesity in childhood is on the rise, as it is among the rest of the American population (Rossner, 1998) such that currently almost one quarter of children in the United States are obese (Bar-Or et al., 1998). If children are getting good food, then they are getting too much of it. Unfortunately, that is not likely all the problem. With the rise of fast food restaurants, more and more families eat out on a regular basis. The food served in these establishments is largely high fat. A quarter-pound cheeseburger may contain as many as 60 grams of fat, and along with french fries and a milk shake, the caloric value of this single meal might exceed 1,000 calories.

As time in front of the television has increased, active play has declined, resulting in children who are overweight and less fit (Bar-Or et al., 1998). The advertisements during children's programming are largely devoted to high-sugar cereals, candy bars, snack foods, or toys. Children focus more on food and may seek to satisfy hunger with these foods of choice. In spite of this social phenomenon, public schools have reduced the time devoted to physical education and free play in elementary schools such that children may spend as many as 6 hours per day at school with no physical exercise. Although this response was a result of a decline in test scores and perceived need to return to the basics, the physical dimension has been overlooked.

Well, if good food is not guaranteed, what about a safe environment? Statistics show that unintentional injuries are the most likely cause of death among children between 5 and 19 years of age (Sells & Blum, 1996). Despite seat belt laws in almost every state, children are still at great risk from car accidents. Child safety seats are often not installed correctly, resulting in injury during even minor accidents. Front-seat air bags have also caused the death of children, which has generated a change in automobile design to allow the air bag to be disconnected if a child is a passenger in the front seat.

Not all of the news regarding children's health is bad (Walthall, 1998). A study of the status of children commissioned by President Clinton revealed that harmful lead levels in small children had dropped from 82% in 1976–1980 to 6.2% in 1988–1994. There was also a record low infant mortality rate, immunizations of toddlers had increased to 77%, and teen birth rates were down nationwide. However, even among this good news, it was found that increasing numbers of teens are smoking, drinking, and using illicit drugs.

The problem of violence on school campuses is of national concern. During a 6-month period in 1997–1998 there were five major shooting episodes in which students brought firearms to school and killed or injured classmates and teachers. These young men killed 17 and wounded 44 others in Mississippi, Kentucky, Arkansas, Pennsylvania, and Oregon (Cloud, 1998; Hornblower, 1998; Labi, 1998a, Witkin, Thorp, Schrof, Toch, & Scattarella, 1998). The perpetrators in these shooting sprees ranged from 11 to 15 years of age.

While in general juvenile crime is on the decline (Alter et al., 1998), the trend for other school violence is on the rise. Data reported by the Bureau of Justice Statistics and the National Center for Education Statistics ("Gangs, Violence Rise," 1998) revealed that the number of students victimized by violent crime rose by nearly 25% between 1989 and 1995. Surveys of youths 12 to 19 years of age showed that 28.4% had seen gangs in their schools in 1995 compared with 15.3% in 1989. Physical attacks and robbery also increased to 4.2% in 1995 compared with 3.4% in 1989 ("Gangs, Violence Rise," 1998).

For girls, violence is often associated with dating ("U.S. Girls Report," 1998). The Girls Report commissioned by the National Council for Research on Women found that from one fourth to one third of girls ages 15 to 19 had experienced sexual violence. Most rapists were family members, friends, or acquaintances. C. Roberts and Roberts (1998) also recognized that while the Girls Report did show some progress in test scores and athletics participation, problems remained. They said:

> But there is another finding in the "Girls Report" that makes us believe there still is a long way to go before girls feel very powerful or even good about themselves. Here is where they still are very different from boys: Girls are twice as likely to be depressed. They attempt suicide more often and suffer from eating disorders. . . . And a lot of girls report that the reason they smoke is to hold down their weight. (p. 17A)

We have already addressed the problem of lack of physical education in public schools, but what else is right or wrong with public education? In a pathfinding study of effective teaching, D. Aspy and Roebuck (1996) found that students of teachers who offered high-level empathic conditions were more likely to be at school, to achieve higher test scores, to have fewer discipline problems, and to improve academic achievement. Even though these skills could be taught to teachers, without training, teachers scored an average of 1.7 where a score of 3 was minimally facilitative (D. Aspy, 1986; D. Aspy & Roebuck, 1984). These findings have been substantiated by numerous researchers, including Goodlad (1984) and Sizer (1984).

Our final recommendation for the elements contributing to healthy child rearing is plenty of love and affection, and we address this issue in the next section. However, the preceding sections paint a grim picture of child rearing in the United States today. We are increasingly a society of haves and have-nots, and more children live in poverty than ever before. Wicker (1996) reported that in 1976, 25 million Americans lived in poverty, and by 1983, nearly 33 million were defined as poor. The trend has continued upward, and in 1993, nearly 36.5 million Americans (13.7% of the population) were below the poverty level. Unfortunately, children are overrepresented with a poverty rate of 20.5 (Famighetti, 1998).

Dysfunctional Family

In the late 1950s and early 1960s, television portrayed the idealized American family in shows such as *Ozzie & Harriet*, *The Donna Reed Show*, and *Leave It to Beaver*. Each family had a father, two or more children, and a stay-at-home mom whose primary responsibility was to solve the problem of "what's for dinner?" This was a serene, perhaps idealized world, not troubled by drugs, gangs, or promiscuous sexual behavior, and for the most part it mirrored the family structure of the times. However, Lipset (1996) suggested that a longer view of history would judge this period as an anomaly and not the way America always was.

In 1963, the percentage of households containing married couples with children was at an all-time high of 51.5%. In 1997, that number was 35.7% ("American Families," 1998). Single-parent families have been on the increase since 1970 and in 1997 the proportion was about 14%. However, the rate doubled between 1970 and 1990 from 6% to 12% but increased only about 2% between 1990 and 1997 ("American Families," 1998). This change in single-parent families is due in part to the divorce rate, which also increased during that time period. However, the divorce rate has declined since 1985, and in 1997 was 4.1 per 1,000 people ("American Families," 1998).

When poverty is considered, differences can be found. In 1996, about 10% of poor White children lived with both parents, compared with 28% of poor Black children. Children who lived with their mother only included 27% of poor White children and 44% of poor Black children. Translated into financial status, for these female-headed households, 27% of White families and 44% of Black families were classified as poor (Famighetti, 1998).

Births to single women have steadily increased from 26.6% in 1990 to 32.6% in 1994. This trend tends to be typical of other wealthy nations ("Home Alone," 1993, Popenoe, 1988; N. Wood, 1993) and may be due to less frequent marriage, cohabitation for younger unmarried couples, and marriage later in life (Lipset, 1996).

Given that the structure of the American family has changed, what impact has that phenomenon had on the quality of life for children? We know that increasingly more children are living in poverty, and that poverty brings with it a worldview that is less hopeful for the future. Poverty also increases the likelihood that children (a) do not receive good health care, (b) have a less enriching home environment that may delay their reading skills, (c) may live in higher crime neighborhoods, and (d) have more anxiety at home because of the stress of poverty and a more chaotic environment.

It is difficult to determine whether children are in fact receiving the kind of nurturing they require for healthy development regardless of the conditions of the home life from which they come. We can only surmise that those children who do not successfully exit childhood with a positive self-identity and goals for the future did not receive all the love, discipline, and affection required for healthy development.

We do know that in homes in which compulsive behaviors such as alcoholism, gambling, and drug addiction are present, children are more likely to internalize the chaos of the environment and develop emotional or mental health problems (Woititz, 1983). It is estimated that there are at least 10 million alcoholics in the United States and that they have a catastrophic impact on the workforce, their families, and themselves (Woititz, 1983).

Child abuse is also rampant in the United States, and almost every community can identify a recent tragedy in which parents have fatally injured a child. Usually after the death of the child, investigations reveal that he or she has been beaten repeatedly, sometimes treated, and then returned to the parents who ultimately cause the child's death. The cases that come to light are shocking in their violence, and yet child abuse is a secret crime, perpetrated on the weakest members of society who cannot speak in their own behalf.

Dysfunctional Religious System

One of the most dearly held rights in the United States is the freedom to practice the religion of choice without interference or prejudice by the government. This is a sacred right and one that does not lend itself easily to analysis and evaluation. However, there are some criteria that can be used to test all religious organizations. These criteria are not meant to be evaluative for any individual but provide for the individual a framework for applying individual values.

Racial or Ethnic Cleansing

Many religions exist within the context of a particular racial or ethnic group. This interpretation of the Divine for a single group may provide comfort and security and a sense of family. However, difficulties arise when one religious group sees its purpose as the destruction of another racial or ethnic group. In recent years, we have seen such difficulties in Iraq, Bosnia, Ireland, and Somalia. This use of religion as an excuse for ethnic cleansing, political power, or tribal warfare may leave its followers with a dysfunctional worldview.

Counselors who work with female clients from these parts of the world or those who may have grown up in religious communities in the United States that hold unique views of race and ethnicity should be aware of the role that religion has played in the development of the client's view of herself within the confines of her religion. Individuals who have experienced the turmoil of war or terrorism in the name of religion may be particularly resistant to change and may act out their aggression toward other groups when the original group is no longer accessible.

Gender Inequity

There are many religions in the world today that hold a patriarchal view of women. From the account of creation in the Judeo-Christian Bible, many have interpreted that women are inferior to men, and in Aristotle's view women rank somewhere between animals and slaves. This interpretation of the world order as ordained by God makes it impervious to change.

Because gender inequity is common in the United States today, it is also common in many religions in varying forms. The Roman Catholic Church (RCC) does not allow women to be priests. The RCC also defines divorce, birth control, and abortion as sins against God. For Catholic women who may have committed one of these supposed sins, the guilt may be extreme, and they may also be estranged from the support previously provided by the church.

At a national meeting in June 1998, the Southern Baptists adopted a proclamation that "a wife is to submit graciously to the servant leadership of her husband, even as the church willingly submits to the headship of Christ" (Moulton, 1998). Mabel Claire Maddrey, a 91-year-old Southern Baptist, voiced the concern of many women when she stated that she could not understand why, in 1998, "any woman would vote to sacrifice the independence of other women" (Bragg, 1998, p. 13A). Frank Ruff, a Roman Catholic priest, suggested that this statement would hurt the Baptists in their evangelizing since "the word 'submit' has come to mean oppressive domination" (Moulton, 1998, p. 19).

Women who have grown up in such religions may also hold this view, and for them it may be dysfunctional as they strive to develop their talents and abilities. For these women, counseling should provide a means for articulating competing values and selecting a hierarchy with which the woman can live her life in growth and contentment. Ultimately, the problem for women in religions that do not allow them to assume leadership roles is how to integrate their beliefs about women's roles while at the same time developing their professional or work identities.

Separatist or Cult Movements

One of the most controversial cults of recent times was the Branch Davidians who set up a compound near Waco, Texas. When a warrant for the leader of this cult, David Koresh, was served, a violent clash ensued in which lives were lost by both the FBI (4 killed and 15 wounded) and the cult (unknown). Following this initial clash, a 51-day standoff was televised on a daily basis. Finally, the FBI attempted to end the standoff on April 19, 1993, and the compound burned (Scruggs et al., 1993). There were 75 lives lost, including 25 children, and this, too, was the lead story for the evening news that night.

This cult led a separatist life-style as a religious community. However, there were reports of illegal sexual practices involving both children and adults. Children who may have been raised in such environments provide a difficult challenge for counselors. Their ideas of God, adults, power, authority, and reasonable expectations for treatment are intertwined, and counselors must help such clients sort through these concepts layer by layer to ensure that prejudice does not emerge, usually in the victim state.

All individuals learn about the world through the environments in which they grow and this reality makes the status quo very difficult to change. Socialization or engenderment can take many destructive forms for the individual who comes to believe that she is less worthy because she is a woman. Empowerment is a process by which an individual can, despite her previous socialization, come to believe that the way things are is not the way they have to be—that change can occur and that it can be good.

The MMPPR uses five phases that cycle through individual issues, then social issues, and finally political issues. In the following dialogue, Helen and her counselor are initially in Phase 3 and move into Phase 5 as Helen develops a program of action to change the social environment that gave rise to the prejudicial situation of which she was a victim. By taking action to change her view of an appropriate social order, Helen will be empowered and will thus shape the environments in which she will participate in the future. The dialogue between Helen and her counselor highlights this process.

The Case of Helen

Counselor: You've worked very hard these past few weeks on your personal issues, how are things progressing with your school work?

Helen: I haven't done anything other than to continue my course work. I don't know what else I can do really.

Counselor: You're conflicted between wanting justice and pursuing it.

Helen: I was so discouraged after talking with my husband about the suit—it would just be such a big mess that I know I can't do that. But to think that he [the professor] is getting away with this makes me furious! How many other women will he affect if I don't do something? That's really my dilemma. I don't want to just continue my studies knowing that next year or the year after, he'll discriminate against another woman and she may not have the resources I do.

Counselor: You feel compelled to make the situation better for those who will come after you.

Helen: (Laughs.) You know, I never really thought of myself as a feminist or anything like that. I grew up in a home that was ruled by men, and I just accepted my "wifely" role without question. Now that Bill and I have worked through these issues, I can't believe I was so stupid. If we have a girl, I don't want to raise her with those values, I want her to feel like she can do anything her heart desires—and so does Bill. So, yes, I have to do something. I talked with several of the other women in the program and we are planning to meet each week to talk about our problems and at least try to support one another. Maybe we could do something as a group. (Pauses) You know, maybe we really could! They are much more likely to listen to us as a group than if any one of us goes in to complain!

Counselor: You're really excited that this may be the direction to take.

Helen: I feel like a weight has been lifted! I don't feel very powerful myself, but there are some really strong women in our program, and I am sure that we can make something happen together!

[A session about 2 weeks later.]

Counselor: What kind of progress has your women's group made?

Helen: We had a real breakthrough yesterday! We finally had a meeting with the department chair, and it was very helpful. He suggested that we file a grievance—my case was just one of many this man has created—with the dean to put everything into a formal process. The dean will assign a committee to hear the grievance, and we have all agreed to abide by their decision. No one has ever filed a grievance against him before, and that is really amazing. He has been there 6 years, and the stories we have been collecting are appalling. It really makes you wonder why women just accept the treatment and go on, but I guess I should speak only for myself. A year ago, I wouldn't have done this, but somehow the thought of having a daughter has made me look at the world from a different perspective.

Counselor: You are proud of your new-found courage.

Helen: More than you could ever imagine! I feel like a new person — the future is hopeful. I believe that Bill and I will raise our daughter so that she will always feel this way. She will always believe that she is valuable and that how she is treated is important.

Summary

The social and cultural factors that contribute to prejudice include negative social and cultural identity, negative intergroup experience, negative child rearing, dysfunctional families, and dysfunctional religious systems. Each of these areas contributes to the likelihood that individuals experiencing them will be at a much greater risk of prejudice either as a victim or a perpetrator.

Unfortunately, the number of children exposed to these factors is on the rise, and we can expect future concomitant increases in prejudicial behaviors in the future. The main strategy for eliminating these negative social and cultural factors involves education with prevention in mind. There are programs that have been shown to be effective in each problem area. What we need is an avenue for delivering the educational programs to children at the developmentally appropriate time. School counselors can have a major role in addressing these issues in the school curriculum or referring children and families to community agencies for assistance.

Helen was empowered by her rejection of powerlessness that had been part of her engenderment as less important because she was female. The process of rejecting this role was difficult and required the support of her counselor, her husband, and other women graduate students. The effect of her empowerment will cross generations as she provides an environment for her daughter that will socialize her into new expectations for equality.

Counselors have an important role in changing the future of women by addressing the social ills that contribute to unhealthy individual behavior. Every female client who refuses to accept destructive actions from others changes the future for those who come after her. Through education as well as therapy, counselors can change expectations for equity, and once these expectations have been raised, society will never be the same.

Applications for Counselors

Counselors who help women overcome the socialization process and engenderment will make these women aware of their own behaviors that perpetuate these processes in themselves, their friends, and their families.

Change processes at the social level may involve counselor or client activities such as:

- Becoming a mentor or leader for a girls' organization such as scouting, church youth group, service club, and vocational or professional organizations.
- Working for social justice by organizing or participating in lobbying of state and federal legislators.
- Volunteering at a women's shelter.
- Developing a literacy program for immigrant women.
- Organizing a "clothes closet" for poor women who need more professional clothing for interviews and new jobs.
- Reading community development literature or Web sites to understand positive ways to influence asset development within a community. (The Search Institute literature and Web site are especially helpful. They also have a listserv at http://www.searchinstitute.org.)

6

Political Strategies
for Prejudice Prevention
and Reduction

I t is difficult to define the term *politics*. Of course, there are
multiple definitions in various reference books, but the real-
world question is, What does it mean in daily life? That is, how
does politics work in the space where I live?

Politics is about power. To individuals, power is about using
personal assets to make things happen in the external world.
Recently, several news sources reported that Bill Gates, chairman of Microsoft, is worth $51 billion. That makes him the
world's richest man. He has financial power. Wherever money
is a critical component in decision making, Bill Gates can exert
considerable power. He can make things happen.

Michael DeBakey is a renowned heart surgeon who developed the coronary artery bypass graft surgical procedure that

has saved many thousands of lives during the latter part of the 20th century. When Boris Yeltsin, president of Russia, was gravely ill with heart problems, the Russian officials invited Dr. DeBakey to advise them. In this situation, in which technical expertise in medicine was required, Dr. DeBakey was very powerful, but because money was not at issue, Bill Gates had no standing.

The point is that power is relative to the situation, and frequently, there are many sources of power. The power derived from politics is the ability to orchestrate the factors that bear upon a decision so that a desired outcome is achieved. In this sense, politics must be understood in terms of the roles of the disparate elements that participate in a decision-making situation.

The purpose of this chapter is to provide an overview of types and sources of power. To be empowered, women must understand how power is used in the political or decision processes. This understanding is key because power is only operationalized in decisions. Therefore, we provide a seven-step process for operationalizing power through the decision process. We begin, however, with a definition of power.

Power

If politics is about power, then it is necessary to understand power. Thurow (1996) wrote:

> In democratic-capitalistic societies power comes from two sources—wealth and political position. Over the past two centuries two factors have allowed these two power systems based on antithetical principles about the right distribution of power to co-exist. First, it has always been possible to convert economic power into political power or, conversely, political power into economic power. Few held one without the other. Second, government has been used actively to alter market outcomes and generate a more equal distribution of income than would have been produced in the market if it had been left alone. (p. 242)

Thurow (1996) explained the articulation between economic power and political power by stating, "the politician's power can substitute for his lack of money, and the businessman's economic power can substitute for his lack of political power" (p. 251).

West (1993) took an activist view of power and described how citizens could influence its flow. West offered "the new cultural politics of difference," which he contended "embraces the distinct articulations of talented contributors to culture who desire to align themselves with demoralized, demobilized, depoliticized and disorganized people in order to empower and enable social action and, if possible, to enlist collective insurgency for the expansion of freedom, democracy, and individuality" (p. 4).

West (1993) explained that participants in the new cultural politics faced three challenges: intellectual, existential, and political. The intellectual trap was composed of reductionism on one side and aestheticism on the other. The existential challenge is the problem of gaining enough resources to effectively call for reform, and the political challenge is the formation of alliances of people who are able to bring about reform. In this vein, West (1993) cautioned, "In a world in which most of the resources, wealth and power are centered in huge corporations and supportive political elites, the new cultural politics of difference may appear to be solely visionary, utopian and fanciful" (p. 31). Nevertheless, West continued with this assertion:

> The time has come for critics and artists of the new cultural politics of difference to cast their nets widely, flex their muscles broadly and thereby refuse to limit their visions, analyses and praxis to their particular terrains. The aim is to dare to recast, redefine and revise the very notions of "modernity," "mainstream," "margins," "difference," "otherness." (p. 31)

Essentially, West's call is to use intellectual and political means to alter the current structures so that they include more, perhaps all, of humanity.

The Unpopularity of Politics

Politics is concerned with power, yet it is an unpopular topic. DiOnne (1991) asserted, "Americans have come to hate politics . . . the faith of the American people in their democratic institutions has declined, and Americans have begun to doubt their ability to improve the world through politics. . . we still praise democracy incessantly and recommend democracy to the world. But at home, we do little to promote the virtues that self-government requires or encourage citizens to believe that public engagement is worth the time" (p. 10). Johnson (1994) wrote, "There are many reasons the political system remains under siege. An elemental one is that the American political system has produced a generation of politicians in both parties who can't, or won't, tell the truth, because if they do, they will not win; and that lies permeate American politics" (p. 329). In this same vein, Wolfe (1998) stated:

> Those who carry out the actions of government, especially politicians, are transformed into people who lose a sense of impact their actions have on others. There are four aspects of the way politicians act that stand in striking sharp contrast to the ways we act with our friends and neighbors: To capture and remain in power, they have to compromise, become dependent on wealth, speak in loud rather than soft tones, and substitute ideology for common sense. (pp. 293 – 294)

The Necessity of Politics

Despite its unpopularity, the political process is essential for a democracy, and for women to be empowered, they must become increasingly involved in politics and in the struggle for change that will provide equal representation and equality for women. Recognizing the importance of politics and the decline of the process in our time, Johnson (1994) wrote:

> What politicians define as good politics is the ability of opposing camps to sit down and forge common interests through debate and

arduous efforts to arrive at consensus. Americans increasingly do the opposite. They attempt to resolve questions by taking them to the courts instead of permitting the political system to solve them. Thus, litigation strategies replace political strategies; too often, conflict rather than compromise is the chosen political path. . . . All of which leads to what Cain [Berkeley political scientist] calls the decline of effective politics through greater polarization on issues dividing public life, a polarization in which well-financed groups representing sharply differing ideological positions dominate the increasingly rancorous debates. (p. 332)

In short, the political process has been corrupted from what it ought to be as well as what democracy needs it to be and requires restoration. Because women tend to work more effectively within teams, they are ideal candidates to influence the political process to a more consensus-building approach. In the following sections, we outline a seven-step model that women can use to influence effective political processes.

Step I: Multidimensional Thinking

Musical solos are interesting and, depending on the talent of the soloist, may be entertaining, even inspiring. The same may be said of duets, trios, quartets, quintets, sextets, and so on. A symphony orchestra can be awesome. But, each increment in the number of instruments increases the complexity of the conductor's task. As more players enter the production, the greater is the sum of the elements to be orchestrated into a total product. Thus, successful symphony orchestra conductors such as Segei Ozawa are capable of synchronizing a vast array of elements into a dynamic harmony. When the harmony breaks down, the conductors are able to restore it because they understand how it operates. They comprehend multidimensional space, which is to say simply that many factors are operating simultaneously.

In politics, democracy has expanded the significance of multidimensional thinking in terms of decision making. Where power is centralized, such as in a dictatorship, the almost singular concern is to influence the dictator who acts unilaterally. In many instances, this is referred to as "sucking up" to power. But, in a democracy, where power is dispersed, the task of influencing the various contributors to decisions is more complex and requires multidimensional thought.

Multidimensional thinking is largely a matter of visualizing an object in motion and then of comprehending the array of forces that contribute to its movement. The operative word is *forces*. The plural form indicates that the observer recognizes that the event is a product of a variety of factors. In a sense, this indicates that the person has matured beyond the level of attributing occurrences to a single, capricious, and all-powerful individual.

Step 2: Diagnose the Present Situation

Multidimensional thinking leads to an analysis of the factors that influence a decision. This process begins with a diagnosis in the form of a clear statement of the status quo. For instance, at the outset of President Clinton's 1998 trip to China, the American policy was one of engagement, which was widely interpreted as a willingness to enter into exchanges that are beneficial to both parties. If engagement is an unsatisfactory policy to a certain group, then that group can embark on an effort to change the policy which, in America, involves political means. But, it is important that the group must first identify the starting point. The members must be certain of the point of their disagreement.

Step 3: Analyze the Why of the Present Situation

The next step is to analyze why the policy (decision) was made. Essentially, there are two components to that question: Who made the decision and why did they make it? The *who* element is answered by specifying the participants in the decision, and the *why* element is a matter of discerning the reasons for their views. This reduces to an enumeration of the interests that led to the opinions that produced the decision. An example of this analysis for a school board decision to offer only softball and basketball to girls can be found in Table 6.1 .

Step 4: State a Goal

Having specified the current policy and the reasons for it, members of the change group must identify the decision or policy they favor. This is simply to articulate what is wanted. It is one thing to know what is not wanted but it is quite another to state clearly what is desired. Translated into action terms, it means to know what one is for. This allows the group to become proactive rather than reactive.

Step 5: Design a Program

If a group (or individual) knows what decision it wants, then it can articulate the precise shifts that are needed to attain the preferred choice. That is, it knows what must be done. The change procedures must specify the alterations that are to occur to alter the decision makers' choices to the ones the change group desires. In short, the question becomes, How can we change the views of the decision makers or how can we

TABLE 6.1
Decision Analysis Example

Issues for the Special Interest Group	Issues for the Majority or Status Quo Group
• Opportunities for girls to participate in a variety of team sports • Equal treatment for girls and boys • Increased visibility for female athletes could mean additional college scholarships	• Costs for additional teams owing to personnel, travel, uniforms, referees, etc. • Fear of community reprisal for budget reductions in male sports • Belief that continued debate could lead to community dissatisfaction and continued polarization

change the structure of the decision-making process? Thus, the procedure specifies the subgoals to be accomplished.

When goals are identified, the next assignment is to devise tasks that will attain those goals. For example, if the goal is to get Organization A to change its stance to Position X, then the problem is to select the tasks that will lead to that goal. When all the tasks are defined and aligned, they constitute the program the change group can implement to accomplish its objective. In many instances the program is called a campaign.

Step 6: Select Tactics or Means

Power is seen mainly in terms of money and political position, but it comes in a wide variety of forms. For instance, during the civil rights movement Martin Luther King, Jr., employed nonviolent resistance, which was epitomized by tactics such as not riding the public transportation facilities in Montgomery, Alabama, and boycotting restaurants. Also, in the civil rights effort, Jesse Jackson organized voter registration drives and others attended the world's finest universities to gain access to "the establishment." So, the task is to identify one's power and to use it effectively with the assumption that everyone has some power.

It is said that Sol Alinsky, famed advisor to civil rights groups, spoke to some Black activists in Chicago and told them that their skin color was a source of great power. Of course, many of them believed their blackness was their deficit. Alinsky explained that one of the White middle class's major fears was that their daughters would become "involved" with Black men. He continued by stating that Black men should use that fear by "hanging around" the places where White girls recreated so that their White fathers would become concerned about the activities of the African American men. From such tactics came many social efforts such as recreation centers and better schools for African American citizens.

Athletics is a source of social power. Americans want to do well in Olympic competition so they rather handsomely subsidize some of the athletes who can enhance the United States' scoring total. Likewise, professional athletes are paid exorbitant salaries to perform tasks that elude "ordinary" people. The remuneration and its fringe benefits enable professional athletes to develop sources of power.

Access to media is a source of power. Various social and political marches have followed that path. When masses of people gather to support a cause, the media usually cover the event and give spokespersons access to the media.

Embarrassment is a source of power. Small children learn of that power early on. Often in public places they flop on the floor and throw a tantrum so that their embarrassed parents concede anything just to keep the youngster from attracting more negative attention. In a similar vein, a pastor of a large, affluent Protestant church got into a controversy with his governing board about whether or not to relocate the downtown church to a suburban area. The board voted to move, but the pastor refused to budge. When the board cut funds to upgrade the present structure, the pastor initiated a campaign in which people brought pennies in jars to save the church. Each Sunday, while on local TV, the children paraded past the pastor and dropped their jars into a bucket. This maneuver so embarrassed the affluent congregation that it reneged on its budget cuts and acceded to the pastor's demand to stay downtown.

A major error in selecting means is to overestimate the giant sources of power and to underestimate the small ones. For instance, small events have influenced history greatly. Gerald Ford's campaign for president was influenced drastically when he bumped his head, slipped, and fell down the steps while disembarking from a helicopter. That incident underscored the perception that he was a clumsy clod. Michael Dukakis's presidential effort never recovered from the picture of him wearing a helmet while standing in the turret of a tank. It depicted him as a clown. Then, there was the moment during a national presidential debate when an ordinary-looking lady asked George Bush if he knew the cost of a loaf of bread. When he did not give a reasonable answer, it reinforced the image that he was out of touch with the average person.

Another example of the appropriate selection of tactics involved a school board's decision to auction off a small building that was no longer in use. One bidder who owned a bar wanted to convert the premises into another bar for working men. A second bidder wanted to convert the place into a mission church for low-income people. It was one of those moments when good and evil seemed to collide head on. The mission group had only $400 to bid. The bar owner had extensive funds and a solid line of credit at the bank. But the woman who was bidding for the mission group had a source of power and a tactic for using it.

The bidding opened and the bar owner bid $300. The woman bidding for the mission group said, "$400." Then, she walked to the first bidder, whispered into his ear, and returned to her seat. The auctioneer called for more bids but none came. The room fell silent as the auctioneer stood incredulous. He said, "I can't believe a building of this quality would sell for $400." Still, there were no more bids. Finally, the auctioneer pounded the gavel and said, "Sold." What did the woman whisper to the bar owner? No one knows, but whatever it was, it had power, and the woman used it effectively to achieve her goal.

A state committee hired a consulting team to produce a list of recommendations that would upgrade the state's juvenile justice system. The entire committee gathered to listen to the consultants' report, which focused on rehabilitating rather than punishing juvenile offenders. The details were rather ingenious and held a great deal of promise for an educational approach to juvenile justice.

As the report unfolded, the committee members' resistance increased noticeably. The statement had dire implications for the existing system. Whole power domains were threatened. For instance, one juvenile incarceration institution was to be closed and if it was, it meant that the town's only bank would close because most of its deposits came from the juvenile justice center. One of the committee's members also served on the bank's board.

The committee broke for lunch, and the chairperson told the head consultant that things looked bleak. Immediately after lunch the committee members bombarded the consultants with searing questions. All seemed lost until the head consultant made her concluding remarks during which she observed, "I am surprised at this group's reaction. I have heard many comments about economics and even inconvenience. But, I have heard nothing about what is good for kids. This report is good for kids." Then she sat down.

The report was accepted unanimously. The head consultant understood and used the power of conviction that when something is morally right, it deserves a voice. She could make her statement because she was fully convinced that the report was good for children and that her silence would leave them with no advocate. Conviction and the courage to give it voice are essential if women are to be politically effective.

Step 7: Know the Rules and Make Them Work for You

It seems rather fundamental that participants should know the rules that govern their activity, but many fail that very test. It is not that they are totally ignorant of the rules but rather that they have not mastered them. Yet, in politics, it is essential to know the rules.

Rules describe the field of play. Activity outside those lines is illegal but everything inside them is legal. However, there usually are two sets of rules: theoretical and actual. For instance, the police usually give drivers a bit of leeway in traffic speed. The legal speed limit is the theoretical rule, but the actual speed limit is the rule that is enforced. It is important to know both.

Lyman Johnson, famed civil rights worker in Louisville, Kentucky, was an avid student of civil rights legislation. His catchphrase was to "know the rules and play hard inside them." During proceedings, he was apt to call his opponents' hands at any point that fell outside the lines (personal communication, March 24, 1988).

Playing hard inside the lines is a critical corollary of knowing the rules, especially if one's strategy is geared to the rules of the game. Small exceptions can be crucial. For example, attorneys often "sneak" in a comment that is outside the rules just to send a message to the jury. The opponent's objection does not always remove the idea from the jury's mind.

Playing hard is a dynamic quality in that it occurs during the process. Unless one plays hard, planning and preparation may be pointless. In fact, the best plan can be defeated by poor execution. Politics often is a rough, competitive activity, and the participants must be prepared physically, intellectually, and emotionally to engage in it.

For women, the socialization process puts them at a disadvantage in confrontations. Women are taught and expected to be polite, patient, and never to interrupt; to play by the rules; and to be gracious at all costs. However, the games of power require that women step out of their socialization to achieve equal stature. When the rules are unfair, then usually a political process is required to change them. In the case of Helen, by working with other women graduate students, Helen was able to reframe the problem from an individual one to a much broader one. She worked with this group to achieve success by using current rules as a standard for measuring the equity of the interview process and holding her professor accountable for his actions. The following case summary describes the strategy by which she was able to use the political process for her benefit.

The Case of Helen

Helen asked for assistance because she felt powerless in a situation that was clearly unfair. Through the counseling process, she came to understand that certain components of her situation were beyond her, namely, the rules of the job interview process were part of the problem. As a result of Phase 4 in the

Multidimensional Model for Prejudice Prevention and Reduction (MMPPR), Helen decided that she wanted to change the rules of the interview process. At that point, her counselor used Phase 5 of the MMPPR, which uses behavioral techniques to support behavioral change. From her expertise, the counselor explained the seven steps of political action and consulted with Helen as she implemented them. The counselor asked herself:

1. Is Helen thinking multidimensionally?
2. Is Helen diagnosing the present situation?
3. Is Helen diagnosing the causes of the present situation?
4. Is Helen certain of what she wants?
5. Does Helen have a program to accomplish her goals?
6. Is Helen considering a range of ways to accomplish her goals?
7. Does Helen know the rules of the process?

Implicit in the entire process is the counselor's concern for Helen's fundamental preparation for the effort. Is she physically, emotionally, and intellectually fit enough to undertake the project of altering something beyond herself? If not, then the counselor must help Helen understand that she must accept that her choices are either to diminish her chances of success or to take time to prepare herself adequately for the effort.

Summary

Politics is about power. It is the ability to orchestrate the decision-making process in a desired direction, and it is especially important in democratic situations. To participate effectively in politics, participants should know the following:

1. How to think multidimensionally
2. What the present situation is (diagnosis)
3. How the present situation got to be the way it is (analysis)
4. What is wanted (goal)

5. How to accomplish what is wanted (program)
6. How to generate and evaluate a variety of ways to achieve the goal (tactics)
7. What rules govern these activities (implementation)

Success in politics is determined by three basic dimensions: diagnosis, goal setting, and a program for action. In addition, there is a need for skillful execution of the program that includes using feedback to alter the activities as they unfold.

Applications for Counselors

Because power is achieved through influencing decisions, counselors may recommend exercises or activities for clients to help them develop a sense of personal power. Exercises might include:

- Participating in a neighborhood association to influence city zoning decisions.
- Running for political office or helping another woman run for office.
- Lobbying on behalf of a personally meaningful cause before local, state, or federal authorities.
- Influencing a meaningful change within the family or work environment.

Counselors might also encourage clients to use the seven-step model to make one significant change in their own lives to further develop their sense of personal power.

Section III

Competencies Required for Gender Equity

When Rudyard Kipling defined the components of manhood in his poem, "If," he stressed the stoic qualities of the warrior. Although some of Kipling's metaphors do not speak to women, the message in his poem is the notion of the cause-and-effect relationships among behavior, attitude, planning, and outcome. His message was essentially that if you believe in yourself, if you act in accordance with those beliefs, and if you plan for all contingencies, then you will become a mature individual (whether male or female). This section is devoted to exactly those same ends with a caveat that our purpose is to help counselors facilitate the empowerment of women to achieve equity in the new millennium.

We believe there are competencies that will contribute to the successful growth and development of young women if they have the opportunity to develop them. We have categorized these competencies into the physical, emotional, intellectual, and spiritual, because these areas of development have been tested across the centuries as the basic building blocks of character. We have Maslow to thank for articulating the needs that drive us to improve, beginning with the physical. The emotional life is one that is less well studied because notions of the unconscious are relatively recent. The intellectual ability to plan and problem solve is essential to effective, independent action. Finally, although in fact, the spiritual area is truly first, individuals must each decide why they are here and how they will live to accomplish the mission that they adopt as their own. Each person must learn how to weave these seemingly disparate pieces into a life.

We begin this section with the physical competencies because physical stamina limits one's good intentions. Whatever individuals hope to achieve must be accomplished by the whole body. Of course, we can think of tremendous contributions that were made by individuals who had significant illness or disability. These events may not be within an individual's control; however, to the degree that individuals maintain their bodies at the highest level possible, the effects of whatever illness or disability that befalls them will be lessened because they were healthy at the outset.

We define the physical skills as understanding health and how the body works, promoting health and preventing disease, conditioning, and participating in sports. Each of these areas contributes to a woman's ability to make the most of her innate talents in all areas; to find the strength and stamina to meet life's daily challenges and not be diverted from her path; and, finally, to provide the degrees of freedom essential for making choices.

The emotions reflect how people experience the world, and the emotional skills people have defined facilitate the interpretation of those experiences so that they can be used to relate in a healthy way to themselves as well as others. They help connect a person to others like herself or himself and join together in common purpose. For women, the "feminine" and the "emotional" were often believed to be interchangeable, as if women were only emotional beings. There is truth in the statement, but not the truth that is usually expected. The emotions are integral to all human functioning, and understanding their contribution to the intellectual and physical dimensions is related to mental health.

We define the emotional skills as intrapersonal, interpersonal, and networking. These areas address a woman's ability to relate to herself in a healthy way, to relate to others, and to establish and maintain mutually supportive groups. The skills in each of these areas are critical for encouraging healthy emotional development. Women (as well as men) must learn to define their emotions and the events that precipitate them.

Never before in the history of time has so much information been available to so many. The World Wide Web and the Internet have linked people globally in meaningful ways. Professionally, problems and solutions are shared with individuals one has never met. The written materials that cross workers' desks in a month are equal to what our grandparents saw in a lifetime. The intellectual skills are those that help a person problem solve in multidimensional ways so that he or she can reach solutions that match the extent of the problem.

We define the intellectual skills as processing data, communication, conquering a substantive content area, learning how to learn, and thinking critically. Increasingly, the knowledge base or content area in every field changes rapidly as a result of research and technological development. One can no longer memorize a content area and depend on that expertise for effective performance for the long term. Once conquered, a content area will change, and learning skills become critical as each person must become her or his own teacher throughout one's lifetime. Communicating one's expertise and thinking critically remain the stalwart components of the intellectual dimension.

The spiritual component of life has been associated with the higher life, how one relates to God or a higher power, or the mystical dimension of the soul. While acknowledging these levels, we believe that the spiritual competencies are related to how one comes to terms with why one is here, what one's purpose is in life, and how one should relate to others. We have defined these competencies as establishing a mission, defining values and virtues, choosing personal values and virtues, living one's values and virtues, and coming to terms with faith.

These competencies translate the spiritual dimension into practical aspects of daily living. A person is faced with hundreds of choices each day, including the tremendous variety of foods, media, newspapers, and the Internet. Without a guiding principle, he or she would be lost. By defining and adopting values and virtues, the person knows how to choose efficiently and effectively. Finally, we address the issue of faith and how it is related to the other competencies we have defined.

The concept of competencies is an important one, because everyone can devote time and energy to their development. People will not all arrive at the same place, but each person can invest in herself or himself, and this investment will pay big dividends as people work toward the accomplishment of their individual missions.

7

Physical Competencies

Physical competencies are the baseline essentials for gender equity because the energy for the struggle is either available or not. Historically, women were often viewed as the "gentler sex," and strenuous physical activity was considered unladylike except for the very few who excelled in a specific sport. Muscles and femininity did not mix, and schools did not offer the same level of physical training for girls as they did for boys (American Alliance for Health, Physical Education, Recreation, and Dance, 1995). Although progress has been made, equity has not been achieved. Executive director of the Women's Sports Foundation, Donna Lopiano, PhD, said, "The downside is it's taken 25 years, and the treatment of athletes is still uneven" (J. Lee, 1997, p. 38).

The American Alliance for Health, Physical Education, Recreation, and Dance (1995) defined gender equity as "the provision of opportunity and access and the realization of equality of results for all students based on individual aptitudes" (p. 3). The progress that has been achieved can be traced to Title IX legislation, which prohibits sex discrimination in any educational institution receiving federal funds. This legislation "applies to all programs in schools, including physical education and sport" (American Alliance for Health, Physical Education, Recreation, and Dance, 1995, p. 4).

However, to achieve the highest level of health possible, every girl and every woman must take charge of their bodies and plan for physical health. At the most basic level, making dreams a reality requires physical stamina. Clients arrive with many problems and varying amounts of energy to address them. Physical competency means having the necessary stamina to meet life's demands. As Vince Lombardi, the coach of the Green Bay Packers, said, "Fatigue makes cowards of us all."

Most of us take our health for granted. Particularly when we are young, the thought of disease or incapacity is far away, and yet the beliefs and habits that we form in our youth are so critical to the level of health we will achieve throughout our lives. For adolescents, body image has become so important that the pressure to achieve the svelte, almost emaciated look of a model has been associated with eating disorders such as anorexia nervosa and bulimia (Halmi, 1998). Firoz (1995) suggested that the pressure to be thin in order to be happy is continually reinforced through the media. She also reported a study by Luppino that indicated "that children would choose to be crippled rather than be fat" (p. 168).

A study by Children Now and the Kaiser Family Foundation found that 71% of girls ages 16 and 17 years thought that female characters on television were unrealistically thin (Labi, 1998b). She stated, "Recognizing gender stereotyping is one thing, but successfully resisting it is quite another" (p. 62). Katch and McArdle (1993) noted that the emaciated look currently associated with models is a recent trend. They said, "In 1967, professional models weighed only 8% less than the average American woman. Today their average weight is 23% lower than the national average for women" (p. 303).

Although these disorders have a complex psychological component, it is important to help young women develop an affinity for health beyond the current body image fad. For indeed, the popular look of the 1950s is now considered somewhat chubby (Edlin, Golanty, & Brown, 1998).

This chapter is organized around four competencies: (a) understanding health and how the body works, (b) health promotion and disease prevention, (c) conditioning, and (d) sports participation. Each of these areas contributes to a woman's ability to meet the demands of life by addressing those factors that will either build or diminish stamina.

Understanding Health

The first competency related to physical functioning begins with an understanding of how one's body works and what health is. Many definitions have been proffered, but the World Health Organization (1986) defined health as:

> a state of complete physical, psychological, and social well being and not simply the absence of disease or infirmity to reach which, an individual or group must be able to identify and realize aspirations, satisfy needs, and change or cope with the environment. (p. iii)

Mold (1993), a physician, offered a more expansive notion of health in his definition. He said that health is:

> defined as a process rather than a state. Features of this process of health include physical maturation and differentiation, self-actualization, development of greater adaptability and better coping skills, and the acquisition of wisdom in its broadest possible sense. (p. 2)

Peck (1993), also a physician, described health as "an ongo-ing process, often painful, of an organism becoming the most—the best—it can be" (p. 11). All of these definitions reflect a view of health that goes vastly beyond not being sick. These descriptions of health stand in sharp contrast to the mainstream medical definition of health as "The absence of discomfort, disease, or dysfunction; physical and psychological normalcy; the absence of health problems" (Mold, 1993, p. 1).

Although health professionals may define these concepts of health for their patients, research has shown that individuals may not reflect the same definitions. Colantonio (1988) studied the concepts of health of 100 participants stratified by age and sex. She interviewed all participants and used content analysis to discover six distinct definitions of health among these partic-ipants. The definitions included (a) being fit ("able to do what one needs to do"), (b) feeling well ("feeling happy" and "full of life"), (c) not being ill ("not needing medical attention"), (d) having good health behaviors ("eating well" and "getting enough rest"), (e) looking well ("good complexion" and "not overweight"), and (f) living in a healthy environment ("clean air" and "having enough money)" (pp. 4-5).

Whatever definition of health one chooses, the responsibility remains for each individual to translate that vision of health into day-by-day actions to achieve her or his own aspirations. The difficulty with this process may develop from a lack of knowledge about goal setting (see Chapter 12) or it may stem from a lack of knowledge about how the body works.

Most of us learned what we know about how the body functions by studying each system (digestive, musculatory, cardiovascular, pulmonary, etc.) in health class, and a general knowledge in this area is probably sufficient for most people. However, for women, there are three areas that need more exposition: (a) the hormonal cycle and its effect on emotions and perceptions, (b) the effect of stress on health and illness, and (c) reproduction.

For centuries, words such as *the curse* have described the menstruation cycle (Delaney, Lupton, & Toth, 1977). In some cultures in the past and in other cultures even now, women are isolated during the bleeding portion of the cycle. In many cultures, women are prohibited from visiting a temple or church during menstruation. The mystery associated with the process and paraphernalia required to contain it have long provided young girls with fears of "accidents" or rejection. A clear understanding of the stages in the cycle and an understanding of what abnormality is can help to ease these fears.

Less clearly understood are the emotional and perceptual changes that may interfere with a woman's normal cognitive and emotional functioning often included under the label of premenstrual syndrome (PMS; Rittenhouse, 1991). She noted that the social status of women has been undermined by the designation of premenstrual tension as a biological phenomenon associated with menstruation. In recent times, the three letters, PMS, have served to further disqualify women from positions of leadership and responsibility. Lorber (1994) stated, "Another example of discrimination against women on the basis of their physiology is the use of menstruation to call into question women's intellectual and physical capabilities" (p. 47).

While changes are real, they can be managed like other conditions, such as diabetes mellitus, and should not result in emotional outbursts or uncontrolled rage and truly disqualify women from any job for which they are otherwise qualified. "Know thyself" is the operative course of action. By keeping a menstrual diary, a woman can chart the presence of a number of symptoms across the monthly cycle. Patterns will be revealed across several months, and this knowledge, along with appropriate interventions, can be used to mitigate the negative effects of the hormonal cycle.

Stress and illness, or the mind-body connection, has been recognized for centuries. In the late 1950s, Hans Selyee, an endocrinologist, studied the phenomenon and defined stress as "the nonspecific response of the body to any demand made upon it" (Locke & Colligan, 1986). Selye (1956) further differentiated between stress and eustress to denote negative and positive stressors, respectively. Selye demonstrated that chronic stress can take a measurable toll on the body.

The stress response is left over from prehistoric times when humans needed the "flight or fight" capability. Today, life's challenges seldom require people to run from wild animals or fight them, but their minds still perceive threats that they cannot or should not act on and it prepares the bodies for battle. The result of this process is anxiety and the by-products of adrenaline, which make people more susceptible to disease.

Stress management is a skill to maintain health. It begins with identification of the signs of stress, such as moodiness, anxiety, depression, sleep changes, tension headaches, fatigue, and increased muscle tension. Finding the cause of the stress is the next step. Most often, stress is related to incomplete problem solving. When something goes awry in people's lives, they may not know how to correct it, so they try to cope with the changes at the same time they resist them. Pain may then become a distraction that keeps them from focusing on the real problem (Schwartz, 1995). By defining the problem and deciding on a course of action, one's anxiety is reduced, concentration improves, and ultimately stress responses decline. People cannot control the events that come into their lives, but they can manage their responses. Learning to listen to one's body, resting when one is tired, and eating when one is hungry allows one to act to prevent the negative consequences of stress.

Benson and Stuart (1992) explored the benefits of meditation on high blood pressure and discovered significant improvement after several weeks of meditation. Benson came to believe that transcendental meditation was not the only method of relaxation that could be effective, and this led to the development of specific procedures he identified as the relaxation response. To engage this response, one could, H. Benson (1975) believed, practice progressive tensing and relaxation of specific muscle groups. After the relaxation response was learned, it could be invoked in a time of stress by intentionally tensing and then relaxing the stressed muscle group. Although the research has shown varying results regarding the long-term benefits of these techniques, anecdotal evidence is very positive.

In addition to effective problem solving, exercise is an excellent way to metabolize the by-products of stress and increase the endorphins that give people a sense of well-being. Exercise will be addressed in greater detail in a later section, but it is important that every woman learn firsthand the benefits of a regular exercise and fitness program.

Childbearing is a natural process for women, but not every woman's body is equally nurturing for a fetus. The things women eat, drink, or smoke today may affect the health of a fetus at some time in the future. Smoking during pregnancy has the most convincing support in the literature as a relative risk factor for low birth weight (LBW) babies (Brook, Anderson, Bland, Peacock, & Stewart, 1989; Ferraz, Gray, & Cunha, 1990; Infante-Rivard, Fernandez, Gauthier, David, & Rivard, 1993; H. C. Miller & Jekel, 1987; Naeye, 1981). Any smoking on a daily basis will contribute to LBW risk (H. C. Miller & Jekel, 1987).

A well-executed study by Infante-Rivard et al. (1993) gives strong support for the notion that caffeine intake during pregnancy is associated with fetal loss. From the Seattle longitudinal prospective study on alcohol and pregnancy, evidence suggested that alcohol is related to impaired fetal growth (Hanson, Streissguth, & Smith, 1978; Streissguth, Martin, Martin, & Barr, 1981). Lack of folic acid in the diet may also lead to neural tube defects (Menard, 1997; Rayburn, Stanley, & Garrett, 1996).

Counselors may use a variety of techniques when working with adolescent girls or women of any age to help them develop an understanding of how their bodies work. This understanding is essential for them to be proactive in preventing problems before they happen and, if that is not possible, then to be able to respond to the problems that may interfere with optimal functioning. Prevention and problem solving are the actions that will enhance the quality of life of all women and girls. Learning these skills in adolescence will prevent the development of ineffective coping mechanisms that will have to be unlearned sometime in the future.

The current educational efforts may not be effective in defining for girls and young women those behaviors that will ensure their ability to accept gender equity. The American Alliance for Health, Physical Education, Recreation, and Dance (1995) stated, "A socially and educationally imposed hidden curriculum has taught some that being born female means the acceptance of gender appropriate behavior prioritized by compliancy, dependency, cooperation, and general physical malaise" (p. 4).

Health Promotion and Disease Prevention

Adolescence and young adulthood bring many changes into the lives of young women. Chief among the dangers at this stage of life are the high-risk behaviors of sexual activity, illegal drugs, and alcohol. Group norms and expectations bring about peer pressure to conform. In the movie, *Star Trek: First Contact* (Berman & Frakes, 1996), the Federation starship battles with the Borg who bragged, "Resistance is futile. You will be assimilated." Many young girls feel this is exactly the way things must be and that conformity is safer than resisting. However, each of these high-risk behaviors can be life threatening.

S. Scott (1986) described the skills of peer pressure reversal, or how to say no and keep one's friends. She identified the following three steps: (a) check out the scene (look and listen and ask, "Is this trouble?"); (b) make a good decision (weigh both sides and decide to stop or go); and (c) act to avoid trouble. Peer pressure is difficult for youths to handle, but these techniques were 80% effective with a group of first offenders who received the training.

Griffin, Linder, Logan-El, and Carkhuff (1987) also identified skills for handling negative peer pressure. They suggested five levels or responses to negative peer pressure. The first, Getting Caught, meant having to do what the group wants. The second level was Getting Away Negative or getting away at any cost, usually in a way that is bad for everyone. Level 3 is Getting Away Clean or getting away with the least amount of trouble for everyone. Level 4, Getting Away Positive, means getting out of a bad situation and leaving peers with a positive feeling. Level 5, Getting Away Helpful, is the highest level in handling negative peer pressure. At this level, the youth helps others as well as herself to attain positive goals.

Sexual activity among teens is much more prevalent today than it was a generation ago (Sells & Blum, 1996). With the potential for HIV infection in addition to pregnancy, the price is much higher. Many programs today focus on teaching teens to postpone sexual involvement rather than decrying sexual activity as evil. This is more than semantics. It is encouraging responsible decision making, respecting the dignity of each individual, and empowering individuals to choose wisely. Programs using this model have been highly successful (Kirby, Korpi, Barth, & Cagampang, 1997).

Although there are cases of teenage girls who became pregnant while in high school finishing their degrees, marrying responsible husbands, and successfully raising happy, well-adjusted children, this is not the modal picture. Most teenage mothers are single moms who live in poverty. They are under-educated for their abilities and are often unfit mothers because of the stress of the life-style they live. Their children may not have the resources available to them to grow up healthy and psychologically well. And the cycle may continue. One of the saddest examples of this phenomenon we have witnessed was a family of five generations of women, the oldest (age 80) and the youngest (age only 3). In between were the mother (age 19), grandmother (age 41), and great-grandmother (age 62). Each of them had raised their children in the chaos of the ghetto without the assistance of a father. The women were bright and capable, but these aspects of their personality had not been developed. However, each had paid a high price for her life-style, and all but the 19- and 3-year-old had chronic illnesses, including diabetes, hypertension, cancer, dementia, and multiple treatments for sexually transmitted disease.

An assembly sponsored by SADD (Students Against Driving Drunk) at a large, midwestern high school brought together the father of a victim and a female perpetrator of drunk driving. They told their stories of pain, loss, and recovery and left an indelible message. All their suffering was needless because it was so easily prevented.

As they left the gym, the students' faces told the story. They were sad. Some identified with the young girl whose life was snuffed out by a drunken man who was not even aware that he had killed her. Others identified with the perpetrator, a woman who had celebrated her birthday with one too many drinks and caused a man who was changing a tire on the side of the road to live out his life with only one leg. Though hard to handle, exposure to the real-life pain and suffering caused by a few moments of bad judgment is a testimony for sobriety and is an effective tool.

Conditioning

Every athlete understands the need for conditioning to reduce injury and provide stamina for the sport. This concept can easily be applied to every individual. The better the "condition," the more likely an individual can achieve her highest level of functioning both intellectually and emotionally. Maslow (1968) described the physical dimension as fundamental to achievement of higher orders of functioning, and until physical needs are met, other levels cannot be attained.

In the United States today, an estimated 55% of adults are overweight (Shapiro, 1998). This is a phenomenal statement given that this excess weight stands as a barrier to sustained performance in other dimensions of life and has been associated with diabetes mellitus, hypertension, asthma, and heart disease. The energy to solve problems and respond creatively to life's demands may not be available to many women because they are overweight and not conditioned. Every woman should have a physical fitness program to ensure that she will become the best that she can be. When working with clients, one of the most important assessments for counselors is whether or not the clients are sufficiently conditioned to meet the challenges of growth. The following sections outline the necessary information for assisting clients in developing a conditioning program. Remember that, as a counselor, you may call on other professionals to help in this process. For example, a client may need to work with a dietitian or a physical trainer to devise daily strategies to accomplish conditioning.

Any conditioning program should address two areas: diet and exercise. A local news program discussed (tongue in cheek) how an elephant got so large. The answer was, "He eats a lot and exercises little!" This summarizes the dilemma for many women who may seek shortcuts to weight loss through medications, herbs, creams, surgery, liposuction, and so forth. Unfortunately, the recent problems with the drug "Fen-Phen" (Fluoxetine and Phenfloramine) that resulted in its removal from the market can be a by-product of the "easy fix." Although these drugs were designed to treat obesity, many women with only 10 to 20 pounds to lose begged their physicians for this treatment. In some cases, this decision was fatal.

The most basic diet concept is to eat what the body needs to be healthy, no more or no less. If a person eats more food than the body can use to maintain itself and provide energy for activities, then the body will store the excess in the form of fat. The only way to remove fat is to make the body take fat from storage for its daily supply of energy. This can be done by eating less or exercising more.

A quick measure of obesity can be determined by the body mass index (BMI). Shapiro (1998) explained, "BMI is a single number representing height and weight without regard to gender: a person who is 5 feet 6 inches and weighs 137 pounds, for example, has a BMI of 22" (p. 55). The formula for computing a BMI is:

$$\frac{703 \times (\text{weight in pounds})}{(\text{height in inches})^2}$$

While the National Center for Health Statistics defines *over-weight* as above 27, the National, Heart, Lung, and Blood Institute uses 25 as the cutoff point (Shapiro, 1998).

By far, the fastest way to cut down on the calories consumed is to switch from high-fat foods to low-fat ones (Katch & McArdle, 1993). Every gram of fat contains 9 calories of energy, whereas carbohydrates and proteins contain only 4. By eating more carbohydrates and proteins, one can cut calories from one's diet without sacrificing quantity. The number of calories consumed each day depends on one's ideal body weight and activity. A quick method for determining ideal body weight for women has been recommended by H. Benson and Stuart (1992):

> Take 100 pounds for the first five feet and add five pounds for each additional inch. Once this number is determined, subtract 10 percent and add 10 percent to calculate ideal-body-weight range. (p. 156)

Weight loss should be in the range of 1 to 2 pounds per week to ensure that the loss is fat rather than muscle. The best method of weight loss involves reducing calories through eating smaller portions and less fat while increasing exercise. Aerobic exercise at least four times a week for about 20 to 30 minutes per session should be sufficient to induce weight loss (H. Benson & Stuart, 1992).

Exercise has been shown to be effective across the life span in improving quality of life (Hassmen & Koivula, 1997; Ruuska-nen & Ruoppila, 1995). It is also an investment in a person's functionality here and now by helping the person achieve the highest level of her ability. A fit body aids the mind as well as the emotions (Deuster, 1996; Pinto, Marcus, & Clark, 1996) and has been shown to positively affect PMS (Peters, 1997).

Counselors need not be experts in conditioning to aid their clients, but they may need to develop a list of resources for referral, such as the local YMCA or other physical conditioning experts. Counselors must also be aware of the role they play in modeling desired behaviors for their clients. It is difficult to advocate for physical fitness when one is not a practitioner.

Sports Participation

Since the implementation of Title IX and, thus, increased access to organized sports programs for women, participation in sports has been increasing across the life span. Young (1990) suggested that girls were often socialized into being less participative in sports because they were taught to be more restrictive with their bodies. Thus, tennis and golf once dominated the sports enjoyed by most women because a woman could still be "ladylike" and participate. Today, these notions have changed, and women participate in sports across the life span; even teams for soccer, softball, and basketball are abundant.

The notion of women fully participating in sports is a relatively recent phenomenon. In fact, Baron Pierre de Coubertin, the founder of the Modern Olympic Games, believed that women were "unsuited physiologically and psychologically for the stresses of elite international athletic competitions" (Lucas, 1992, p. 2).

The first World Olympics in which women participated was in 1900 when they competed in golf and tennis. Each Olympics since that time, women's participation has increased significantly, and this visibility has done a great deal to refute the confused and unscientific notion that women and sports should not mix. For example, in the 1912 Olympics in Stockholm, Sweden, only 57 women competed, whereas the 1996 Olympics in Atlanta, Georgia, had 2,447 women competitors (Lucas, 1992). Although only the young and most fit compete in the Olympics, women (as men have for years) can continue sports participation across the life span not only for the pleasure of the sport but also for fitness.

One of the major benefits of team sports participation is the opportunity to learn the skills of teamwork. For years, women were not viewed as "team players." Although that criticism may have been used as a form of bias, it was also true that few women had ever participated actively in team sports. The whole notion of team building and the psychology of this process were foreign to most women. Since Title IX, things have changed drastically. Labi (1998b) said, "Today, a record 2.5 million girls compete on high school teams, compared with 300,000 in the early 70s" (p. 62). The American Alliance for Health, Physical Education, Recreation, and Dance (1995) recognized that 35% of all high school athletes are girls and attributed the change to Title IX.

Sports participation should be a lifetime commitment. A sport that is enjoyable and allows for skill development is much more likely to keep one involved in the activity across a number of years. Swimming, biking, golf, hiking, and tennis are particularly suited for individuals of all ages because the intensity of participation can be controlled. Some individuals may participate in more vigorous sports such as mountain climbing well into advanced age. Fitness rather than age seems to be the only limiting factor.

The habit of regular participation in sports if started in childhood will change children's lives. The advantage of just a little exercise over a sedentary life-style has been documented (Deuster, 1996; Pinto et al., 1996). Children who spend hours watching television every day are more likely to be obese and to perform less well academically (Bar-Or et al., 1998). Sports participation can contribute to weight control as well as cardiovascular fitness. Girls need models of women in sports. The Women's National Basketball Association (WNBA) may well fill the need. Labi (1998b) described a ritual at every WNBA game involving a ball exchange.

> Each player hits the court with a basketball that she hands off to a girl from the stands, and it's hard to tell who is more thrilled—the fan, who gets to shake hands with her sports hero, or the player, who still can't quite believe that she *is* a sports hero. (p. 62)

Summary

The physical competencies are (a) knowledge of how the body works, (b) health promotion and disease prevention, (c) conditioning, and (d) sports participation. Each of these areas is a building block to help young girls and women find the stamina they need to meet the demands of their lives. As Maslow stated, this is the basic level of functioning and provides the energy on which all other growth and development must occur.

Being prepared for gender equity begins with the physical capacity to meet life's challenges. The battle for equity continues, and every girl and every woman who would win it must start with being physically competent. The American Alliance for Health, Physical Education, Recreation, and Dance (1995) described the struggle: "Change will not happen readily. Purging a society of discriminatory practices challenges ingrained values, beliefs, and attitudes—all of which demonstrate stubborn resistance to the winds of change" (p. 12).

Applications for Counselors

Counselors can help women become physically competent by assessing their physical capacity through the following question: Does this client have the physical stamina sufficient to provide a foundation for the growth and development desired?

- If the answer is "No," then further assessment must address the source of the problem to identify either knowledge or conditioning as the primary target.
- If the answer is "Yes," then the client may work on health promotion and disease prevention and finding a sport for participation.

Expertise to address a client's physical competencies may come from sources other than counselors; however, each counselor should be able to provide an appropriate referral to a resource for:

- Weight reduction (e.g., Weight Watchers, TOPS [Take Off Pounds Sensibly], a family physician, diet workshop, the Cooper Clinic).

- Conditioning (e.g., YMCA, school or church-sponsored aerobics classes, personal trainers).
- Books for clients to read to provide knowledge about body functioning.
- Sports clubs or leagues for women.

8

Emotional Competencies

Inscribed on the Temple of Apollo at Delphi are the words, "Know Thyself." Indeed, this is one of the most important pieces of advice ever given to humankind. Understanding the source of one's emotions allows a person to remove the chaos of emotionality so that the person can be fully integrated. A child who is crying because she has fallen and skinned her knee seems to be responding appropriately to her setting. A healthy child who is crying because she is afraid to die would cause some concern if the threat of death was not imminent. In either case, the behavior of "crying" must be interpreted in terms of the larger context and the internal world of the child.

To become emotionally competent, every woman must first realize that she has the ability to take charge of her emotional life and that this is accomplished through (a) intrapersonal skills (the ability to care about and facilitate oneself), (b) interpersonal skills (the ability to care about and relate effectively to others), and (c) networking (the ability to establish and maintain groups to mutually facilitate the members). Although these concepts are complex, they can be defined and acquired through skill development. It is essential that clients, especially young girls, believe that they can learn the things they need to accomplish their dreams. Almost any aspiration can be characterized by smaller steps that can be accomplished through effort. Time is the primary barrier. The first step is to understand how to facilitate emotionally healthy development.

Each person is a unique individual because of the combination of genes inherited from parents and the unique environment in which a person has grown. People also have characteristics in common with their species that make them kindred with one another. All humans feel emotions, such as joy, sadness, anger, and fear, but they express them to different degrees in response to differing situations. How one expresses feelings is a function of one's uniqueness as well as the cues one has learned from the environment.

The ability to express affect appropriately and spontaneously is certainly characteristic of emotionally healthy individuals. These individuals are not playing roles or "acting" to achieve approval from the group. When they are sad, they cry; when they are happy, they laugh. Understanding how one feels and why one feels that way is the basic process for developing intrapersonal skills. However, having the skills to be emotionally healthy extends beyond experiencing emotion. It also involves an understanding of one's motivation, which is a key component of intrapersonal skills.

As a result of their individuality and the opportunities of their environment, children develop preferences. These priorities are modified through experiences and time and are sought out in new environments when they are encountered. The desire to achieve these preferences in any environment may be defined as a need. Maslow (1968) categorized needs into a hierarchy to include the physical, love and belongingness, competence, and self-actualization. He contended that healthy human development proceeds sequentially through these stages unless it is blocked by circumstances that may cause an individual to fixate or regress.

However, we must emphasize the contribution of gender role socialization in the process that guides the emotional world of children. Children learn very early in their lives that associated with anatomical differences are ways of dressing, acting, and relating (Bem, 1989), and they are often punished for acting outside of cultural expectations. For example, little boys are encouraged to be rough and tough, and little girls are expected to be sweet and kind. The emotional behaviors for women suggest that crying is acceptable, anger is not. This socialization is based on stereotypes rather than any genetic gender difference. In fact, gender research has shown that "despite all the multiple conditions in our society that push girls and boys, and then women and men, into different spheres, there simply is no getting around the fact that the differences so painstakingly identified are small indeed" (Lott, 1996).

Erikson (1964) described the developmental tasks of children as industry versus inferiority and those of adolescence as identity versus role confusion. Healthy adolescents emerge from childhood with a sense of their competency. Even though this is primarily a result of the parenting each child receives, schools also have a role in this process, especially if remediation is required. A successful adolescence will provide an individual with a strong sense of who she is and what she hopes to achieve. The ability to plan ahead to achieve goals is part of this healthy development.

Erikson (1963, 1968) described the developmental task of young adults as choosing between intimacy and isolation. Humans are social creatures and need to be able to help others achieve their goals in addition to achieving their own. The ability to care and facilitate others is also an emotional skill that we address in this chapter as interpersonal skills.

The third area required to be emotionally competent is the ability to network with others to either achieve shared goals or mutually facilitate the accomplishment of individual goals. For men, the "good old boy network" was the process by which men identified those individuals who were part of their group and should be facilitated. Needless to say, most women did not have access to this kind of facilitation. Therefore, women must learn how to develop healthy networks to facilitate one another's development. A woman may receive help from the network or work as a mentor.

It is important to note that these skills, although addressed separately in this chapter, are in fact integrated and developmental. An individual must begin with intrapersonal skills and progress beyond herself to help others through her interpersonal and networking skills. As Carkhuff (1981) stated, "In the end, however, those who do not get outside of themselves in their motivation for living do not actualize their human potential" (p. 80)

Intrapersonal Skills

The first intrapersonal skill is the ability to listen to one's own "self-talk" to determine what one is trying to talk oneself into or out of as the case may be. Think of the teenager who continually tells herself, "I am so clumsy I can never make the team." This same girl may fantasize about making the final basket to win the championship game. The incongruity of these are lost unless the girl can learn to listen to her self-talk as well as her fantasies and at some point act to make the reality of her life more consistent with her fantasies.

For example, she might ask herself, "What will really prevent me from making the team, and what can I do to change it?" If she is overweight or out of shape, she can start a diet and exercise program. In fact, almost any person can do something to improve her chances of success with a little effort. However, if she were to probe her self-talk, she may find that clumsiness is really a metaphor for fear of failure. Whatever the problem, the ability to listen and self-reflect is essential if a woman of any age can truly begin to make her dreams a reality.

Reflective statements are helpful in the self-knowing process. For example, a teenager might say, "I feel scared about trying out for the basketball team because I may not make it." Knowing that rejection is the cause of the fear begins the process for exploring rejection. She might use the "worst case scenario" to imagine her response if she were to lose in the tryouts. How would she interpret and respond to this situation? She might be devastated and afraid to go back to school, or she might say simply that there are other things to do. She might also list reasons for risking the tryout and reasons she should not. In any case, activities such as this prepare individuals to be wholly integrated and aware of their strengths and weaknesses and ultimately to find value in their own creation.

The development of self-worth should happen as a result of a healthy emotional environment, and for many young girls, the middle school years are critical to the continued belief in personal value. Resnick et al. (1997) found that there are protective contexts that help adolescents resist high-risk behavior. Among these factors were emotionally stable households as well as connectedness to school and family.

Gilligan (1982) noted that at this stage of development, girls may substitute the masculine view of the world for their individual voices in order to maintain relationships. She said:

> Thus women have traditionally deferred to the judgment of men, although often while intimating a sensibility of their own which is at variance with that judgment. . . . The developmental ordering of these two points of view has been to consider the masculine as more adequate than the feminine and thus as replacing the feminine when the individual moves toward maturity. (p. 69)

Thus, for an adolescent girl, the expectations and approval of boys may become more important than continuing to believe that her individual preferences and beliefs are worthy enough to be manifest. The personal voice is lost before it is fully developed in order to become acceptable or desirable within the constraints of a relationship, primarily with boys. It is possible that boys are not asking for this change nearly as much as girls anticipate that they are. Girls tend to be highly aware of the larger culture and interpret acceptability as acquiescence.

The process of self-reflection may be helpful to young women as they struggle to define themselves apart from the cultural expectations they find reflected in television and movies. Part of this process may include systematically reviewing their talents and abilities to look for areas to develop as part of the self-defining process. Discovering abilities is also reinforcing and may provide the encouragement necessary to take a step toward achievement.

Carkhuff (1981) described intrapersonal motivation as "the conditions that get people mobilized to invest themselves in efforts. In a very real sense, it describes what makes them tick" (p. 78). There are multiple theories about why people do what they do, but common among them is the importance of motivation, and the core of motivation is hope. Most of us develop goals with the belief that we will be able to achieve them—the very essence of hope. However, for some individuals, hope must be acquired through small successes.

Carkhuff (1981) suggested that motivation progresses through five levels: (a) nonincentive, (b) incentive, (c) achievement, (d) self-fulfillment, and (e) mission. The process by which one is motivated essentially defines the motivation level. At the lowest level (no motivation), there is nothing to interest the individual in the effort. Teachers may use the phrase, "She just isn't motivated." Almost no one is equally motivated to mow the lawn or run a marathon. People choose their interests and thus their motivation.

Incentives are needed for individuals with little motivation. For instance, parents may say, "If you want to play basketball, then you will have to maintain a C average." At this level of motivation, an individual is willing to trade something she has for something she wants—studying for basketball. Parents may pay students to make a particular grade. Incentives work for the time that they can be provided. Once basketball season is over, the incentive has vanished. However, if basketball itself becomes a source of achievement, then an incentive may no longer be required.

Achievement is a very frequent source of motivation, and because it is internal rather than external, it is longer lasting and potentially more powerful than extrinsic motivation. Achievement-oriented individuals take pride in their work, and the quality of their products is the source of their motivation. Developing achievement motivation may require designing small challenges so that success can be achieved and then praised. Success becomes the motivation to achieve more. Growth programs must have steps small enough to ensure success and large enough to be of interest.

Beyond the achievement level is self-fulfillment. At this point, individuals work to ensure their own growth. Learning is a vehicle for self-fulfillment, but the focus is internal rather than external. This source of motivation has been used by the military services in their recruitment program that suggests, "Be all that you can be" by enlisting.

An individual can be motivated toward self-fulfillment by recognizing her talent or ability that could be developed and then encouraging perfection of the talent. Encouragement and support may be the critical ingredients at this level of motivation, but because this level is internal, an individual must ultimately adopt this for her own.

The highest level of motivation according to Carkhuff (1981) is that of mission. At this level, an individual is focused on something outside herself to give her life meaning. He said, "this commitment involves nurturing life wherever and whenever it is encountered" (p. 79). Models and mentors may be helpful in focusing the particular direction, but a person with a mission will not be easily dissuaded. This notion of living with such a passion or commitment to others is quite obvious in the individuals who are living it. These individuals are valued and appreciated because they are the ones who remind us that we are a community. Their devotion and commitment make changes in the lives of others.

For the client with no motivation, counselors must explore the client's life situation until they find an incentive—a starting place. Counselors can motivate clients programmatically as far as the achievement level, but for the person with a mission, counselors are limited to asking, "How can I help?"

Interpersonal Skills

Interpersonal skills empower a person to show care for others and a willingness to help others achieve their goals. These skills are crucial to all helping roles as well as for all relationships in which one desires to be constructive. These skills include (a) active listening, (b) accurate responding, and (c) planning change.

Active Listening

The idea that listening is a skill that must be developed is disconcerting to many since everyone presumes that they listen every day. However, active listening implies also hearing and understanding what has been said as well as what was meant. Active listening focuses on total communication, including verbal as well as nonverbal signals.

Nonverbal signals include all aspects of physical presentation, such as posture, facial expressions, and gestures. When people observe these behaviors while listening, they make assumptions or inferences. For example, a young girl twisting her hair and swinging the foot of her crossed leg might be nervous. One would check her facial expression for other clues before making an inference. Even before she has spoken a word, one has some clue about her emotional state.

Verbal clues include both process and content. The words that an individual says form meanings that are further enhanced by the way the words are spoken. Rate of speech, inflection (or lack thereof), pitch, and verbal ticks (such as "you know") all provide information about what is being said. A person near tears or a person on the brink of laughter may say the same words, but the meaning is clearly different. The encoding of the message is part of the communication process, and ignoring it, diminishes the message.

Accurate Responding

Day by day, people send signals to others about the world in which they live hoping that others will receive them, understand them, and help them cope. By accurate responding, one sends a message that, in fact, one has heard and does understand another's experience of the world. Carkhuff (1996) labeled this type of response as an *interchangeable response,* containing both a response to feeling and a response to content or reason for the feeling. His research on this model has been extensive (Carkhuff, 1984, 1986).

The interchangeable response is empathy operationalized, and the benefits of empathic communication were originally proposed by Carl Rogers (1957) as one of three necessary and sufficient conditions for therapeutic personality change. Empathy is the fuel for growth and change within an individual, and it can and should be provided to every individual. Just as people need air to breathe, food to eat, and water to drink to perpetuate life, so do people also need empathy to feed them emotionally. Because the skill is easily learned, it is open to everyone and does not require certification or license.

As one watches and listens to others talk, one gathers data from their physical posture and facial expressions along with their tone of voice, inflection, and rate of speed. One analyzes and synthesizes the information to form an inference about how the person feels and why she feels that way. With this information at hand, one is prepared to make an empathic response in this form: "You feel____ (feeling word) because ____ (reason for the feeling or content)."

For example, a young woman laments to her mother, "You just don't understand how things are now!" A possible empathic response might be, "Your are disappointed because I'm not as helpful as you need right now." The feeling word is *disappointed*, and the reason for the feeling is that her mother is not as helpful as her daughter needs her to be.

The skill of empathic responding is crucial. It is therapeutic in any relationship, and it can be mastered with practice by almost everyone. As part of our academic teaching responsibilities, we have trained hundreds of individuals in empathic responding. We have reviewed thousands of audiotapes and videotapes of counselor–client or doctor–patient interactions. The power of empathy is always evident. Videotapes indicate almost invariably that a client's posture relaxes on receiving an interchangeable response. It is as if clients steel themselves against not being heard, and then when contrary evidence is provided through an empathic response, their bodies relax. Resistance is reduced and clients think, "Here is someone who can be trusted."

This phenomenon is one of the reasons that empathic responding should be used only for the good of the other. Manipulation through the use of empathy is interpersonal dishonesty. Caring for others and interest in their growth are the motivations out of which empathy should be used.

Planning Change

According to Carkhuff (1996), the helping process is defined by exploration, understanding, and then action. An individual explores the problem until she understands where she is and where she wants or needs to be. Then she acts to change herself or the environment to facilitate growth or relieve pain. Knowing what action to take and how to structure the tasks to ensure success are the skills of planning change.

The process by which an individual moves from a current state or condition into a more desirable one is facilitated by a plan. The more specific the plan, the more likely it can be followed. For example, a woman wants to lose weight and has determined that she must cut her daily consumption of food. It is unlikely that a plan that says "Eat less" will accomplish her weight-loss goal. First of all, what is "less" and how much "less" should she eat to lose weight? A good plan includes specific, step-by-step instructions for accomplishing a goal.

The size of the step is another critical component. A plan for weight loss might contain a listing of foods for three meals with a total calorie count of 1,000. For a person who has been consuming 3,000 calories per day, this reduction or step is too large and most likely will not be followed. A girl who is able to run only 100 yards will not be able to run a mile every day regardless of what is stated on the physical fitness plan. Plans must build on current capacity in a steady, developmental way.

For example, a 10th-grade girl might identify a piece of music she will play on her clarinet at solo competition. The piece is a Level 5 (the most difficult) and the current pieces that she is playing are at a Level 3 (moderately difficult). Before she can play a Level 5 piece, she might first develop the skill to play at Level 4. The distance from where she is to where she wants to be can be bridged through careful skill development in a step-by-step way. Some might say that the goal is too lofty, and if the time is short, that is quite likely. However, rather than deny the goal, a good facilitator might suggest smaller steps. For this year, she might select a Level 3 piece, and next year, a Level 4. In her senior year she may be ready for Level 5.

Thus, a good plan will provide a way for an individual to achieve the goal she desires. The steps when implemented will ensure that the goal is accomplished. Steps that are too large may cause failure, and it is more difficult to overcome failure than to celebrate small successes. These small victories are reinforcing and keep an individual involved in the tasks of the plan.

Helping Versus Codependency

It is important to note the difference between helping others and codependency. Codependency is defined as "a mutual dependency such as that between two individuals each of whom is emotionally dependent upon the other" (Reber, 1995, p. 133). The problem with codependency is that the emotional identity of two individuals becomes so enmeshed that neither is free to make healthy, independent decisions. The success of one is dependent on the success of the other rather than on one's own accomplishments.

Codependency operates when one tries to change another to enhance herself. On the other hand, helping behavior is defined as "Providing direct assistance to someone in need" (Reber, 1995, p. 332) and the advantage (if any) to the helper is not considered. While numerous self-help books have been written about codependency, the issue here is the motivation of the helper. To help others to enhance one's own self is not helping behavior by definition. Carkhuff (1984) identified the concept of the exemplar and noted that one can only help others to one's own level of functioning. A person who knows how to speak rudimentary German can only teach others to speak at that level. However, Carkhuff's (1996) conceptof human resource development is continual growth and continual facilitation of others to one's former level of functioning.

Networking

Networking is defined as the ability to establish and maintain groups to mutually facilitate their members. Networking is the skill of bringing together women with similar interests and commitments to their own growth and development whether it is in the career or personal area. Numerous, extensive networks have been established in the interest of facilitating women. These organizations, such as the National Organization for Women, have become so large that their facilitation is not for an individual woman but for the woman collective as they define her. This is not the skill of networking we propose here. Large organizations with political agendas have their place in society, and many of them make great contributions in advocacy for legislation and other equity-promoting processes. However, every woman needs to know how to find women of similar interests to encourage and facilitate her own development.

People as Resources

The first step in the networking process is the adoption of the concept of people as physical, intellectual, and emotional resources. This is not a process of exploitation, but one of recognizing talent and encouraging the development of that talent. It is a cooperative rather than competitive attitude. Women who believe that other women should be helped to grow will relate to them facilitatively.

Implicit in this concept is the notion that every woman (and man) has talents and abilities that are being used at a given level of her (or his) potential. Facilitation first recognizes one's own resources that can be made available to other women to help them develop their own talents and skills. Women need a cooperative pool of talents and abilities from which members can receive help and give assistance to others.

The facilitation process begins as we did at the beginning of this chapter, by recognizing the importance of intrapersonal skills to the development of self-awareness. Once an individual knows what her talents and skills are and how well she functions, then she is not only ready to plan her own change but also prepared to help others who function at levels below hers.

Interpersonal skills are important in meeting other women and determining how best to relate to their needs. The process begins with listening to their stories. What are their hopes and dreams? What resources do they currently have? What do they want to develop in themselves. Finally, ask what role you will take in that process and what other resources (other women) you can find to assist you.

This is the essence of networking: women committed to each other's growth and development and willing to devote time and resources to the process. Some women find luncheon groups especially helpful. Others have dedicated one night per week to the process. Still others use the telephone and e-mail to keep in touch and facilitate one another. The exact nature of the process is variable and open to creative problem solving.

Volunteering

The adage, "To whom much is given, much is required" should be the motto for volunteerism. Or perhaps, "It is more blessed to give than to receive" would be an equally inviting motto. The notion of volunteering as an emotional competency is not a new one. Many individuals have found learning and fulfillment in the process of helping others. Almost every small town paper in the United States honors a "volunteer of the week." Churches do their work through vast networks of volunteers. While those who are helped through volunteerism are better for the process, the volunteer often states that she or he is the one who has benefited most.

Horney used the term *neurotic claim* for "an inappropriate sense of one's superiority such that one feels that others should rightfully fulfill all one's wants and needs" (cited in Reber, 1995, p. 492). This focus on the self is characteristic of most neurotic disorders. Volunteering is a path outside of the self in which good can be accomplished and others' needs experienced, which is health promoting and brings life into perspective.

The choice of a place to volunteer should begin early in adolescence as young girls develop a sense of who they are and what talents, interests, and abilities they have. Nursing homes, hospitals, shelters, food banks, churches, day-care centers, and numerous other organizations offer opportunities for youths to focus outside themselves and experience the process of meeting other people's needs. These are habits of a lifetime, and building them early helps a young woman establish herself as a contributing member of the community. The Search Institute (P. L. Benson, 1996) has defined 40 youth assets that are protective against high-risk behavior. Two of these assets, "constructive use of time" and "community service," can be developed through volunteering.

Mentoring

One of the characteristics of successful academicians is the presence of a mentor who helped to guide their career (Bland

& Schmitz, 1986). We are sure that this phenomenon occurs in other fields as well. Having a mentor to teach the subtle actions that can make the difference between success and failure is critical. Only a few years ago, for women in academe, that mentor was most likely male, because there were very few women and only a small number of them progressed above the lowest academic rank. Now that more women are included in this field, women are assuming mentor roles.

For all fields, whether paid work or not, teaching and guiding those who share one's interests is a critical skill for emotional health. It is as true for the mentor as for the one who is mentored. It is the noncompetitive difference that women can bring to business, medicine, law, teaching, counseling, and all other fields. Women need not perpetuate the competitive drive that required beating coworkers for promotion. If women are to change the workplace, then they must be more like the female ideal than the aggressive male ideal.

Summary

The emotional competencies required for gender equity are intrapersonal skills, interpersonal skills, and networking. These skills are cumulative and developmental, each building on the other. Emotional competencies prepare women to relate in a healthy way not only to themselves but also to other individuals, as well to the groups that will support and facilitate their growth. An emotionally competent woman knows who she is, knows what her strengths are, and is able to use her talents and resources to further her own development while at the same time facilitating the development of others.

Being committed to life, wherever and whenever she finds it, is the essence of the emotionally competent women. She is sure of herself for she has done the work of self-knowledge. She is a volunteer and a mentor; she gives of herself. As Maya Angelou (1993b) said:

The woman who survives intact and happy must be at once tender and tough. She must have convinced herself, or be in the unending process of convincing herself, that she, her values, and her choices are important. . . . The struggle for equality continues unabated, and the woman warrior who is armed with wit and courage will be among the first to celebrate victory. (pp. 6–7)

Applications for Counselors

Intrapersonal and interpersonal skills are the counselor's tools, and most counselors feel able and ready to teach these skills to their clients.

Networking may be a new area for counselors working with women, since the concept applied in this way to women is relatively new. Women have always been involved in groups and have always been volunteers, but the purpose in the past was most often charity, and these groups have done mighty works. However, as women seek to move into political representation and into the highest levels of business and industry, they must learn a new strategy: how to develop "good old women" networks. Strategies for helping women to develop networks may include the following:

• Develop a list of those individuals in one's acquaintance who have similar needs and interests and start a support group. One of the most successful women's groups I (CBA) know is called "Friday Group" from Southern Hills Christian Church in Edmond, Oklahoma. The group consists of about 15 women who have lunch together on Friday in one another's homes and then continue a study, usually on personal or spiritual development. This group has encouraged the development of a remarkably strong group of women who have grown personally, emotionally, and spiritually. Through their process of self-selected study and personal sharing, they have facilitated each other's growth, served as mentors and friends, and each of them is better for her participation.

- Many churches, social clubs, or service organizations already provide a structure for women's groups. Women may join these groups and work toward a more intentional process of personal growth and mutual support.

9

Intellectual Competencies

The entire study of intellectual functioning is undergoing a radical change. During the Industrial Age (1800–1970) there was a premium on repetitive tasks. This meant that a person who was conditioned to expertly repeat the same behavior was the one most fit for the production line. But, with the advent of the Information Age in the mid-1900s, the highest priority is being given to workers who can make effective on-the-spot decisions at their workstation. That is, there has been a shift away from generating all decisions at the top and instead, responsibility is flowing steadily to individuals who serve at the interface between problems and solutions. Information Age organizations are held together by broad policies rather than by standard operating procedure manuals that give detailed prescriptions for all employees.

Why has such a stark change taken place? Primarily because the pace of change is too rapid for decision making to be done at a central location. This point can be demonstrated graphically by the collapse of the Soviet empire, which depended almost entirely on centralized decision making. Another example is the circumstances of a typical family unit in the era of the automobile. Parents can supervise the choices of young children, but when the offspring become teenagers and get into a car with their friends, the possibility of monitoring the choice process is drastically diminished if not entirely eliminated. Thus, the automobile has revamped the role of parents in decision making. The same thing is being replicated throughout society. Thus, more people must be able to make independent, complex, and important choices.

Despite the fact that people are expected to do new and different things with their minds, the anatomy of the human brain remains relatively stable, at least as far as we know. This means that there must be shifts in the way the brain is used. In short, learning new ways to behave is critical for humans' survival both individually and collectively.

Is the brain up to the challenge? The answer is yes. There is considerable consensus among brain researchers such as Marian Diamond (D. Aspy, Aspy, & Roebuck, 1984), Pinker (1997), and Sylwester (1995) that the human brain contains about 100 billion neurons and that each one is capable of interconnecting with 50,000 others, perhaps even more. Not only that, but inside each neuron is an unimaginably complex network of molecules that do amazing things. This adds up to a biological basis for a thinking system whose potential is beyond present-day explanatory models.

Potential and *possibilities* are the key words in considerations of the intellectual functioning of human beings. During the Industrial Age, there was an emphasis on measuring the fixed capacity of a person's brain. Large organizations such as the army needed a quick way to separate "smart" people from "less smart" people and so widely used IQ tests were developed that were designed to produce intelligence labels. Indeed, there was so much confidence in those diagnoses that people were segregated into groups on the basis of them. But, there also was widespread discomfort with the "sorting" process, and investigators kept exploring the limits of the classification system so that eventually, the entire procedure was found to be totally inadequate for the Information Age, though vestiges of it survive even in today's enlightened world.

IQ tests failed to consider the potential of the human brain. They took static pictures of the brain's functioning in a specific context and generalized that photograph to the brain's ability in all settings. But investigations revealed that brain functioning changes and adapts to different environments so that today, the major question is not what the mind is doing at any point in time but rather what can it do (Goleman, 1995). What is its potential? Allied with that issue is the question of how to release the brain's potential. Thus, the Information Age challenge is to develop new ways to nurture the brain so that its vast potential can be actualized.

This chapter is organized to address those competencies required for intellectual functioning in the Information Age and include (a) processing data, (b) communicating, (c) conquering a substantive content area, (d) learning how to learn, and (e) thinking critically. However, before we begin a discussion of these skills, we address the topic of gender differences in intellectual functioning.

Gender Differences in Intellectual Functioning

It is rather popular to attribute differential intellectual functioning to gender differences. However, this approach has inherent problems. First, it is the wrong emphasis at this time in history. In fact, it may well be a red herring that, if chased, will produce only minimal results. In many ways this approach is similar to the work of people such as Herrnstein and Murray (1996) and D'Souza (1996), who gained a great deal of notoriety by underscoring data that suggested race-specific intellectual traits.

A fundamental question is whether or not such investigations are more beneficial than harmful. That is, if gender differences were found, what constructive ends would be served? This is a relevant question because in many instances the motivation behind such information is to "prove" some sort of group superiority, which is rarely of positive value to anyone.

A basic fact is that so little is known about human intellect that any findings based on today's understandings are likely to be rejected in no more than a decade. Currently, the overlap of gender groups is far greater than their unique traits. This means that whatever is said of one group is also attributable to a segment of the other. The variability tends to be more attributable to intragroup factors than to intergroup factors. Apparently, there is more similarity than uniqueness.

Specific gender differences in cognitive functioning have been noted by researchers. Women have been found to perform better than men on tasks of verbal fluency, verbal learning, and symbol substitution (Benton, Hamsher, Varney, & Spreen, 1983), whereas men tend to perform better than women on visuospatial processing tasks (McGee, 1979). Men also tend to have greater lateralization of function than women because verbal function is more organized in the left hemisphere and visuospatial function occurs more in the right hemisphere (Lezak, 1983; McGlone, 1977).

Tests of cognitive performance have also revealed gender differences, but these differences are seldom more than one half of a standard deviation (Ivison, 1977; Wechsler, 1958). This may support the notion that there is more overlap than difference between men and women in cognitive functioning. George, Ketter, Parekh, Herscovitch, and Post (1996) found differences in regional cerebral blood flow at rest and during transient, self-induced sadness. Whatever gender differences were found have not adequately explained behavioral differences. George et al. (1996) concluded, "Thus, it appears likely that gender differences in regional brain activity, if they do exist, are subtle and can be influenced by such variables as imaging modality and tracer used, and importantly by the task during the scan" (p. 868).

Therefore, if we conclude that discovering gender differences will offer only subtle differences, we must explore those factors that are key to future growth and development. We believe the biggest challenge offered by the Information Age is that of developing the brain's ability to adapt to change. *Adapt* is the operative word. Future shifts in the culture may well require vastly different roles of both genders, and if human thinking is tunneled by the notion that gender traits are innate, then, at best, progress will be severely retarded. Human survival depends on cognitive flexibility and any preconceived notions that it is "gender determined" seem dangerous, perhaps lethal.

The Prime Intellectual Task: Processing Data

The human nervous system has three major functions: gathering data, drawing conclusions from the data, and initiating actions on the basis of those conclusions. Sometimes this process is called generating information, which is different from data. Information is a uniquely human product made by combining objective and subjective data to create human meaning.

For example, if the nerve endings receive a message that a bill is due, then, that data is sent to the brain where it is processed and a response is formulated. Subsequently, the brain sends that response to some muscle center to implement the preferred course of action. Reflexes short-circuit the system by bypassing the brain so that the spinal cord initiates an automatic response such as people do when they quickly avoid an automobile crash. This chapter, however, refers primarily to activity involving the cerebral cortex.

Essentially, the brain constantly processes facts: It perpetually integrates incoming data with its stored database and produces conclusions or bottom lines called perceptions or meanings that, in turn, are used to initiate actions. Back in the Industrial Age the rate of incoming data was relatively slow, but it has been accelerated geometrically by the Information Age with its electronic transmission capabilities. And the rate of increase shows no signs of decline, so that the dimensions of the intellectual challenge are expanding. In brief, the brain must work differently and more efficiently.

Some theoreticians have tried with limited success to build computer models of human thinking, but Carkhuff (1986) proposed a model of human processing in which values or human desires (perception) are integrated with objective data (science) through the learning model of exploration, understanding, and action. Carkhuff defined values as the meanings attached to people or things. As with most human transactions, the model begins with a stimulus (S) that is idiosyncratic and must have an idiosyncratic response (R). Between those two events, human processing as defined by Carkhuff describes the interactive processes that translate a person's values and needs into an action plan or response to meet those needs. Because people are not necessarily linear in their approach, Figure 9.1 (Carkhuff, 1986, p. 72) depicts the interactive nature of human processing. According to Carkhuff's model, every cell of this diagram interacts with other cells such that a dynamic process is depicted. This procedure discriminates idiosyncratically among levels of values by defining a specific situation and then specifying an individual's varying levels of satisfaction of that value.

For instance, if a person said that money (salary) was an important factor when considering a job choice, then the task would be to clarify the degree of satisfaction a particular amount of money would represent to that person, as shown in Table 9.1.

Usually, human processing is done intuitively in the sense that decisions are made without publicly articulating the value assessments that are used in the procedure (Pinker, 1997). However, in daily life, it is important to clarify as many factors as possible to understand one's decisions. For instance, emotions may exert an important but hidden influence. In sibling rivalry, a person can stay angry for a lifetime, and it is difficult to discern that component unless it is explicated. Therefore, when making major choices, it is helpful, perhaps critical, to

Figure 9.1

Phases of Processing (Decision Making)

LEVELS OF INPUT	I EXPLORE	II UNDERSTAND	III ACT
VALUES	Define ◄►	Productivity ◄►	Policy
INFORMATION	↕	↕	↕
CONTENT	Analyze ◄►	Synthesize ◄►	Operationalize
PERSON	↕	↕	↕
PERSONAL	Diagnose ◄►	Set Goals ◄►	Program
INTRA-PERSONAL	Respond ◄►	Personalize ◄►	Initiate

S→ ... →R

NOTE From *Human Processing and Human Productivity* (p. 72) by R. R. Carkuff, 1986, Amherst, MA: HRD Press. Copyright 1986 by HRD Press. Reprinted with permission.

explicate the decision-making procedure by listing both the values and the facts involved.

An overarching proposition is because most societal change is being generated by technology, it is appropriate to use a human technology to respond to its challenges. In other words, a preferred course of action is to use the power of a human technology to direct scientific technology toward constructive,

TABLE 9.1

Value Statement: Salary Is Important

Annual Salary	Level of Satisfaction
$100,000	5
$75,000	4
$50,000	3
$25,000	2
Less than $25,000	1

human ends. Short of that, there is a possibility that people can be overwhelmed by the information glut produced by the Information Age. Because the human brain is the chief instrument by which human choices are made, it is incumbent on human beings to develop and use systematic procedures that maintain and sustain human existence in the full sense of those words. Perhaps human uniqueness was expressed well by Mark Twain (1897), who said, "The human being is the only organism that blushes. Or needs to."

Communication in the Information Age

There is a rather strange paradox developing in the Information Age: People can lie more skillfully in an age when truth is more essential. First, the culture has generated a huge capacity to generate and transmit misleading information. This ability is variously called misinformation, disinformation, propaganda, and sometimes, advertising. The crux of it is to mislead others, and the science of deceptive information is highly sophisticated. For instance, politicians often make an ambiguous response to questions so that in the future they can come down on either side of an issue. Brooks Hays, legendary Arkansas legislator, often told the story of a politician who was asked about his position on beverage alcohol. His response was, "If by alcohol you mean the substance that enslaves the mind, then I am unalterably opposed to it. But, on the other hand, if by alcohol you mean the beverage that frees the spirit, then I am unalterably for it. That, sir, is my firm opinion." In a more subtle move, Vice President Al Gore denied that he solicited campaign funds from his White House office and he made it "clear" that he had violated no regulations of a controlling jurisdiction. Thus, that thin veil of judicialese was used to convey an ambiguous idea. In fact, the average person was totally unequipped to discern the difference between general innocence and legal innocence.

Second, society has an increasing need for more precise information. This need is expressed in the phrase "garbage in, garbage out"—if incorrect data are entered into a computer, then the data that come out of it are meaningless. Even worse, actions based on the output will be ineffective or destructive.

Thus, although there is a greater ability to generate misinformation that can mislead people, there is a corresponding need for greater accuracy. The question is, How does one deal with that seeming paradox?

It appears that everyone would prefer accurate data for their own use, but there is an advantage to giving others lies and distortions. Deception of others for personal benefit has been a human trait since time immemorial. Thus, the task is to determine the purpose of one's communication, and when the goal is to communicate honestly, one fundamental rule is essential: Talk or write about what you are trying to communicate. Don't obfuscate the data. Although that notion may seem obvious, it is a rather complex task.

Probably the most common confounding element of human communication is called the "hidden agenda" or "personalized goals" (C. Aspy, 1995). It happens when children try to convince their parents that they should be allowed to do some activity that has been off-limits. However, children are limited in their "doublespeak" vocabulary, and parents, who are much more experienced, easily expose the deceptions. However, along with maturity comes an expanded repertoire of deceptive responses, which often are so reflexive that perpetrators are unaware they are using them. Thus, the first phase of honest communication is to be certain about what one really wants to say.

After a person is certain of what she or he wants to say, the task becomes that of being as precise as possible. This may lead to a preference for numbers. A common axiom is "numbers don't lie." Of course, any accountant can testify to the limits of that putative wisdom. For example, income tax returns are often rife with untruths or half truths. Numbers do not ensure honesty or accurate communication.

Truth in communication rests first on the intent of the communicant. That is, the speaker or writer must *intend* to tell the truth. After intent is established, then the task is to state a core message in terms that distort it least. All human communication is subject to personal interpretations, so the challenge is to reduce misinterpretation as much as possible. This entails the use of words or symbols that have a minimal amount of ambiguity. For instance, the statement "I love you" generates considerable misinterpretation among human beings. It is much more precise to say "I will share all of my income with you and I earn $1,000 a week." The words all and $1,000 are fairly precise, but the word *share* leaves room for a lot of interpretation or misinterpretation.

Redundancy is a third component of honest communication. Back to the example cited above. The statement "I will share all of my income with you, and I earn $1,000 a week" can be restated to say "I will deposit my $1,000 in a bank account and both of us can use it as we see fit." This restatement of the communication is intended to reduce whatever ambiguity the first draft generated. A third iteration may be needed before satisfactory precision is attained.

Communicators are well advised to follow Shakespeare's axiom that "brevity is the soul of wit." In essence, a good communicator frames the core message and refines the statement across several revisions. Wills (1992) wrote that Abraham Lincoln revised the Gettysburg Address numerous times until he finally produced the brief version he delivered. It is often overlooked that Lincoln was preceded at the rostrum by Edward Everitt, who talked for 2 hours, which was the accepted speaking style of that period. In fact, in the debates between Lincoln and Douglas, both men often spoke for 3 hours or more. So, at Gettysburg, Lincoln purposely adapted his speech to give it stark contrast to the extended address that preceded him. Thus, he advanced the communication style more appropriate for the oncoming Information Age. Therefore, summarizing the previous paragraphs, we postulate the following eight rules of honest communication: (a) intend to be honest, (b) frame the core message, (c) state the core message as briefly as possible using precise words, (d) revise the statement of the core message at least three times, (e) practice delivering the core message in either a written or oral format, (f) get feedback from your "editors," (g) use the feedback to revise the statement of the core message, and then (h) deliver the core message to the intended recipient.

Tannen (1994) suggested that in everyday communications, people use particular styles that may or may not match the communication styles of those who are trying to understand them, which sometimes results in serious misunderstandings. She said:

> People have different conversational styles, influenced by the part of the country they grew up in, their ethnic backgrounds and those of their parents, their age, class, and gender. . . . Unaware that these and other aspects of our backgrounds influence our ways of talking, we think we are simply saying what we mean. (p. 11)

Tannen (1994) showed that gender differences in communication style are often perceived to be absolute rather than "a matter of degree and percentages, and as universal rather than culturally mediated" (p. 14). In the workplace and at home, women and men sometimes (and perhaps often) misunderstand each other's messages because of communication style that has been learned as a part of culture rather than because of biological inheritance. Realizing that communication style has as much to do with the results of decision-making conversations around tables as the power of the ideas presented, Tannen (1994) suggested, "Understanding and allowing for style differences should allow more truly powerful ideas to emerge—in meetings as well as other workplace conversations" (p. 306).

Conquering a Substantive Content Area

A person who communicates must have something to communicate, especially in the Information Age. In short, people in the 21st century must conquer substantive content areas. The question is, How does one do that?

There are many notions about the structure of content areas.

One concept looks like a pyramid with big ideas at the top and little details at the bottom. In this image, the learning task is to start either at the top or the bottom and continue upward or downward until there is a grasp of the entire pyramid. This is known as conceptual learning, that is, a person has an intellectual understanding of the structure of a content area. This is typical school learning.

A second type of learning involves a knowledge of how a substantive area can be applied to real-world problems. Essentially, the issue is knowing how to make some intellectual knowledge work for oneself. For example, many people know how an automobile engine works. They can make diagrams of the engine and explain the function of each part. But those same people do not know how to repair an engine when it malfunctions. Conversely, there are others who know very little about the structure of an engine but who can repair it when it breaks down. Fortunately, a few people have mastered both.

The point is that there are two ways of knowing: intellectual and functional. Thus, it is necessary to decide how one wants to know a substantive area. Intellectual learning is a matter of mastering the principles, concepts, and facts in the substantive content. Principles are the "if, then, so that" components. For instance, in the area of biology, one of the principles is this: In sexual reproduction, *if* an egg is united with a sperm *then* a fertilized egg is formed *so that* an offspring can develop. Concepts are if-then statements such as "*if* an egg is united with a sperm *then* a fertilized egg is formed." Egg and sperm are facts.

A second way of knowing a substantive area is functional, which is a mastery of the skills involved in applying the knowledge. In the egg–sperm example, the skills would involve learning to do the behaviors necessary to unite egg and sperm, such as is done in artificial insemination, so as to produce a fertilized egg. In baseball, a functional knowledge of hitting would entail a mastery of the behaviors necessary to bring the bat into contact with the ball.

One of the common criticisms of teachers is that they are "ivory tower" people who know a great deal intellectually but who have mastered few, if any, of the skills necessary to apply or convey their knowledge effectively. Conversely, technicians are accused of being mindless workers who do not know how or why something works, only that it does. True masters of a content area know both the ideational content and the skills essential for application. For instance, most expert musicians know their field both intellectually and functionally. They can both compose and play music.

How does a person master a content area? By delineating and learning the facts, concepts, principles, and skills in a body of knowledge. In short, a person should know how and why a body of knowledge works and how to apply it.

Learning How to Learn

One of the classic stories of parenting is the one wherein parents tell their children they can go swimming when they have learned how to swim. Unfortunately, this rules out one of the greatest sources of learning: experience. Yet, it is risky to try to learn something such as driving simply by jumping into a car and moving into heavy traffic. To be sure, there is a place for experience in the total learning equation, but it must be done in its proper sequence. The basic question remains, "How do I learn?"

During the Information Age, learning must be a lifelong process. Of course, people have different learning styles, but fortunately, many of them have enough commonalties so that broad guidelines about a learning sequence can be stated. First, learning is enhanced when it involves a variety of sensory inputs. That is, learning is more efficient when the learner's abilities to see, hear and touch, and taste and smell are activated. This means that learning is upgraded when the learner is told something, shown something, and allowed to do relevant tasks. This is called the tell, show, and do method.

It is important to enter learning experiences when the person is ready for them. Havighurst (1952) referred to "teachable moments," and Dewey (1965) talked about readiness. Many of us caution ourselves not to "get in over our heads." Thus, for most learners there is an almost innate awareness of an optimal sequencing of learning experiences.

First, learners benefit from discovering where they are in terms of mastering the content area. This is normally called a diagnosis. When learners enter a content area, the teacher can inform them about their current level of mastery. For instance, if a person wants to learn to hit a golf ball, then the instructor can make a diagnosis about the current performance in terms of distance and direction.

Second, learners must be motivated to learn the content that is put before them. If not, the content just lies there meaningless. So, the second phase of learning identifies the learner's benefits gained by mastering the content. If the learning benefits are great enough, then the learner is motivated. For example, if learners discovered that they could increase their income by 25% by mastering some new content, then the motivation might be high enough for them to proceed into the subject matter. If there is not enough motivation, then the learners are not ready to move ahead.

Third, the task is to tell learners about the content and to give them a demonstration of how it can be applied. This then opens their minds to the functional possibilities of the new content they have seen in operation.

Fourth, learners can learn the functional skills by trying to replicate the teacher's demonstration. In medical education, a learning model is see one, do one, teach one. A Chinese proverb says, "I listen and I hear. I watch and I see. I do and I learn." In many teaching situations, the fourth stage is called an exercise or a laboratory experience. It is a hands-on assignment.

Fifth, learners can increase their opportunity for success by planning specifically how to apply their new learning in their "real world." For instance, a person who is learning how to invest money might devise a plan for investing $100 with a local stockbroker. This experience transfers the learning to the person's home turf.

In summary, effective learning involves a variety of the learner's senses—telling, showing, and doing. Effective learning also is sequential in that it begins with a diagnosis, identifies motivation, shows a demonstration, offers a hands-on experience, and provides for optimum transfer to the person's real world. If learners are equipped with knowledge of this learning model, then they are able either to devise their own learning program or to evaluate the work of those who teach them. The appropriate questions are:

1. Do I know my beginning level of mastery of the substantive area?
2. Am I motivated to learn this material?
3. Have I been shown an application of the subject matter?
4. Have I had an opportunity to apply the subject matter?
5. Have I planned an application of the subject matter back in my "home situation"?
6. Has the learning experience provided a variety of sensory inputs?

For example, a person tries to play a piano and discovers she can't (diagnosis). She enrolls in a class to learn to play the piano. The teacher informs her that reasonably skilled piano players can earn as much as $1,000 a week playing for local events such as weddings, funerals, and recitals (motivation). The teacher describes a piano playing skill and demonstrates it for the learner (demonstration). The learner performs the skill while the teacher watches (practice). The learner plans to practice the skill at home on her own piano (transfer). Thus, the learner is able to discern that she has been taught effectively. In that sense, she is in charge of her own learning. She does not know the specific content (piano playing) but she knows how to assess an effective teaching procedure.

Thinking Critically

Education is replete with strategies for criticism. Students in all types of learning situations are intimidated by the thought of receiving grades for assignments they have submitted for evaluation. This model of criticism pervades society so that evaluation time is dreaded almost universally. In politics, evaluations are euphemistically called referendums, and incumbents are often stricken with fear of the electorate's response to their actions.

Thinking critically is far different from being critical. People think critically when they examine both the internal and external attributes of a product. The internal evaluation is a matter of determining whether or not the components of a product enhance, as opposed to lessen, each other. The external phase of critical thinking is a matter of comparing the product to outside criteria such as a similar product or a set of standards for that type of product.

In the internal phase, evaluators assess the manufacturer's orchestration of the components into a harmonious whole. This involves analysis and synthesis during which the separate pieces are taken apart, examined, and put back together until their consistency is determined. For instance, a poodle started to carry a toy around and cry almost continually. She lost her appetite. A review of her diet and activities before the change in behavior revealed that she had been given a monthly tablet for heartworms and that the dosage had been for a 25-pound dog while she weighed only 7 pounds. The overdose had caused the unusual reaction. That is an analysis.

Anything, including plays, operas, stories, families, corporations, and individuals, can be assessed by critical thinking. The following are some relevant questions relating to internal criteria: (a) Do the components function as they were designed? (b) Do the components contribute appropriately to the product's overall function? and (c) How can the components be improved to upgrade the overall function?

Questions to judge external criteria might include these: (a) How does the product compare with other similar products?

(b) How does the product meet specific external criteria? and (c) How can the product be improved?

Critical thinking should produce first a report that indicates the quality of the internal components of a product as well as the degree of harmony between them. Second, it should indicate how the product compares with other similar ones. Both of these phases can be enhanced through the use of outside experts, and at this point a network of resources can contribute to the outcome. That is, it helps to be able to call upon the abilities of people beyond one's immediate circle of friends or acquaintances to expand the available resources in making both quantitative and qualitative judgments.

Summary

There is a shift in studies of intellectual functioning. The emerging emphasis is on human processing, which is the integration of objective data with human values. This change highlights honest and informed human communication because the rate of information exchange is so rapid that disinformation or misinformation renders it dysfunctional.

To participate in Information Age communication, a person must have command of a content area, which means to know its constituent facts, concepts, and principles in addition to the skills required to apply it. Learning the content is facilitated when the learner begins with an accurate diagnosis and pairs it with proper motivation and opportunities to both learn and apply the material.

Critical thinking enhances operations when it includes an analysis and synthesis of the process under consideration. That is, it is beneficial when the person is able to evaluate both the internal and external quality of the product.

While differential cognitive functioning may be attributed to gender factors, the temptation to explore that domain should be resisted until better assessment devices are available. The salient issue in the intellectual domain for at least the early part of the 21st century deals with the development of the adaptability and flexibility of the human brain. Explorations that do not advance that effort may well be more deleterious than productive. In essence, the critical intellectual content pertains to two factors: the ability to acquire data that are needed by self and others and the ability to process the data into information that enhances the data's value.

Applications for Counselors

Counselors can emphasize the multidimensional nature of processing data when teaching clients the importance of using all the data available to them to make better responses.

Because many clients have difficulty in sending and receiving communication, counselors who wish to help clients develop intellectual competencies will be prepared to offer remediation or referral in this area. Some strategies that may be helpful include:

- Role playing important communications so that clients can practice both sending and receiving messages in several communication styles.
- Discussing character communications in popular television shows and movies to practice obtaining messages from different communication styles.

For young women still in the education system, counselors should encourage them to seek out opportunities to enhance their processing skills, critical thinking, learning skills, and development of a substantive content area. For older women, counselors can:

- Encourage them to learn one new personal skill to develop learning skills and increase a sense of accomplishment and self-esteem.
- Provide resources to assist in developing learning and critical thinking skills.
- Help clients define their substantive area and set goals for new learning.

10

Spiritual Competencies

Discussions of spiritual competencies are often avoided in counseling relationships because some professionals consider them inappropriate for the counseling context. But, because 90% of the American population claims some type of religious affiliation, it seems inconsistent to omit a consideration of spiritual competencies in any serious treatment of human existence.

On the other hand, when the topic is opened, there is a concomitant obligation to provide conditions that have been tested and validated across extended time. In short, the spiritual domain is not one for idle speculation.

Most people equate the spiritual dimension with theological matters that include questions such as, Is there a God and, if so, what is my relation to the deity? There are many ways to answer those questions, and after they are resolved, earthly issues remain. One of the critical issues is how to translate the relationship to God into practices with human beings. Essentially, the questions about God determine how people relate to the cosmos, whereas moral issues concern behaviors on Earth.

The purpose of this chapter is to discuss the guidelines that translate the spiritual life into the practical aspects of living effectively with other human beings. We believe these factors include (a) establishing a mission, (b) defining values and virtues, (c) choosing personal values and virtues, (d) living one's values and virtues, and (e) coming to terms with faith. There is an underlying assumption that relations with God are essential but that they must be resolved in each individual's way. Thus, in this chapter, we assume that the clients have settled those matters and are ready to progress to moral issues at the personal and interpersonal levels.

Establishing a Mission

The core of spiritual matters consists of those thoughts that people have about the overarching purpose of life. Wilcox (1997) suggested that the question should be framed as, "Why are you living your life the way you are?" (p. 149). The answer is central for every reflective person who wants to live a meaningful, intentional life. Thomas Aquinas phrased the substantive issue elegantly by stating that only an examined life is worth living. Essentially, every human being confronts the task of contemplating her or his entire existence in the context of everything she or he knows. The product of such a process may be a declaration that, "This is what life is all about and this is my individual purpose for being in it." This, then, is what a mission is in straightforward, unvarnished terms.

If one assumes that a mission is desirable, then the next question is, how do people decide what their mission is? For some, it is a matter of accepting a task that is dictated by the circumstances. For example, future queens or kings of England are born into a set of conditions intended to shape them to accept the role of monarch. Of course, a few heir-apparents have rejected the prescribed role, but most have gone along with the contextual expectancies. Unfortunately, some people arrive in conditions that restrict their expectations to those of enslavement to do menial tasks at the behest of masters who literally slay their possibilities.

On the other hand, wherever people are free to develop their human potentials, they also have the privilege of examining their life space and choosing how to invest their talents across a lifetime. For those fortunate free citizens, the process is one of first, surveying both their personal potential, second, assessing the needs of their situation, and third, determining the point of "best fit" between them. The fortunate ones quickly find that comfortable niche that fulfills their needs, but most people make a succession of tries that progressively seem more right for them. Unfortunately, others never find their place of best fit and spend considerable time endlessly searching and seeking in what becomes a Sisyphean task. Perhaps most people belong in the third group that never locates a comfortable mission—a place and a task that make sense of their life and to which they are committed. Henry David Thoreau said that most human beings are destined to live lives of quiet desperation.

Thus, determining a personal mission is a matter of examining one's world and identifying the work that gives meaning to one's life. Then, the next challenge is exemplified by the biblical phrase, "Whatsoever thy hand findeth to do, do it with thy might." That is, once a mission is identified, the greatest benefits are reaped through a full engagement with the opportunities it offers.

A systematic approach to the establishment of a mission involves a series of four steps that produce a statement that expresses a person's chosen purpose for living. In Step 1, an individual makes a list of her abilities. These may include native talent or developed skills. Step 2 involves a careful listing of the opportunities that are currently available or could be made available with reasonable effort. Step 3 requires a clear listing of the values most important to the individual. Finally, Step 4 consists of the integration of values and abilities with the opportunities available to discover which opportunity will best match values and abilities. This opportunity then becomes the mission. These factors can be placed in a matrix like that found in Table 10.1.

The issue of what opportunities are available does not preclude tasks that are not apparent to others. For example, when Susan B. Anthony framed her mission of securing the vote for women, it probably seemed impossible to most of the people around her. But her vision was uniquely creative and was in fact possible when she was able to configure the factors as she envisioned them. However, there is a thin line between a vision that "stretches the envelope" and one that is sheer fantasy. Those two factors can be discriminated by whether or not a person is working to actualize the goal. A fantasy is characterized by no work to attain it. A dream is a goal that a person is actively trying to make happen.

The term *mission* connotes a rather grandiloquent notion that is prone to fantasy thinking. But missions may be quite down to earth. For instance, parents may establish their mission as the effective rearing of their children. A classroom teacher may assume the mission of teaching students to read. The critical element is that a mission statement frames a life and expresses the central goal toward which persons or organizations have chosen to invest their resources.

TABLE 10.1

Abilities, Opportunities, and Values Matrix

Abilities	Opportunities	Values
1. Oral reading	1. Local drama group	1. Sharing with others
2. Singing	2. Local choral group	2. Pleasure
3. Running	3. Local athletic club	3. Personal health
4. Speaking	4. Local church	4. Educating others
5. Empathic responding	5. Local hospital	5. Comforting others

The strength of the commitment to a mission determines how successful it will be. In the vicissitudes of life, successes and failures are inevitable, and a steadfast commitment to accomplish the goal is the only force that will sustain the effort through the up and downs. Therefore, a person's mission is a profoundly serious matter that requires an intense consideration because it is akin to the message in Robert Frost's (1992) lines, "Two roads diverged in a yellow wood and I—I took the one less traveled by and that has made all the difference" (p. 900). In short, the same mission that opens some doors closes others. That makes it an important decision.

Maya Angelou's grandmother (Angelou, 1993b) often gave her this wisdom in another way. She said, "What you're supposed to do when you don't like a thing is change it. If you can't change it, change the way you think about it. Don't complain" (p. 17).

Defining Values and Virtues

Values are part of the popular culture. However, they also have a solid historical base in the United States. Sandel (1996) traced the path of virtue through the development of modern America. He identified periodic landmarks. For example, he pointed out that in the writing of the U.S. Constitution, the framers tried to codify civic virtue. However, James Madison, who is often called the father of the Constitution, said, "Is there no virtue among us? If there is not, we are in a wretched situation. No theoretical checks, no form of government, can render us secure" (p. 132).

Today, there are best-selling books on the subject of values and virtues, such as Gertrude Himmelfarb's (1995) *The De-Moralization of Society*, William Bennett's (1993) *The Book of Virtues*, and Aaron, Mann, and Taylor's (1994) *Values and Public Policy* published by Washington's prestigious Brookings Institute. Indeed, many groups are conducting extensive discussions about values and virtues. The following sections present brief reviews of some of the major points of view.

The scholarly community is replete with treatises on values and virtues, which have become synonymous terms. Pelligrino and Thomasma (1993) discussed virtues in the medical context. Boonin-Vail (1994) stated, "The person who cultivates virtues minimizes the chances that she will fail to flourish" (p. 201). Himmelfarb (1995) described the deterioration of virtues and values in American society. Wilson (1993) spoke of innate virtues. Wattenberg (1995) stated that values are the most important factors in presidential elections. MacIntyre (1984) investigated the philosophical underpinnings of values and virtues. Carter (1995) contended that America has developed a culture of disbelief in which religiously based values are nonfunctional except on Sundays.

Lipset (1996) described Americans as "Utopian moralists who press hard to institutionalize virtue, to destroy evil people, and eliminate wicked institutions and practices" (p. 63). Kotkin (1992) commented, "The gradual erosion of the Anglo-American hegemony over the past few decades stems from the erosion of many of the core values that drove its ascendance" (p. 7). Huntington (1996) asserted that "the religious resurgence throughout the world is a reaction against secularism, moral relativism, and self-indulgence, and a reaffirmation of the values of order, discipline, work, mutual help and human solidarity" (p. 98). West (1994) made a piercing statement:

> A fully crystallized market culture appeared in which civic institutions such as families, neighborhoods, unions, churches, synagogues, mosques, held less sway, especially among young people. Is it a mere accident that nonmarket values like loyalty, commitment, service, care, concern—even tenderness—can hardly gain a foothold in such a market culture? Or that more and more of our children believe that life is a thoroughly hedonistic and narcissistic affair? (p. 48)

Henry Kissinger (1994) described the role of values in international affairs by stating:

> American leaders have taken their values so much for granted that they rarely recognize how revolutionary and unsettling these values can appear to others. No other society has asserted that the princi-

ples of ethical conduct apply to international conduct in the same way that they do to the individual. . . . No nation has ever imposed the moral demands on itself that America has. And no country has so tormented itself over the gap between its moral values which are by definition absolute, and the imperfections inherent in the concrete solutions to which they must be applied. (pp. 22–23).

H. Johnson (1994) told of the impact of values on everyday life in the United States:

Among Americans I met, the quest for values goes far beyond the political realm and represents much more than the term politicians use to claim superiority for their values over their opponents' unworthy values. . . . For some the search for values takes the form of a yearning for spiritual reassurance, whether from organized religion, popular media-age spiritual "gurus," or cults whose messiahs promise new forms of salvation. For others, the search leads toward a return to tradition, to strict "rules," to literal "truths" of the Bible. For still others, those same "rules" do not apply, nor can they rely on the traditions of the past as guides to the future. (pp. 294–295)

Thurow (1996) discussed the role of values in capitalism. His remarks cast doubt on compatibility between capitalism and values:

Values or preferences are the black hole of capitalism. They are what the system exists to serve, but there are no capitalistic theories of good or bad preferences, capitalistic theories of how values arise, and no capitalistic theories of how values should be altered or controlled. (p. 277)

Thurow (1996) concluded with a question: "How can capitalism promote the values that it needs to sustain itself when it denies that it needs to promote any particular set of values at all?" (pp. 308–309).

Sandel (1996) spoke of a recrudescence of virtue. He contended that during the 1930s there was an emphasis on freedom, but that by the 1990s, "Americans' discontent with their moral and civic condition was too pervasive to ignore" (p. 327). Sandel (1996) concluded that Bill Clinton was elected president because he stressed citizen responsibility as well as rights. Thus, virtues were viewed as a two-edged sword.

Psychology

Many in the psychological community have expressed an enduring interest in values and virtues. May (1953) wrote:

> The human being not only can make choices of values and goals, but he is the animal who must do so if he is to attain integration. For the value—the goal he moves toward—serves him as a psychological center, a kind of core of integration which draws together his powers as a core of a magnet draws the magnet's lines of force together. (p. 175)

Allport (1955) also discussed the function of values:

> The healthy adult develops under the influence of value schemata whose fulfillment he regards as desirable even though it may never be completely attained. . . he selects his perceptions, consults his conscience, inhibits irrelevant or contrary lines of conduct, drops and forms subsystems of habits as they are dissonant with his commitments. (pp. 75–76)

Prescott (1957) added to the dialogue about the meaning of values:

> Values are more than wishes or desires; they are convictions. They are an individual's deepest and most sincere statement to himself of what his life is about, what he believes, aspires to do, bring about, and become. (p. 412)

Prescotting (1957) believed that there were six functions of values: selecting, shaping, and ordering perceptions; shaping one's goals; choosing a sequence of behaviors to accomplish those goals; organizing the core of cognitive and affective life;

helping a person withstand privations; and helping maintain an ability to experience emotions.

Erikson (1964) defined virtues as "certain human qualities of strength" (p. 113). He also offered a developmental taxonomy of virtues:

1. Childhood: hope, will, purpose, and competence;
2. Adolescence: competence; and
3. Adult: love, care, and wisdom. (p. 115)

Maslow (1968) stated that some human values that are intrinsic and biologically based are also fragile. His estimate was that someday therapy would be defined as a search for values (p. 177).

Arbuckle (1970, p. 63) listed three major postulates about human values:

1. One can hardly be human without values. Indeed, the values of the person are the person.
2. To a tremendous degree, our values are the values we have learned, and we usually learn them from the people and the organizations who have most control and most influence over us.
3. The more a person learns he cannot be who and what he is, the more artificial he becomes as a person.

Frankl (1973) contended that values pull a person toward a goal. He added that a person is never driven toward a goal but rather decides to behave morally. Thus, Frankl placed emphasis on the cognitive dimension.

Frankl (1975) identified three groups of values: creative, experiential, and attitudinal. He explained that attitudinal values can convert anything into something positive and creative.

Carl Rogers (1983) proposed a valuing process and attributed two characteristics to it: (a) It has an organismic basis and (b) it is effective in achieving self-enhancement to the degree the individual is open to the experiencing that is going on within.

Carkhuff (1984) specified three types of values: living, learning, and working. He explained that the living values include parents, home, and family. Learning values emphasize growth and development in the community. Working values allow a person to become an independent contributor to the community-at-large.

Combs, Richards, and Richards (1988) stated that values are differentiated frames of reference that serve as guides for seeking or avoiding certain things. They explained that the clarity of those frames of reference differs greatly.

Kelly (1995) defined values as "principles, or criteria, for selecting what is good (or better, or best) among objects, actions, ways of life, and social and political institutions and structure" (p. 648). He explained that values "operate at the levels of individuals, of institutions and of entire societies" (p. 648).

Education

Sizer (1984) stated, "Clearly, schools are expected by most Americans to stand for certain values and to inculcate these in their students. Most of these values have religious roots, if not strict theological identification today. Educators who pretend that these are purely secular values are whistling in the dark" (p. 129).

Bloom (1987), in his famous critique of higher education, *The Closing of the American Mind*, contended that values as proposed by Friedrich Nietzsche were the core cause for the decline of undergraduate schools. Bloom passionately lamented the rise of relativism, which he declared destroyed the pursuit of truth and replaced it with the primacy of experience. He believed that values could lead only to irrational wars because there could be no agreement about which ones were preeminent. That is, they were not subject to systematic testing. Wilshire (1990) agreed in principle with Bloom by stating, "I believe that education is a moral enterprise and that the contemporary university lacks moral direction" (p. xxiii).

Lickona (1993) proposed a character approach to values and emphasized purposeful instruction for them. His stance was that values in the United States were deteriorating significantly and that it was time for intervention. Kohn (1997) described Lickona's proposal as inappropriate indoctrination and came down on the side of procedures that facilitate individual discovery of values.

Ryan (1993) wrote, "What constitutes a 'good person' has paralyzed many sincere educators and non-educators. Because the United States is a multiracial, multiethnic nation, many educators despair of coming up with a shared vision of the good person to guide curriculum builders" (p. 16).

Thomas and Roberts (1994) gave an assessment of the public schools' internal dilemma, "Some argue that character education has no place in public schools. . . . Educators at the other end of the spectrum argue that character education must be taught as a separate subject" (p. 33).

Writing in *Time* magazine, Wright (1996) said:

> It's true that many public schools fail to imbue virtue and that some imbue self-indulgence, self-pity and ersatz self-esteem. It may even be true that mush-minded liberal educators are the reason. Still, moral flabbiness isn't an inherent property of public schools; many of us remember when they were different. . . . In any event, public schools are one of the few remaining vehicles that in theory could help rebuild a moral structure transcending class, ethnicity and religion. (p. 44)

Conservatives

Robert Bork (1996) stated that "American culture is complex and resilient. But it is also not to be denied that there are aspects of almost every branch of our culture that are worse than ever before and that the rot is spreading" (p. 2).

Robertson (1993) was more sanguine than Bork when he wrote, "Traditional family values grew sharply and significantly between 1989 and 1991. . . . This trend toward traditional family values, family life, clean entertainment, simpler lifestyles, and religious faith is accelerating rapidly" (p. 163).

Colson (1987) stated, "A destructive philosophical trend has gripped American intellectuals. The long fuse lit by the ideas of Nietzsche, Freud, and Darwin finally set off an explosion of relativism. All moral distinctions were equally valid and equally invalid since all were equally subjective" (p. 468).

D'Souza (1996) contended, "A new liberal paradigm is emerging which seeks a transformation of basic American institutions. It seeks to implement new rules of political organization, new regulations, for the work force, new approaches to education, indeed, a new American dream and a new way of life" (p. 21).

Barna (1994) observed, "To understand a group of people, the most insightful information is that which reveals their values. . . . Busters (X-generation) concur with their elders that the most important elements of life are the family and their health" (pp. 59–60).

Wilson (1993) stated, "humans have a moral sense, one that emerges as naturally as the sense of beauty or ritual and that will affect [their] behavior, though not always and in some cases not obviously" (p. 25).

Liberals

Kozol (1991) asserted, "Conservatives are generally the ones who speak most passionately of patriotic values . . . but they reduce America to something tight and mean and sour, and they make the flag less beautiful than it should be" (p. 173). Later he added, "equity in education represents a formidable threat to other values held by many affluent Americans. It will be resisted as bitterly as school desegregation" (p. 222).

Schlessinger (1992) contended:

> We don't have to believe that our values are absolutely better than the next fellow's or the next country's, but we have no doubt that they are better for us, reared as we are — and are worthy of living by and worth dying for. For our values are not matters of whim and happenstance. History has given them to us. They are anchored in

our national experience, in our great national documents, in our heroes, in our folkways, traditions, and standards. People with a different history will have different values. But we believe that our own are better for us. They work for us; and for that reason, we live and die for them. (p. 137)

Hill and Jordan (1995) wrote, "we have learned that perspective informs judgment, that problems must be understood not only from the posture of privilege but from the point of view of the displaced, and that the displaced do not themselves all share the same point of view" (p. 201).

Pedersen (1994) stated:

Values are more often products of a person's subjective culture. . . . Attempts to treat values as objective verifiable facts have not been very successful. . . . Value differences may result from different national affiliations, different ethnic identities, or different social roles. . . . The description of cultures by their values suggests that culture is a trait or "disposition" to do one thing and not do another. (p. 124)

Glazer (1997) said, "It is clear that scholarly and scientific authority does not carry the weight it once did among nonexperts . . . no one really insists that truth is the only criterion for judgment on curriculum in social studies. . . truth is an uncertain and incomplete guide" (p. 39); "difficult as it is to implement them at the lower grades, and indeed in high school, we cannot escape 'multiple perspectives'" (p. 41).

The proliferation of writing about values and virtues is prima facie evidence of the widespread interest in the topic. A warranted conclusion is that the United States is deeply concerned about the state of its values and virtues, and a variety of proposals have been set forth. However, no concerted action has been taken or planned, which seems to indicate that the citizens are not ready to move rapidly in any direction. This relative inaction may suggest that the ongoing dialogue about values satisfies a palpable unease that is being expressed widely.

A second strand that is emerging from the discussion is that the proponents tend to cluster into two distinct groups. First are the advocates of traditional values, such as loyalty, honesty, and hard work. Second are the people who are placing a new emphasis on equity, diversity, and separate-but-equal orientations. Many members of this latter group express their common interests under the aegis of multiculturalism. In a sense, the momentum comes from the concern that marginal groups are being left out of the "main event" or power sharing in U.S. society. Said bluntly, their hope is to be included in the decision-making process.

The conventional tension between absolutism and relativism is somewhat obscured by the higher profiles of race and gender issues that more directly affect the marketplace. Discussions of affirmative action also mask the more intellectual underpinnings of the differences between those orientations.

In general, the United States is engaged in a rather spirited dialogue between those who have it pretty good under the present state of affairs (conservatives) and those who think society could do better if things were changed (liberals). Both groups agree that values shifts are key factors in cultural alterations and both have vested interests in seeing what changes are made. Changers are attacking the traditional values and "status quoers" are defending them. This is certainly not an unusual situation, but it is a somewhat disquieting one.

Choosing Personal Values or Virtues

Within the larger cultural context lies the individual task of choosing personal virtues or values. Aaron et al. (1994) contended that values and virtues have become so intertwined in the public's mind that they now are used interchangeably. But Woodward (1994) suggested different definitions for each term. He proposed that *virtues* are qualities of character by which individuals habitually recognize and do the right thing and that *values* are morally neutral terms that merely indicate preferences. For instance, the classical Greeks supported the virtues of courage, justice, temperance, and wisdom, whereas the Judeo-Christian virtues are faith, hope, and love. On the other hand, values may be as mundane as preferring steak over ham.

The notion of differentiating virtues from values is a good one because it allows a person to consider both enduring and temporary goals. In this conception, virtues can be classified as character traits a person wishes to cultivate in herself or himself across a lifetime, whereas values include the relatively short-range goals a person wants to attain.

Virtues, then, are enduring matters that deal with the kind of person an individual wants to become. For instance, trustworthiness is not something a person can establish immediately. It takes an extended period of time to confront a series of situations in which trustworthiness is validated so that one can say to oneself, "I was trustworthy." On the other hand, individuals can set trustworthiness as a goal toward which they strive. In that sense, trustworthiness becomes a guideline for a series of choices. The sequence of events is that a person enters a situation with the intent of being trustworthy. Second, a choice point is reached and the person is either trustworthy or not. Third, the person can review her or his behavior and determine if she or he was trustworthy. Thus, trustworthiness is functional both as a guideline during ongoing events and as a standard for assessing past behavior.

Choosing Virtues

Where or how does a person select virtues? Three different sources of virtues are supported by various theorists: innate, environment, and self-selection. Maslow (1968) and Rogers (1983), among others, contended that human beings are born with tendencies toward personal integration. That is, children are moral in that they tend to naturally seek experiences that are "good" for them. Wilson (1993) contended that people have an innate moral sense that competes with other senses for ascendancy. He wrote, "people have a natural moral sense, a sense that is formed out of the interaction of their innate dispositions with their familial experiences" (p. 2).

The most widely held view is that people get their virtues or values from their interpersonal environment. Rogers (1983) wrote very directly and poignantly on this subject:

> I believe that individuals with values mostly introjected, held as fixed concepts, rarely examined or tested, is the picture of most of us. By taking over the conceptions of others as our own, we lose contact with the potential wisdom of our own functioning and lose confidence in ourselves. Since these value constructs are often sharply at variance with what is going on in our own experiencing, we have in a very basic way divorced ourselves from ourselves, and this accounts for much of modern strain and insecurity. This fundamental discrepancy between the individual's concepts and what she is experiencing, between the intellectual structure of her values and the valuing process going on unrecognized within—this is a part of the fundamental estrangement of the modern person from his or her self. (p. 261)

Certainly, churches and all other values instruction agencies favor a virtues indoctrination process (Lickona, 1991). It also is reasonable to conclude that every society has common values it strives to teach its members. Maslow (1968) contended that in addition to their innate values, people have to learn some values from the environment. Therefore, there is considerable reason to conclude that some virtues originate in the culture rather than in the individual.

The third source of virtues is within the person's mental apparatus. That is, people can select some virtues. The suggestion is that at some point along the continuum of individual development, a person can pause to assess her or his status and choose to either alter or affirm specific virtues. In this sense, free people have an opportunity to reset their moral compass.

Reorienting oneself can be a matter of assessing the effectiveness of one's guideposts. The operative question is whether or not the present ones are helping the individual be the kind of person she or he wants to be. For instance, a person who wishes to become an effective parent may on reflection discover that she or he is currently placing too much value on work. Thus, at that point, the person can reorient herself or himself toward a different standard that will take her or him more directly to the desired goal.

Virtue shifts may occur swiftly through insight or through some type of conversion experience. They may also be accomplished systematically by stating the desired trait in behavioral terms and following a growth program composed of incremental steps. For instance, if work is the desired virtue, then it might be defined as fulfilling one's labor contracts (formal or informal) that spell out an obligation to do specific tasks. A review of a person's labor contracts might reveal that at present only 5 of 10 of them are being fulfilled, so the person then could choose to increase that number by one each month across a 5-month period. Thus, at the end of 5 months, the person would have behaviorally enhanced her or his practice of the virtue of work.

Thus, human beings get their virtues from innate and environmental sources, and at some point in their development they may have the opportunity to review their virtues and to alter them by means of cognitive and systematic procedures. The choice of specific virtues can be done by stating the kind of person one wants to be and determining which virtues attain that goal.

Choosing Values

Values are relatively short-term goals such as buying a home, going to college, or raising a family. They guide actions in a more immediate sense than do missions and virtues but, ideally, they are consistent with them. If a person's mission, preferred virtues, and values are in harmony, then the chances for satisfying all of them are enhanced. For instance, if one's mission is to reduce ignorance, then both the preferred virtues and the values are limited to the range of activities that facilitate the overall objective. The general notion is that people are more effective when their overarching purpose is integrated with the kind of person they want to be as well as the short-term objectives. It is comparable to aligning a ship's course according to the stars as well as to more immediate landmarks.

Living One's Values

Living one's values is the "real-life" test of character that is sometimes defined as doing what is right when no one sees you. That's a great idea, but how does a person do it? The truth is that no one does it perfectly. Allport (1955) wrote, "Few if any of our value-orientations hold the prospect of complete fulfillment. . . . Even the most integrated of personalities do not act always consistent with their schemata of value. Irresistible impulse, threads of infantilism, violations of conscience are factors to be reckoned with in every life" (pp. 76–77). Even the apostle Paul said, "That which I would not do, I do." Given that it is difficult to live one's values, it is reasonable to contend that they should be chosen carefully.

One relevant rule is that it is easier to keep a commitment that is made publicly than one that is held privately. For this reason, it is helpful to make one's values known to at least one other person. For example, one of the underlying principles of Weight Watchers and Alcoholics Anonymous is to create a support group that not only reinforces desired behavior but also indirectly holds a member responsible for "bad" behavior. Indeed, the effect of social pressure has been known since time immemorial.

One group of human development specialists convened annually with the expressed purpose of sharing their past year's work with each other. Each member took a turn explaining her or his projects across the preceding year. It was a moment of truth—something like a class reunion. Members used to prepare physically, intellectually, and emotionally for the conference where activities called for each set of skills.

At one family's annual Christmas party, each member informally reviewed how the year had gone. Always the father would ask someone this question—"I hear what you are doing, but what are you doing with the life God gave you?" By this, he meant, How are you investing your talents? That is a provocative question for all families.

Other groups such as church school classes can serve the same function. The core understanding is that "no person is an island" and that everyone's practice of their values can be enhanced by feedback and support from a constructive group or an individual.

The steps are, first, to state one's preferred virtues and self-selected goals (values) to a group of constructive people and, second, to report back to them about the degree of success attained. In other words, it helps to make a public commitment to a mission, a set of virtues, and one's values and to accept the responsibility for reporting (sharing) how well those goals have been accomplished. Perhaps the President's oath of office is the prototype of this type of commitment, and in a more personal sense, the wedding vow is akin to it.

The story is often told that when Bill Clinton met Hillary Rodham, he related to her that he wanted to be President of the United States some day. It is said that she shared his value (a relatively short-term goal). Together they attained that objective. Now, a good question is this: Do they have a mission? Is there something such as increasing women's participation in government that is their lifetime mission? And, if so, have they accomplished it, or is there still more to do? Then, there are Jimmy and Rosalyn Carter. Obviously, at some time they decided he would try to be President, which they accomplished. Now that they are out of the White House, it is equally clear that the Carters have a mission of upgrading the plight of the poor and homeless. It still motivates them and matches both what they do and the kind of people they are. There is a consistency among their mission, their virtues, and their values.

Living one's values is a matter of choosing short-term goals that are consistent with both the way one wishes to live (virtues) and the overarching goal one wants to achieve (mission). The next step is to make them public to constructive people and to be accountable to that group for striving toward one's goals. Remember, Jimmy Carter used to greet people by saying. "I'm Jimmy Carter and I'm running for President." In fact, those were the words that opened his acceptance address to the 1976 Democratic National Convention. That's the model. Perhaps it might help all of us to introduce ourselves to some groups by saying "this is who I am and this is what I'm trying to do with my life." If not publicly, then perhaps to a mirror.

Coming to Terms With Faith

Faith is the belief that one's way of explaining events is sufficient to cope with future happenings. The key word is *future*. Faith is focused on the future. The past is known and the present is unfolding. But faith is needed to face the future. Of course, the degree of faith varies from complete to none, and the amount of related anxiety is directly proportional to the level of faith.

Most people probably associate faith with "religion." Many women raised in patriarchal religions may feel excluded, marginalized, and put down by their religions (Wilcox, 1997). Wilcox, a counselor, minister, and woman, recounted stories of women whose pastors told them "to return to battering husbands and 'pray harder,' that it was the woman's fault for provoking the husband to anger" (p. 20). It is her contention that religious teaching has implications for self-esteem. She warned that theology can be and often is corrupted to maintain cultural traditions. Despite these realities, Wilcox (1997) suggested, "Under the haze of patriarchy, status quo, and tradition, shines a beacon of hope. Many cannot resist its pull and endure many abuses, trying to connect with their spiritual selves" (p. 27).

Thibault (1993) characterized the task of mature adulthood as developing an intense, mutual, and loving relationship with God. She expanded the notion of faith into the idea that the gift of the spirit is in all of life, both positive and negative events. She said:

> No suffering in itself is or ever will be gift. . . . All tragedies, all negative events can be transformed into gift if we have the desire to become aware of the gift. This does not mean that we glibly

deny pain and suffering. It means that we allow ourselves to experience it completely, become aware of all of it, acknowledge it, accept it, then go beyond it to a new meaning. (pp. 34-35)

If a person believes that her or his way of explaining events (usually religion or science or a combination of the two) is sufficient to cope with future events, then she or he faces oncoming occurrences with confidence. On the other hand, to the degree that there is doubt about the sufficiency of one's response system, the person experiences anxiety. Thus, a task faced by every person is to develop a faith that is sufficient to cope with future possibilities.

Faith development is a process that evolves from innocent trust to experiential validation. A newly born child assumes security until events generate doubt, at which time the individual begins to probe the environment to discover sources of security. As those new sources fulfill the need for security, the person develops faith in them and gains confidence to move into the future. In this quest for security, many people discover science as a way to cope with normal activities, and then religion becomes the means by which they can face the imponderables such as death, the great unknown.

The major point is that faith is built by successive approximations. That is, it is constructed either by trial and error or by systematic testing of hypotheses about the ability of certain devices to cope with subsequent events. As those hypotheses are confirmed, they are transformed into a repertoire of available responses that enable a person to live comfortably in a reasonably predictable life space. Thus, people progressively gain faith in their response repertoire, which includes a capacity for inventing new responses to fit novel circumstances.

A body of unknowns persists in all lives, and often, people adopt religious positions designed to cope with those mysterious situations. Thus, most mature persons have a faith in a personalized response repertoire that is based on both science and religion. This means that they believe that their response system is sufficient to cope with the future. If the confidence is eroded seriously, then emotional difficulties may ensue, and often, counseling and therapy are used as means to regain or establish the person's faith in her or his response repertoire.

Ultimately, faith is the ability to rise in the morning with a full understanding that even though life is fraught with uncertainty, one will accept the risk and continue with one's work because of the belief that one's way of explaining things will see one through. For some, that means a total reliance on science. For some, it means a total reliance on religion. For others, it means a reliance on some combination of both science and religion. Whatever the basis, the product is a faith that enables the person to use her or his abilities in a task that is consistent with the person's mission, preferred virtues, and self-selected values. In short, it empowers a human being to be a person.

Summary

This chapter discussed the spiritual dimension of human existence. Our general thesis is that there are three levels of spiritual concerns: mission, virtues, and values. Missions are the overarching purpose of a life. Virtues are the traits a person wishes to cultivate as a part of her being—the kind of person an individual wants to be. Values are the relatively short-term goals a person wants to accomplish, such as buying a home, starting a business, or parenting a family. The core position has been that human effectiveness is enhanced when the mission, virtues, and values are consistent.

We contend that a free people are able to select their missions by assessing the available opportunities and finding a best-fit opportunity and the individual's abilities and interests. The discriminating factor is the person's unique cluster of values, which indicate what is immediately important. It is as if a free world offers a smorgasbord of opportunities, and people's unique talents and desires permit them to select the one item that fulfills them most adequately.

The spiritual dimension is concerned primarily with generating harmony within one's life. As it develops, it aligns the larger purposes with the smaller tasks so that one's dreams and hopes are consistent with one's actions. It is achieving an integration that includes internal and external factors and is expressed in harmonious living variously called inner peace and calm.

Applications for Counselors

- Every client should have a personal mission statement. For many women, this exercise will be difficult because it requires a woman to define her life individually and not just as a part of a family. This does not mean that caring for her family cannot be part of her mission, but that a woman must come to terms with her self-selected rather than society-dictated goals.
- Who an individual will become is also a process of defining, selecting, and living a set of values and virtues. Counselors can assist clients in this process by providing a list of virtues. Bennett (1993) identified 10 key virtues, but every woman must be clear about which virtues are critical to her. She must define those for herself and develop a way to determine if they are reflected in her daily life. These activities fall within usual counseling methodologies.
- Counselors may feel unqualified to help individuals come to terms with faith because this area may be viewed more as the responsibility of clergy. However, counselors should feel qualified to address this area as "preventive screening." The notion of screening for potential risks comes from the medical model but has application here. Physicians ask patients about life-style as well as family illnesses to determine the need for intervention, and counselors should ask clients if they have come to a personally satisfying answer to their own faith questions. If a client has not found a meaningful answer, then the counselor can use homework assignments to help her find appropriate activities to resolve her questions. Such assignments might include a referral to a spiritual advisor or books to read to help in the client's exploration process.

Section IV

Case Examples of Equity Achievement

There have always been women who, despite the difficulties of their situation, managed to achieve equity in her own time. Marie Curie was a great scientist in a time when very few women even considered the possibility. Elizabeth Blackwell was the first woman to complete medical school in the United States (in 1849) and practice as a physician (Caelleigh, 1996). The belle of Amherst, Emily Dickinson, gave us wonderful poetry; Georgia O'Keeffe has filled our lives with the beauty of her paintings. Our advantage in looking back in time is that we know their contributions were great. At the time that they lived and struggled, they may not have experienced equity as positively as women do today. They paid a price to blaze a trail.

The four women profiled in this section have achieved success at the highest level of their fields. Other women have followed their lead, but these four women were first, and being first is in itself a cause for anxiety requiring great courage to overcome. Each of them—Sandra Day O'Connor, Maya Angelou, Sally Ride, and Betty Lentz Siegel—brings to this text a wonderful story, rich in texture of the possibilities of womanhood fully developed.

These women are amazingly different, and yet there are similarities in the way their lives unfolded. All of them carried within themselves a strong belief in their own talents. They prepared themselves so that when the opportunity came, they were ready to accept it. They worked hard. They learned about how the world works and did not accept that as the final reality. They risked. They acted. They won.

From Sandra Day O'Connor, we learn the persistence of believing in oneself when others do not. Her first job offer after graduating third in her law class at Stanford University was as a secretary in a major law firm, not as an attorney. It is obvious that she was bright and talented, but the world of the 1950s did not anticipate the likelihood of a woman Supreme Court Justice in the making.

Maya Angelou at age 16 was pregnant and unmarried at a time when such things were not as common as they are today. The distance between her life in San Francisco in 1949 and that of the woman reading her poem to not only the nation but also the world on the west side of the U.S. Capitol on Inauguration Day, 1992, is almost too great to imagine. From Maya Angelou, we learn about having great faith and persistence, studying, developing talent, accepting challenge, learning, and loving. Whatever the challenge, she did not lose sight of who she was and the talents she had been given.

Sally Ride grew up amid the turmoil of the 1960s. The struggles for civil rights and women's rights were front page news. She grew up in a home that practiced the beliefs so many others were struggling for, and she internalized the notion that ability, not gender or race, should determine a person's opportunities. Sally Ride followed her interests, first in tennis, and then in physics. She worked for perfection and did not settle easily for less. When opportunity came, Sally was ready and perfectly prepared to take advantage of it, and it was a great adventure.

Betty Lentz Siegel also grew up in a home that valued education, dreaming dreams, then working to achieve them. Her love of the arts began with daily exposure to the movies and a broader world beyond her Applachian home. She is a woman of many firsts in the educational world, including becoming the first woman to assume the role of president of a college in the Georgia university system. Her awards and honors are legion because she has lived the principles (respect, trust, optimism, and intentionality) of an organization that she cofounded that is dedicated to invitational education. She has worked hard and blazed a trail for many women to follow.

It has always been possible for *some* women to achieve all that they desire. The models in this chapter demonstrate this reality, and these women are good models. However, there are thousands of women who could have taken their places—they just did not have the opportunity. Other women can learn from the four in this section and apply that learning to their own lives with the belief that good things will happen. Each of us has opportunities that come our way because of timing. These women met the challenge of their opportunities.

11

Sandra Day O'Connor: U.S. Supreme Court Justice

In 1952, two Arizonans, William Rehnquist and Sandra Day, graduated from Stanford University's Law School. He was ranked first and she was ranked third. He went to work as a law clerk for U.S. Supreme Court Justice Robert Jackson, (William Rehnquist, 1998), and she was offered employment as a legal secretary. The discrepancy between their professional opportunities was enormous. When one asks why this difference existed, the answer seems to devolve down to sex biases of that time. However, an equally important issue is how Sandra Day (O'Connor) coped with those inequities to become a justice on the U.S. Supreme Court.

Growing Up

Sandra Day was born on March 26, 1930, on a ranch that covered 300 square miles near the border of Arizona and New Mexico. On that Lazy B Ranch, there were no phones, neighbors were far away, and the closest town was a 25-mile trip (Morris-Lipsman, 1990). People had to be self-sufficient, a trait Sandra learned from both her mother, Ada Mae Wilkey Day, and her father, Harry A. Day, a reputed conservative. By her teenage years, Sandra could ride horses, shoot rifles, and brand steer (Smolla, 1995).

College and Career

Self-reliance remained one of Sandra's chief character traits during her school days in El Paso, Texas. Because Sandra was very bright and the local schools were quite limited, her parents sent her to live with her grandparents in El Paso, where she could enroll in a private school (Morris-Lipsman, 1990). Sandra excelled in high school, and proceeded to enroll at Stanford University for both undergraduate and law school, where she served as editor of the prestigious *Stanford Law Review* (Cannon, 1996). Quite probably, one of her inspirations at Stanford was classmate John Jay O'Connor, who became her husband and father of their three sons, Scott, Brian, and Jay.

After graduation from Stanford, Sandra entered the job market with great expectations. She applied to several top West Coast law firms, which she later referred to as "white shoe firms." However, her only offer was to be a legal secretary in a large company. Sandra opted for a position as a law clerk for San Mateo County in California, but her obviously superior ability led to a promotion as the deputy county attorney. Nevertheless, the early rejection by the prestigious law firms left a deep and indelible impression in Sandra's mind (Morris-Lipsman, 1990). At that time, her husband's military career took him to an overseas assignment in Germany, and Sandra accompanied him. When John's military obligation was completed, the family settled in Phoenix, Arizona, where he joined an upscale law firm, but in the face of the same conditions she had found on the West Coast, Sandra decided to care for her children and, later, to start her own private practice in Maryville, Arizona.

In 1965, perhaps because of the limited opportunities in private practice, Sandra entered public law practice as an assistant attorney general. She must have drawn attention because in 1969, Governor John Williams appointed her to an empty seat in the Arizona State Senate. Subsequently, she was elected to two more terms.

Sandra stepped indirectly into national affairs in 1972, when she cochaired Richard Nixon's Arizona reelection campaign. During the following year, she was the first woman to become majority leader of Arizona's Republican-dominated State Senate.

Her storybook rise in state politics continued in 1975 when she was elected judge of Maricopa County Superior Court. Two years later, in 1979, a democrat, Governor Bruce Babbitt, appointed her to the Arizona Court of Appeals. Thus, she stood near the pinnacle of the state's legal system.

It is interesting that Sandra Day O'Connor's early professional career had some important similarities with as well as differences from that of William Rehnquist. At undergraduate school, Sandra graduated magna cum laude from Stanford while William was Phi Beta Kappa at Harvard. Both attended Stanford Law School, where they did exceptionally well academically. In 1952, William went to Washington for a clerkship at the Supreme Court while Sandra accompanied her husband to an overseas military assignment (Cannon, 1996).

By the late 1950s and early 1960s, both were in Phoenix pursuing separate private law practices, but each also was active in local Republican politics, where Senator Barry Goldwater was emerging as a national figure. Both Sandra and William participated in Goldwater's 1964 presidential campaign. However, in 1969, Rehnquist left Phoenix permanently when he was appointed by President Nixon as the Assistant U.S. Attorney General for the Office of Legal Counsel. From that position,

Rehnquist participated in many high-profile legal affairs in which he consistently assumed a firm conservative stance (Sandra Day O'Connor, 1998).

Circumstances gave Sandra's career a dramatic shift one month before election day in 1980. While Ronald Reagan was campaigning for president, his pollster, Richard Wirthlin, reported that for the first time, Jimmy Carter was slightly ahead. Reagan's political advisors suggested that he announce that he was going to appoint a woman to the Supreme Court. The next day he made that announcement. It is important to note that Reagan never trailed again (Cannon, 1996).

Justice Potter Stewart retired during Reagan's first year in office, thus paving the way for the President to keep his promise to appoint a woman to the Supreme Court. Reagan asked for a list of four possible nominees, and his first interview was with O'Connor, who had been recommended by Senator Barry Goldwater. Subsequently, the other meetings were canceled and O'Connor's name was sent up to the U.S. Senate on July 7, 1981. The Senate confirmed her unanimously, and she was officially appointed on September 25, 1981. Not everyone was happy, however. Reverend Jerry Falwell, a conservative religious political activist, said that "All good Christians should be concerned," to which Senator Goldwater replied, "Every good Christian ought to kick Falwell right in the ass" (Cannon, 1996, p. 55).

On the day of her swearing in, President Reagan went to the Supreme Court to view the historic proceedings. This was a rare exception in procedure because the brief ceremony had no role for the President. So, President and Nancy Reagan sat quietly on the front row while Sandra Day O'Connor took her oath of office as the first female justice at the U.S. Supreme Court. The significance of that event was clear to all and was underscored by the President's attendance.

An interesting sidebar is that the Supreme Court was preparing itself for the arrival of the first woman justice. Justice Byron White called the court's attention to its tradition of signing its decisions "Mr. Justice _____." White suggested, and his cohorts concurred, that the court should start a new tradition by signing "Justice _____." The "Mr." was deleted in anticipation of the addition of women to the Supreme Court. In a real sense, it was a civilized recognition of the changing patterns in American society.

Ironically, William French Smith was President Reagan's Attorney General when Sandra was nominated to the Supreme Court. It was his responsibility to call her to ask if she would accept a nomination for the justice position. Back in 1952, Smith was the person who had offered Sandra a legal secretary's position when she sought to join his law firm as an associate. The irony of the situation in 1981 was so striking that Sandra was compelled to ask Smith if he was calling to offer her another secretaryship.

In retrospect, O'Connor's path to the Supreme Court seems somewhat matter of fact, especially in light of her superior credentials. But it was not so, in sharper focus. Two of the customary credentials were missing: She had not been on her state's supreme court, nor had she served in the federal court system. In fact, the person whom many expected to be the first female member of the Supreme Court was someone else: Shirley Hufstedtler. President Johnson had appointed Hufstedtler to the Ninth Circuit Court, and it was assumed that President Carter would nominate her to the Supreme Court, except that no vacancies occurred during his term.

Existing traditions menaced O'Connor's Supreme Court appointment. In the 1870s, Susan B. Anthony stood trial for voting. In 1875, Lavinia Goodell was fighting to be admitted to the bar in Wisconsin. Her case failed in the State supreme Court. In 1965, when Judith Lichtman graduated from the Wisconsin Law School, there were only two women in a class of 150 (Cannon, 1996). Thus, the weight of tradition was against O'Connor.

O'Connor's impressive intellectual credentials were not her only attributes. Her distinction among her fellow justices is that of a fence-mender. She is referred to as a swing vote, which means that she can build majorities of five. In this capacity, she has succeeded Justice William Brennan as the court's pragmatic legal mind. However, she must also transcend the temptation to cater to the differing demands of both conservatives and liberals. In short, she must be at the same time both independent and integrative.

Another of O'Connor's qualities is courage. In 1988, she underwent a mastectomy, which was followed by chemotherapy. She scheduled her treatments on Fridays so that the ensuing weakness and nausea would not interfere with her regular duties (Cannon, 1996). In addition, she endured her surgery without informing her siblings until it was over.

To add balance to her personal life, O'Connor joined the MPU, or Mobile Party Unit, which schedules activities in which no husbands are allowed. On one such outing, this 5 foot 8 inch legal giant danced the night away with an Idaho cowboy moving to the strains of country music (Cannon, 1996).

O'Connor has not monopolized the credit for either her own professional progress or that of women in general in the legal profession. She commented, "I wouldn't be here if it weren't for what. . . other women have done. It's not my accomplishments but theirs that made it possible" (Smolla, 1995, p. 16). Regardless of her modesty, Justice O'Connor has participated in some very important shifts in women's roles in the legal profession:

1. Women now constitute 50% of every major law school class.
2. Women are becoming partners in big law firms.
3. Women serve as general counsels to almost every major agency in the federal government.

In general, the role of women in the legal profession has been transformed, and history will assign Sandra Day O'Connor a major role in the shift of that tectonic plate.

Many social conservatives assumed that President Reagan appointed Justice O'Connor to the Supreme Court so that she could help repeal *Roe v. Wade*, which legalized abortion. But in 1983 when that issue faced the court, O'Connor took the position that the changing membership of the court was not sufficient reason to overturn a previous decision (McCloskey, 1994). With this almost ingenious stance, the first female member of the Supreme Court incurred the wrath of social conservatives.

There were other hard choices for Justice O'Connor. On matters of religion, she rejected the traditional establishment clause based in *Lemon v. Kurtzman* in which a statute is invalid if it has a primary purpose or effect of advancing or inhibiting religion or if it causes excessive government entanglement with religion. O'Connor substituted the question of whether government intends or is presumed to endorse religion (Hall, 1992, p. 604).

Perhaps the knottiest social problem of the late 1900s is affirmative action, and Justice O'Connor has been right in the middle of the action. Her position has been that such programs should be tested under strict scrutiny to show a remedial need for the program to rectify prior government (rather than just social) discrimination.

All of Justice O'Connor's decisions in the pressure-packed legal situations have generated discomfort among many groups. She has drawn upon her physical, emotional, and intellectual resources to demonstrate that a woman can stand in the fires of legal conflict and continue to produce judgments that have furthered the basic principles of freedom and justice that are embedded in the U.S. Constitution. As she has performed her duties, she has brought honor to all women, even those who disagree with her judgments. In short, Justice Sandra Day O'Connor was prepared for the opportunity that history has offered her.

Summary

In many ways, Sandra Day O'Connor is an American success story. She emerged from the sandy soil of the western United States to progress through the educational system and public service until she stands atop the legal profession. It seems that she was destined for high office and yet, her ascension was marked by points that seemed to be blind alleys—no professional job after law school graduation, overseas travels (professional detours) with her husband, private practice which appeared unremarkable, rather pedestrian roles in political campaigns, and, perhaps most encumbering, a network of traditions that presumed women would be assigned low-profile tasks. Her experiences had many of the appearances of a path to an unfulfilled potential.

The main question is, How did O'Connor progress to the U.S. Supreme Court? Hard work? Talent? Yes, but more than that. She persistently did her best in the situations she was in. This meant that she accepted many challenging opportunities where the risk was great. There were chances to fail in grand style. Yet, she stepped forward and learned new ways of doing things. For example, when she was called to Washington to be interviewed by President Reagan, she had never been to Washington and did not know how to get to the White House. Her visit with the President in the Oval Office was the first time she had been there. She was not afraid to succeed, even though some writers have said that she is shy in social gatherings (Smolla, 1995, p. 16).

How did Sandra Day O'Connor succeed? By being prepared physically, emotionally, and intellectually and by being willing to meet her date with destiny. She stands in contrast to many others who also dreamed of wonderful things but who shrank not only from preparation but also from the moment of truth. Perhaps her childhood days on the ranch taught her how to show up for the "high-noon shoot-outs" in the middle of the street where the stakes are high. Certainly, branding a young bull is a test of one's mettle and refines it for higher purposes.

12

Maya Angelou: Poet Laureate

On the brisk afternoon of January 20, 1993, Maya Angelou became the first woman and first African American to read her work at a presidential inauguration. Her poem, "On the Pulse of Morning" (Angelou, 1993a) celebrates the diversity of both the American and world communities and calls on them to work together to create a better future. The poem concludes with:

Here on the pulse of this new day
You may have the grace to look up and out
And into your sister's eyes,
And into your brother's face,
Your country.

And say simply
Very simply
With hope —
Good morning.

In some ways, Maya's appearance at the inauguration was almost inevitable. The incoming president, William Jefferson Clinton, referred to her as his favorite living poet (Maya Angelou, 1998), and Maya had spent most of her early childhood in rural Arkansas where she was reared by her cherished paternal grandmother she called "Momma." On the other hand, Maya's voyage from Stamps, Arkansas, to the west side of the nation's Capitol on Inauguration Day, 1993, was fiercely circuitous and almost wildly unpredictable.

Growing Up

On April 4, 1928, Bailey and Vivian Baxter Johnson became parents of Marguerita Johnson in St. Louis, Missouri (S. Williams, 1996). The newborn's beloved brother, Bailey, Jr., one year her senior, bestowed the name "Maya" on his sister because he preferred it to "Marguerita." Quite probably, it also was easier for the lad to pronounce. Anyway, the melodious name has stuck for more than half a century.

Maya and her brother were sent to Stamps, Arkansas, because her mother's marriage ended (Angelou, 1970). What seemed like a near-tragedy in some quarters became a blessing in the hands of Maya's grandmother. Momma was extremely religious and "invited" all her friends to the local Methodist Episcopal Church, which served only African Americans. In addition to Momma, the Sunday entourage regularly included her neighbor Mrs. Flowers, Maya, Bailey, and Uncle Willie, Momma's handicapped brother and longtime resident in her home (Angelou, 1970). This community of strong African American women gave Maya powerful role models of courage, grace, compassion, and love that would become the foundation of her character.

Through the week, the family ran the only general supply store in the Black part of the little town. Momma's extended business dealings included renting property to White tenants, and in segregated Stamps, this was not an easy alliance (Angelou, 1970).

Momma had a reputation for helping people. In that vein, she, along with Mrs. Flowers, encouraged Maya's reading while she was a student at Lafayette County Training School. Maya loved Mrs. Flowers, who lived alone and was one of the few true gentlewomen Maya had known. Those senior women endured as positive influences in Maya's life. In a sense, they provided Maya with her concepts of home and family.

At age 8, Maya's life received a devastating shock. Her father took her to visit her mother in St. Louis, where one of her mother's friends raped Maya (Schomburg Center, 1998). She told her brother what happened and, subsequently, the rapist was tried and convicted but did not serve time. Instead, he was killed by unidentified assailants, but it was rumored that Maya's uncles had secured revenge. There is some uncertainty about the details of the rapist's death, but Maya interpreted it as a result of her telling about it. She was so distraught by the events that she stopped talking for several years. During that silent period, Mrs. Flowers encouraged Maya to speak and Momma prayed for her. Finally, Maya spoke sometime after Mrs. Flowers told her that she ought to speak the poetry she loved so dearly (Angelou, 1970).

Education and Career

In 1940, at age 12, Maya moved to San Francisco with her mother. Then, in 1945, just after her high school graduation, Maya gave birth to a son named Clyde who later was called Guy. Unwed at 16, she worked odd jobs such as cabaret dancing, singing, and acting (Angelou, 1970).

In 1952, Maya married Tosh Angelos, a sailor of Greek decent. But serious relationship struggles developed. Tosh was an avid atheist whereas Maya was a devout Christian, and the resulting tension dissolved the marriage. However, Maya was not a quitter, so she took a job singing and dancing at the Purple Onion, a club in San Francisco, where contacts led to a role in *Porgy and Bess* with a company that toured internationally. By this time, Maya had changed her name to Maya Angelou, perhaps as a result of her marriage to Tosh Angelos. (Maya Angelou, 1998).

When she returned in 1958, Maya, accompanied by her son Clyde, traveled to New York, where good things happened. She sang in clubs including the Apollo Theater in Harlem. She practiced her writing skills with the Harlem Literary Guild, where she met James Baldwin. She worked with Godfrey Cambridge to produce the *Cabaret for Freedom*, an off-Broadway production for the benefit of the Southern Christian Leadership Conference (SCLC). Then, in 1959, her flair for leadership skills led to her appointment to succeed Bayard Rustin as the northern coordinator for the SCLC headed by Martin Luther King, Jr. (Schomburg Center, 1998).

Maya met and married Vusumzi Make, a South African freedom fighter, and moved with him to Cairo, Egypt, where she became the associate editor of the *Arab Observer*, the only English-language news weekly in the Middle East. However, by 1963, this marriage ended (Schomburg Center, 1998).

Maya had decided to stay in Africa, so she migrated to Ghana to be the administrator of the School of Music and Drama at the University of Ghana. She was the feature editor of the *African Review*. Perhaps most important, Maya felt at home (Angelou, 1986).

During the late 1960s and 1970s, Maya's writing career blossomed. In 1970, she published *I Know Why the Caged Bird Sings*, which was an account of her childhood up to the birth of her son. This work became a bestseller and was nominated for a national book award. It also was a 2-hour special on CBS-TV.

A partial listing of her works includes the following: *Just Give Me a Cool Drink of Water 'fore I Diiie: The Poetry of Maya Angelou* (1971); *Gather Together in My Name* (1974); *Oh Pray My Wings Are Going to Fit Me Well* (1975); *Singin' and Swingin' and Gettin' Merry Like Christmas* (1976); *And Still I Rise* (1976); *The Heart of a Woman* (1981); *Shaker, Why Don't You Sing?* (1983); *All God's Children Need Traveling Shoes* (1986); *Now Sheba Sings the Song* (1987); *I Shall Be Moved* (1990); and *Wouldn't Take Nothing for My Journey Now* (1993; S. Williams, 1996).

Large portions of Maya's work are autobiographical. *Gather Together in My Name* describes her search for survival as a young, unwed mother. *Singin' and Swingin' and Gettin' Merry Like Christmas* tells of her business career. *The Heart of a Woman* speaks of her emergence as a writer and political activist. *All God's Children Need Traveling Shoes* described her time in Ghana and the relationship between Africa and African American culture (The Schomburg Center, 1998)

Things were happening on many fronts. President Gerald Ford nominated Maya to the Bicentennial Commission. President Jimmy Carter appointed her to the National Commission on the Observance of International Women's Year. In film-making, Maya wrote scripts and directed so that she opened doors for other Black women. She wrote several prize-winning documentaries for PBS, including *Afro-Americans in the Arts,* which received the Golden Eagle Award. Her acting role in *Roots* was nominated for an Emmy Award while her screenplay *Georgia, Georgia,* was the first by a Black woman to be filmed (S. Williams, 1996).

In May 1997, Maya addressed the annual conference of the American Counseling Association in Orlando, Florida. In a yellow dress and flowing headpiece, this strikingly handsome woman stood tall in many ways as she spoke eloquently to a hushed, almost reverent audience of counselors who rose repeatedly to applaud her words of compassionate wisdom. Her message was true to her life: Keep the faith and love your human uniqueness.

For the Million Man March that gathered on the plaza in Washington, D.C., in October 1996, Maya contributed a poem, which she read to the participants. Still, her activity continues to grow. She lectures in the United States as well as abroad and, as a Reynolds Professor, teaches at Wake Forest University in North Carolina (Maya Angelou, 1998).

The best spokesperson for Maya Angelou is Maya Angelou. So, it is appropriate to quote from an interview Maya granted to Ken Kelley (1995). Here are excerpts from that interview session:

Question: How does spirituality fit into the American way of life?

Angelou: Somehow we have come to the erroneous belief that we are all but flesh, blood, and bones, and that's all. So we direct our values to material things. We become what writer Beah Richards calls "exiled to things." If we have three cars, rather than two, we'll live a little longer. If we have four more titles, we'll live longer still. And, especially, if we have more money than the next guy, we'll live longer than he. It's so sad.

Question: Does embracing spirituality allow you to be an optimist, who can undespairingly ask, as you do in one of your poems, "Why do Black children hope? Who will bring them peas and lambchops and one more morning?"

Angelou: Those Black children are the bravest, without knowing it, representatives of us all. The Black kids, the poor white kids, Spanish-speaking kids, and Asian kids in the U.S.—in the face of everything to the contrary, they still bop and bump, shout and go to school somehow. And dare not only to love somebody else, and even to accept love in return, but dare to love themselves—that's what is most amazing. Their optimism gives me hope.

Question: You think the spirit of youthful optimism will let today's kids rise above the violence on the streets?

Angelou: Yes, and rise above the oblique and direct negligence.

Question: Meaning?

Angelou: When the human race neglects its weaker members, when the family neglects its weakest one—it's the first blow in a suicidal movement. I see the neglect in cities around the country, in poor White children in West Virginia and Virginia and Kentucky—in big cities, too, for that matter. I see neglect of Native American children in the concentration camps called reservations.

The powerful say, "Pull up your bootstraps." But they don't really believe that those living on denuded reservations, or on strip-mined hills, or in ghettoes that are destinations for drugs from Colombia and Iraq, can somehow pull themselves up. What they're really saying is, "If you can, do, but, if you can't, forget it." It's the most pernicious of all acts of segregation, because it is so subtle.

Question: A generation after the Civil Rights Act, how much progress has America made in the fight against racial discrimination?

Angelou: We've made a lot of progress—it's dangerous not to say so, because if we don't say so, we tell young people, implicitly or explicitly, that there can be no change. Then they compute: "You mean the life and death and work of Malcolm X and Martin Luther King, the Kennedys, Medgar Evers, Fannie Lou Hamer, the life and struggle of Rosa Parks—they did all that and nothing has changed? Well, then, what in the hell am I doing? There's no point for me to do anything." The truth is, a lot has changed—for the good. And it's gonna keep getting better, according to how we put our courage forward, and thrust our hearts forth.

Question: If you were a 16-year-old today, what would you be doing to find your place in a world that can seem so bleak?

Angelou: I would read. That's what I did. I would read everybody, all the time. I would read Dickens, and I would read Kenzaburo Oe for his almost painful insight. I would read James Baldwin for his unqualified love and beautiful writing.

Summary

Because of her outstanding accomplishments, it is tempting to dismiss Maya Angelou as one of those rare exceptions to every rule of life. In that posture, a person can say, "If I had had those talents I would have done some great things, too." A more honest assessment is to delineate the processes Maya uses and to measure one's lifestyle against them. First, she has courage. She battles back from adversity. Second, she has desire. She establishes goals and works to achieve them. Third, she has compassion. She takes the time to enter others' lives empathically and to understand their struggle. Fourth, she has self-love. She accepts and values herself as a person who has struggled and fallen and risen to struggle again. Indeed, it is the struggle she values most. Fifth, Maya lives in a space with all of humanity. Some call that religion, others call it universality. Whatever, Maya transcends the temporary and the compartmentalized and joins the overlapping and timeless well from which springs the force that enriches and ennobles human existence.

Courage, desire, compassion, self-love, transcendence, and role models who guided her journey—these are the secrets of Maya Angelou's success. Through those "windows," she sees beyond the probabilities that limit life, and she grasps the possibilities that are there for all who will reach for them both individually and collectively. No one can capture Maya in space or in mind because she has seen the unlimited potential within herself. Life is so affirmed that she struggles to free it in others. In that sense, she is free and she soars toward the limits that may or may not be there.

13

Sally Ride: First American Woman in Space

E very life is a story in which the events that unfold are only a part of the whole. The story is grander by far than mere events. Sally Ride's story is also grander than the events because there is much to learn about empowerment for women, even though she would be the last to lay claim to such an influence. Her very reluctance to be a metaphor for successful women gives credence to the worldview that made it possible for her to achieve the success she has gained. The events of her story are powerful images of success for any person, but Sally Ride was the first American woman to achieve them, and that made her contribution special. She blazed a trail that others would follow—she made the impossible possible. What characteristics does Sally Ride possess that allowed her to make such a monumental contribution to the right of women to participate in a field that had previously been denied to them? Here, the events of her life provide the clues.

Growing Up

Sally Kristen Ride was born in Los Angeles, California, on May 26, 1951. Her father was a political science professor at Santa Monica College and her mother was a teacher. Sally has a younger sister, Karen. By all accounts, her household was one in which education was emphasized. Reading was appreciated, encouraged, and modeled, especially by her mother, who was a voracious reader. Sally's parents encouraged their children, but they also believed that it was important for them to explore life for themselves (Camp, 1997).

Sally was able to read by the age of 5 and was not only interested but also talented in sports. Her father reported that Sally read the sports pages from age 5 on and had a remarkable memory for baseball statistics (Hurwitz & Hurwitz, 1989). It was also notable that Sally excelled in sports and was so good in softball and football that she was often the only girl selected to play in the neighborhood games organized by boys.

When she was 9, Sally's father took a sabbatical to Europe with his family. This was a tremendously enriching experience for Sally and Karen. When they returned, they often entertained individuals from other countries and different cultures. These experiences gave Sally a much larger context for understanding the world.

Sally was a good student who focused intently on those things that interested her and ignored those that did not. She was not interested in playing the piano and refused to take the lessons her mother wanted for her (Camp, 1997). She was not particularly outgoing, and one teacher described her as quiet and very private (Hurwitz & Hurwitz, 1989). In fact, she almost passed through elementary and middle school unnoticed (Camp, 1997). When asked about her parents' influence on her academic career, she remarked that they did not interfere "except to make sure I studied and brought home the right kind of grades" (Golden, 1983, p. 57).

Besides being a good student, Sally's love of sports helped her discover her talent for tennis. Beyond talent, she also brought the discipline of practice and a determination for excellence. She would practice for hours and eventually studied with four-time women's national champion, Alice Marble (Camp, 1997). Eventually, Sally was the 18th-ranked junior player in the United States while still in high school.

Her skill at tennis was the source of a scholarship to a small, exclusive private high school in Los Angeles, Westlake School for Girls. There she continued to develop her tennis skills and became well known as a fierce competitor. While still a good student, Sally was also known for her personal motivation. Her mother said of her, "If she was bored in the classroom. . . she would not make an effort. It irritated some teachers" (Blacknall, 1984, p. 16).

Westlake was a life-changing experience for Sally, for it was there that she met Dr. Elizabeth Mommaerts and discovered her love for science. Under Dr. Mommaerts' tutelage, Sally discovered the scientific method of problem solving, and this process made exceeding sense to her logical mind. She graduated from Westlake in 1969 at the age of 17 as one of the top six students in the class.

Sally was not affected by society's differing rules about proper work for men and women. She assumed that she could do anything that interested her. Her parents had raised her as a child with abilities, talents, and interests; and they had encouraged her to explore them to the fullest. This attitude was a significant one that led her to follow her interests completely, never asking permission, just believing in her ability to pursue her dreams.

College and Career

Sally Ride began college at Swarthmore College in Pennsylvania in 1969. She majored in physics and continued playing tennis. She won the Eastern Intercollegiate Women's Tennis championship twice, but eventually decided to return to California because Swarthmore did not have indoor tennis courts, which made tennis a seasonal game. Sally transferred to Stanford and continued her study of physics and her devotion to tennis.

At this time in her life, Sally was pulled toward tennis as a profession. She had gained national attention, and Billie Jean King encouraged her to give up science for tennis. And she might have done just that except that Sally was not convinced that she had what it takes to be a tennis professional. Her standards were very high, and she wanted to be able to control every serve and every return. But she couldn't, and that reality propelled her to stay in school and study science. However, Sally continued to train physically by running every day.

As a junior at Stanford, Sally made another major discovery: She loved Shakespeare. For her, his writing style was another problem to solve (without equations), and she loved the change of pace from her science classes. She viewed Shakespeare as a puzzle to be solved and enjoyed the process of figuring out what he was trying to say (Camp, 1997).

Molly Tyson, a friend of Sally's from college, described her this way, "I've never seen Sally trip on or off the court, physically or intellectually" (Golden, 1983, p. 58). She also described Sally as being a succinct writer and discussant who would turn in three-page papers to her English professors.

Upon completion of her undergraduate degree at Stanford, Sally Ride stayed to complete a master's of science degree in physics in 1975 and doctor of philosophy degree in astrophysics in 1978. Astrophysics was a field traditionally occupied by men, and her research on the X-rays given off by stars was pathfinding. It was her work with lasers that helped her acquire a place in the astronaut program (Camp, 1997).

As she struggled with her next career move, Sally inadvertently came across an advertisement in the Stanford University newspaper announcing open applications for a new shuttle astronaut class. The astounding thing to Sally Ride was that not only did they want scientists, but they were also encouraging women and ethnic/racial minorities to apply (Hurwitz & Hurwitz, 1989). There were more than 6,000 applicants from around the country and 1,251 were women (Chaikin, 1996). In January 1978, 35 new astronaut candidates were announced, and 6 of them were women, including Sally Ride.

All of the women held doctorates: There were two medical doctors, a biochemist, an electrical engineer, a geophysicist, and an astrophysicist, and all of them had high-powered scientific credentials. Despite their expertise, however, these women were unlike their male counterparts who (for the most part) had wanted to be astronauts from childhood. "[T]hat possibility had never occurred to most of the women until NASA's 1976 announcement" (Chaikin, 1996, p. 45)

The training for the new astronauts was grueling, for both the men and the women. And there were battles to fight as these women made a place for themselves in a previously male-only club. These special women demonstrated to everyone's satisfaction that they were competent. Once, when an engineer complained that one of the female astronauts had argued with him about a technical matter, Carolyn Huntoon, later director of the Houston Space Center, replied, "They're acting just like the guys do" (Chaikin, 1996, p. 45). This was probably the most telling statement about the mental attitude of Sally Ride and her female colleagues. They were professionals doing their jobs and wanted to be regarded as such.

Another first for Sally Ride was that she and fellow astronaut Steven Hawley were married in July 1982, the first astronaut couple to marry. They were never assigned to the same mission, but each had their opportunities to develop their skills and participate in the space program.

Sally Ride along with colleague, John Fabian, was a specialist with the Remote Manipulator System that was used to launch and pick up satellites. When the crew was selected for the seventh space shuttle flight, Sally and John were included. For Sally, it was important for people to believe that she was selected because she was competent. She said, "It's important to me that people don't think I was picked for the flight because I am a woman and it's time for NASA to send one" (Adler, 1983, p. 36). George W. S. Abbey, NASA's director of operations, said this about her selection:

> Sally Ride is smart in a very special way. You get people who can sit in the lab and think like an Einstein, but they can't do anything with it. Sally can get everything she knows together and bring it to bear where you need it. (Hurwitz & Hurwitz, 1989, pp. 41–42)

An additional pressure for Sally Ride was that the careers of all the female astronauts would be affected by her performance. If she should fail in any way, it would be unlikely that the other women would have a chance to prove themselves. This pressure in addition to the usual preflight jitters could have been overwhelming. Although Sally refused to get caught up in the media frenzy, she was very aware of the conditions imposed on her because she was the first American woman in space. She said, "I wanted to make sure that there wasn't anything associated with the flight that I could be criticized for. People were going to be watching what I did really closely" (Chaikin, 1996, p. 46).

The actual mission was much like others except that for the first time a woman was aboard. The work went on as usual, but there were those who thought that the tone of the communication between astronauts and ground control was changed forever. One source of the change was Sally Ride's extraordinary sense of humor. She took her view of the world with her into space, and she used it as a way of changing the nature of the dialogue between the Challenger crew and ground control from the previous rather stuffy, technical jargon to good-natured kidding around (Fox, 1984).

The media blitz was enormous, especially when Sally returned from the very successful mission in June 1983. She completed the tours and public appearances as required of all astronauts, but she was not comfortable as a status symbol for women. She thought of herself as a physicist and an astronaut before she thought about being a woman. She said, "I'm not historic material" (Bruning, 1983, p. 9).

Sally's next space adventure came in October 1984, when NASA launched its 100th space flight. The media frenzy had died down considerably since women in space were no longer an unusual event. On this flight, there were two women, Sally Ride and Kathryn Sullivan. This mission was as successful as the first even though there were many more technical difficulties (Camp, 1997).

Sally again participated in the round of public appearances that always followed upon the return of the space shuttle from a mission. She received many awards, including the Lindberg Eagle Award and the Jefferson Award from the American Institute of Public Service, and she was honored during the Salute to the American Hero event at Disneyland (Camp, 1997). However, Sally continued to believe that she had not done anything special because she was a woman, but that all of her colleagues had worked hard at their jobs, which just happened to be being an astronaut.

It is very likely that Sally Ride would have made other trips into space if it had not been for the tragedy that occurred on January 28, 1986. Seventy-three seconds after liftoff, the Challenger exploded and all six astronauts and the first teacher in space, Christa McAuliffe, died. Judith Resnik, one of the first six women astronauts, was aboard that day, sitting in the same seat that Sally Ride had occupied in her previous shuttle mission. All shuttle missions were put on hold while NASA tried to determine exactly what had caused this terrible event.

President Reagan appointed a commission to investigate the tragedy and asked William Rogers, former secretary of state, to head it. Sally Ride was also selected, and she spent many hours studying videotapes, photographs, and shuttle debris. She and the other members of the commission also interviewed all those individuals who were involved in the launch. It was their decision that there was a major design flaw with the shuttle, that it was well known to NASA staff, and that the Challenger disaster probably could have been prevented (Hurwitz & Hurwitz, 1989). Reagan ordered NASA to change the priorities of the shuttle program and to discontinue launching satellites.

The reality of NASA's management strategies and the discontinuation of satellite launching probably contributed to Sally Ride's acceptance of reassignment to NASA headquarters in Washington, D.C. She was special assistant to the administrator for strategic planning, and one of the most important activities for her was the publication of a report on leadership at NASA titled "Leadership and America's Future in Space" (Ride, 1987). In this report, she proposed goals that would broaden NASA's purpose. She suggested four major areas of focus: (a) mission to planet Earth: using the perspective of space to study our home planet; (b) exploration of the solar system; (c) outpost on the moon; and (d) humans to Mars.

During this time, she also helped to create the Office of Exploration and was its administrator. In addition, she toured Europe, addressed the United Nations, and was inducted into the National Women's Hall of Fame. Sally Ride used her public speeches to encourage girls and women to become scientists. She had finally realized that she was a role model, and she wanted to be a good one. She said:

> When I go out and give talks at schools and an eight-year-old girl in the audience raises her hand to ask me what she needs to do to become an astronaut, I like that. It's neat! Because now there really is a way. Now it's possible. (O'Connor, 1983, p. 9)

In 1987, Sally Ride left NASA to return to Stanford as a science fellow at the Center for International Security and Arms Control. This was a difficult time for Sally because she was also divorced from her husband, Steven Hawley. After 2 years of training scientists in how their inventions were being used by the military, she left Stanford for San Diego, where she became director of the California Space Institute at the University of California. Here she was primarily a physicist, free to pursue her research interests (Camp, 1997).

One of her accomplishments has been to develop an innovative science education program call "KidSAT: Mission Operations" (Camp, 1997). She has also written three books for children: *To*

Space and Back (1986), *Voyager: An Adventure to the Edge of the Solar System* (1992), and *The Third Planet: Exploring the Earth From Space* (1994). In 1996, Sally Ride left the California Space Institute as director and returned to the physics department, where she focuses on developing creative and innovative science education strategies for public education.

Summary

Why was Sally Ride so successful in a career that had previously been occupied only by men? If one looks back over her life, there are some clear recommendations for parents and educators who would empower women for equity.

Early environment seems critical in focusing less on gender and more on the talents and abilities of the child. Encouraging curiosity and exploration also were crucial in her parents' support of their daughter's interests. Sally never asked if a woman should or could be an astrophysicist. She believed in her own ability and worked hard to achieve her goals.

Another characteristic of Sally Ride was preparation. She was physically fit, first through athletics and then later through fitness training. She believed that fitness was important and was disciplined in working toward it. She prepared herself intellectually and emotionally for the rigors of astronaut training. She studied hard and learned well. She kept her focus on the task at hand rather than on the rewards and honors she would receive. When the media would have distracted her, she was able to say no to their requests. This dedication was crucial. She knew when to work and when to play, and play did not come first.

Another key to Sally Ride was her ability to use humor to relax herself and put others at ease. This ability to gain perspective during difficult times is certainly one of the skills of serenity (K. T. Roberts & Aspy, 1995). Being a trailblazer is difficult work, and by maintaining the long view of things, Sally Ride was able to handle the stress caused not only by the rigors of her work but also by the focus of the media and the public.

Sally Ride was also in the right place at the right time. Such a fortunate marriage of preparation and opportunity can only happen when one is prepared to take advantage of whatever develops. All of the women who became astronauts had prepared themselves through higher education and discipline. When NASA opened the job of astronaut to them, they were qualified and ready.

Sally Ride was more interested in doing the work of an astronaut than the glory and attention it provided her. She loved what she did and fought to devote her time to those aspects to ensure that she could perform the job at the highest level possible. She was prepared because she worked. She was successful because she was prepared. Her life attests to her devotion to physics, space exploration, and problem solving. She blazed the trail for the women who followed her into space and provided a positive image of a woman scientist so that all young girls could dream a new dream. She said, "Before I flew, before the six of us did, if you were an 11-year old girl, when you turned on the TV you didn't see any women astronauts" (Chaikin, 1996, p. 46). Sally Ride became the image of possibility for all young girls who dared to dream of a future as astronauts.

14

Betty Lentz Siegel:
First Woman University
President in the Georgia
University System

Betty Lentz was born to Carl Nicholas Lentz and Vera
Hogg Lentz in Cumberland, Kentucky, in the heart of
Appalachian coal country. Her ancestors had settled this part
of Kentucky more than a hundred years before her birth, and
their strength and courage to persevere were as much a part of
their gifts to her as were the physical things that were her
inheritance.

Early Childhood

Betty has deep roots in the Appalachian community in which
she was born. Her great-grandmother and grandmother both
lived nearby, and Betty was afforded the unique opportunity to

observe three generations of women meeting the challenges of life. Each of these women gave her unique views of the world and strategies for resolving life's dilemmas.

Great-grandmother Leah Lewis was highly respected by her community. However, she was not a woman who tolerated foolishness, and she focused her energy on her personal mission, which was to ensure that government was held accountable for its actions and that wrongs were righted. It was not uncommon for her to flag down the train with her crisp, white apron so that she could travel to Frankfort (the capital of Kentucky) to ensure that justice was served. She was austere, and it was respect (and perhaps fear) that characterized Betty's relationship with her great-grandmother.

Generations often embody opposites, and so it was with Betty's grandmother, Rose Creech Hogg. She had nothing of the severity of her mother and was known as the saint of the community for her caring efforts on behalf of others. For Grandmother Rose, suffering and need were her personal enemies, and her energies were targeted toward eliminating them with the work of her hands. She taught compassion and responsibility to the community by example rather than pedagogy, and her example was an effective one.

Betty's mother, Vera Hogg Lentz, was raised to be the fulfillment of the women before her, and when she eloped with her high school sweetheart, the dream was postponed. Betty was the firstborn of Nick and Vera, and 2 years later, a sister was born. Betty was welcomed into the community of her ancestors to learn the lessons of family and society. For her mother, the primary lesson for her children was that of individual integrity and the need to live a life beyond reproach. Not only did she live this example, but she reminded Betty and her sister often of the importance of integrity to a well-lived life.

Betty's father provided another view of life. He was a rakish entrepreneur who always carried a hundred-dollar bill in his wallet and knew that whatever happened, someday he would be financially successful. He understood coal mining and bought, worked, and sold multiple mines before his destiny was achieved when Betty was in college. His gift to her was an incredible optimism and perseverance directed toward his goal.

Life in a small town where everybody knows not only one's name but one's lineage can lead to expectations that make it difficult to achieve one's own goals. This was not the case for Betty because she really lived in two worlds. Vera was an expert pianist and played daily at the local movie theater. From the time she was 3, Betty went to the movies 5 days a week. Her other world was the larger-than-life movies of her day, and she has seen *Gone With the Wind* no less than 43 times. Even though her community had no orchestra, ballet company, or opera season, she saw and heard this world through the eyes and ears of the characters in movies. This exposure created a lifelong passion for the arts and opening nights. She rarely misses the first-night release of important new movies and volunteers on the boards for the Atlanta opera, orchestra, and ballet.

Betty's life was focused around her extended family, church, and school activities. She was an avid reader, and the importance placed on study by her mother was evidenced by the fact that while she was reading or studying, Betty was never interrupted to help around the house. There were no sermons on the importance of education, but by her actions, Betty's mother communicated volumes.

Betty always knew she would go to college, and after capturing all the accolades available at her high school graduation, she chose Cumberland College in Kentucky, where her uncle had been president. Her career plans were uncertain, but one dream wherein she was a beloved physician for the people of Appalachia, fording the streams and driving narrow mountain trails to reach those in need, was forever shattered on the first day of chemistry class.

Her professor, surprised that a woman would enroll in chemistry, began to ask Betty questions about chemistry to test her qualifications. Betty knew nothing about chemistry because her high school did not offer such a course, but she was confident that she could master any subject and knew that chemistry was a requirement for a pre-med major. Her professor continued to interrogate her before the other students, and when he was sure that he had proved her ignorant, he suggested that women did not belong in chemistry. For Betty, the lesson of this experience was a personal one. Like Scarlett O'Hara's life-changing declaration never again to be hungry, Betty vowed that she would never again be treated with disdain. She left this professor's class immediately and enrolled in another course, and that change in path has made all the difference.

Betty transferred to Wake Forest University after 2 years to complete her bachelor's degree in English and history. Her academic achievements were stellar. Upon graduation, she moved to the University of North Carolina at Chapel Hill for a master's degree, which she completed in 9 months! Throughout her educational experiences, Betty was never mentored by a woman because, with very few exceptions, all her professors were men. Her master's thesis was the first of many activities in her academic life to focus on self-concept.

For her doctoral work, Betty went to Florida State University to study child psychology. Her work focused on administration and child and adolescent development. Always one to view the forest (as well as the trees), Betty understood early that change in any institution, if it is to be effective, must be systemic. She saw administrative skills as preparation for an effective role in any organization. Upon completion of her doctoral work, Betty spent 2 years at Indiana University completing postdoctoral study in clinical child psychology.

Marriage and Children

During her study at Indiana University, Betty met and married Joel Siegel, who shared her vision and was also an academic. During the next 3 years, they became parents of two sons, David and Michael, both of whom have followed in their mother's footsteps and are pursuing doctorates in higher education.

Career

Betty's first academic appointment was at the University of Florida in the Department of Educational Foundations. She was the only woman among 35 men. When she arrived, she was 6 months pregnant and caused her chairman much dismay. It was 1967, and pregnant women were expected to take leave of their professional lives and remove themselves from public view. When her chairman expressed doubt about her ability to perform her duties, she informed him that everything would be all right and continued with her responsibilities.

And she was right. She was named teacher of the year the following year and in 1971, she became dean of academic affairs for continuing education at the University of Florida. Five years later, she was appointed Dean of the School of Education and Psychology at Western Carolina University, the first woman to hold that position.

This was not the last time Betty would be a "first." In 1981, she was named president of Kennesaw College, the first woman to lead an institution in the 24-unit university system of Georgia. At the time she became president, Kennesaw had an enrollment of 4,000 students and 15 baccalaureate-degree programs. In 1996, Kennesaw achieved university status, and current enrollments are over 13,000 with 50 undergraduate- and graduate-degree programs.

Betty Siegel has always been a student of leadership. She understood the principles of successful leadership practices as they applied to male-run institutions. She also understood that as the first woman leader of a Georgia college, she had the opportunity to implement other principles that more nearly reflected her own hypotheses about effective organizations. These principles were intuitive for Betty. She knew that women have long been nourished by bringing individuals into community, by using systemic models such that everything can interact and create synergy.

In an environment of trust, individuals are freed to be creative risk takers and effective problem solvers. This atmosphere was her goal, and the university was her laboratory. She achieved her goal by inviting participation and cheering the successes. These skills are not female or male but human in their dimensions, and Betty tested them in the fires of academia, and her results prove them effective.

Founding IAIE

When Betty and her colleague William Purkey were both faculty members at the University of Florida, they shared a mutual interest in studying self-concept and its relationship to learning. They felt that a theory that could be translated into actual practice was essential. They pursued funding and, with a series of Noyes Foundation grants, began to address the problem of defining the effect of self-concept on the instructional process. Betty addressed her studies to administrators while William focused on teachers.

In 1981, Betty and William along with their spouses went to the mountains of North Carolina for a weekend retreat to address the future direction of their work. They left fully committed to creating a national organization of colleagues who shared their vision. From this planning session, the International Alliance for Invitational Education (IAIE), a nonprofit North Carolina corporation, was created. The four qualities that characterize invitational education—respect, trust, optimism, and intentionality—are also those that guide both Betty's personal and professional relationships. Today this organization has over 1,200 members from around the world. The organization now supports a refereed journal, *The Journal of Invitational Theory and Practice*, which is published twice yearly. Every other year, the organization sponsors a World Conference on Invitational Education, at which Betty and William continue to invite others into their view of education.

Awards

Betty's awards are numerous. She holds honorary doctorates from four colleges and universities and recently received the

OAK award, which is given to an outstanding alumni in the state of Kentucky. She was Cobb County Citizen of the Year in 1996 and the 1997 Georgia Woman of the Year. Turner Broadcasting recognized her as a "Super 17" winner for voluntarily working to improve education in Georgia. These awards are testimonials to her commitment to making life better through education.

Most Significant Accomplishment

For Betty, the opportunity to try out her organizational theories and see them work even better than she had hoped is her most significant accomplishment. Throughout her tenure at Kennesaw State University, Betty has applied the four tenets of invitational theory—respect, trust, optimism, and intentionality—to the five environmental factors of people, places, policies, programs, and processes such that Kennesaw would become the most "inviting" university in the United States. She has presided over its transformation from a closed, homogeneous institution with little awareness of its potential mission to a stellar public, democratic, diverse institution dedicated to entrepreneurial excellence with strong roots in the community that also reaches out to students from around the world.

Betty has used the concept of a "summit" conference to direct attention and creativity toward needs within the university. The process is similar to the New England town meeting that calls for communitywide participation in identifying and solving community problems. In 1997-1998, Kennesaw State University focused on "The Year of the Arts" as a result of a previous summit that brought together university staff, faculty, and students; community and business leaders from many areas; and experts from around the country. This integrated problem solving was replicated, and in 1998-1999, the university has created "The Year of Honoring Service," wherein all students will be involved in some aspect of community service as a part of their educational experience. The opportunity to be creative in addressing the education of young people and thus have an impact on the future is one of the reasons that Betty has dedicated herself to the invitational process.

Summary

What made it possible for a young woman from Appalachia to achieve at the highest levels of her profession? Betty, in characteristic humility, would attribute her success to hard work as well as good fortune. She studied and prepared; she was blessed with many talents. She had the good fortune to be ready for leadership at a time when women were being actively recruited to diversify educational administrations. She has continued to work hard in her professional role and in service to her community through participation on countless boards and committees. She is much in demand as a speaker and travels the country to meet these obligations. Her life speaks to other women who aspire to educational leadership. She has ventured into uncharted waters and has mapped them for other women to follow. She would advise them, however, to trust their talents and abilities and to check the map only when lost.

Section V

Instruments for Measuring Attitudes Toward Gender Roles and Gender Equity

As the previous sections have shown, women have historically been denied par excellence status with men in all spheres of life. Stereotypes abound to ensure that women have a lower status. That women are inferior to men is a belief that has pervaded human society since time immemorial. Confucius contended that women and those of low birth are difficult to deal with. Aristotle suggested that a woman is an unfinished man. American Puritans asserted that women are less intelligent than men (Lauer, 1998). When things go wrong, the blame falls on women as evidenced by "Eve's syndrome," which credits Eve with causing Adam's disobedience to God (Tavris, 1991). Tertullian described women this way: "You are the devil's gateway. . . . How easily you destroyed man, the image of God. Because of the death you brought upon us even the Son of God had to die."

Unfortunately, gender bias includes all stages of the human life span, starting from the gender socialization of a child to gender-related problems in the classroom to the choice of a vocation to gender-specific roles in intimate relationships. Men and women have been described as two different creatures in terms of their innate needs, motivations, and capabilities. The differences between men and women are characterized as so great that it is believed that if men are from Mars, then women are from Venus (J. Gray, 1992). The traditional stereotypes portray women as more emotional and less logical compared to men. They are also considered more passive, more fragile, and more dependent (Tauris, 1991). When women do not act in accordance with these stereotyped expectations, they are often criticized and denied the successes they have earned (Fiske, Bersoff, Borgida, Deaux, & Heilman, 1991).

Both qualitative and quantitative studies have consistently reported that there are significant differences in the attitudes of men and women toward sex roles (Osmond & Martin, 1975). Sadly, many beliefs about women as a weaker sex have been perpetuated without evidence and are really blemishes on human history and an outright affront to women and their dignity (Lauer, 1998).

A person's perceptions about gender differences play an important role consciously and unconsciously in determining his or her attitudes, behaviors, and worldviews toward the other sex. Also, the expectations of gender differences lead to gender differences in behaviors, as they both emerge from stratified social roles. It is clear that gender divisions in labor exist, and as long as they do, these divisions make people expect gender roles to be congruent with social behaviors and vice versa (Eagley, 1987).

Because differences in attitudes, beliefs, and values determine different worldviews and thus different priorities and behaviors with different consequences for clients, it is important that counselors, psychologists, and other mental health professionals are cognizant of these differences. One of the major tasks for counselors is to facilitate the change of men and women's attitudes, beliefs, and values to bring about a more equitable social order. To assist in this process, one must have reliable and solid measures of attitudes available (Dempewolff, 1974).

To acquire adequate knowledge about individual and social behavior, quality measuring instruments are crucial. The field of women's studies is no exception (Beere, 1979). This section on gender equity instruments is our attempt to fulfill this very important need. We encourage counselors to use these instruments to assess clients' attitudes regarding gender equity for both men and women before tailoring strategies to combat sexism. It is our earnest hope that this compendium of instruments will also be useful to further investigation in the areas of gender bias and gender discrimination.

We selected five instruments that counselors may find helpful in studying gender equity perceptions as well as for exploring particular biases in their clients. For each scale, we have provided a description of the instrument, administration and scoring instructions, directions for administration, and factors or subscales when appropriate. Cronbach's alpha is also reported for each scale and subscale.

As a caution, we suggest that readers receive necessary copyright permission and updated validity and reliability data information, results of recent studies, and any other pertinent information from the developers of these instruments. The names and addresses of these developers are provided at the end of this section.

Table of Contents for Gender Equity Instruments

Scale	Authors
Gender Equity Perception Scale	Daya Singh Sandhu and Angelia Bryant (1998)
Quick Discrimination Index or Social Attitude Survey Factor 3: Attitudes Toward Women's Equity	Ingrid Grieger and Joseph G. Ponterotto (1998)

Workplace Perceived Prejudice Scale
    Subscale 2: Perceived Sexism In the Workplace
    Factor 1: Women in Authority Positions
    Factor 2: Work-Related Gender Bias (Exploitation of Women)
    Factor 3: Sexual Attraction
	Daya Singh Sandhu and Cheryl B. Aspy (1997)

The Situational Attitude Scale for Women	William E. Sedlacek (1973)
Sex Role Attitude Scale	Marie W. Osmond and Patricia Y. Martin (1975)

Gender Equity Perception Scale

Daya Singh Sandhu and Angelia Bryant (1998)

The Gender Equity Perception Scale (GEPS) is a Likert-type scale that consists of 32 statements designed to assess participants' contemporary attitudes toward gender equity issues. The total scores range from 32 to 180. The higher scores are indicative of bias toward men or women. This bias could be positive or negative.

Administration and Scoring

The GEPS is self-administered and generally takes only 12–15 minutes. All statements are equally weighted. The total score can be obtained by adding all the responses. There are three subscales: Male Controllability (Male Superiority), Priorities or

Preferences for Male Roles, and Bias Against Women (Oppression Against Women). The scores on each subscale can also be computed by adding the responses of each statement. The overall Cronbach alpha for this scale is .78. The Cronbach alpha coefficient for each subscale is also provided.

Directions for Administration

This scale is designed to assess the prevalent attitude toward gender equality. There are no right or wrong answers. However, for the data to be meaningful, you must answer each statement. Also, it is important that you express your true feelings. Please rate the following statements as:

Strongly disagree = 1, *Disagree* = 2, *Not sure* = 3,
Agree = 4, and *Strongly agree* = 5

In general, I think that:

1. Men make better business decisions than women.
2. Educators tend to treat male students more seriously than female students.
3. The number of women holding governmental offices is very small.
4. Women's opportunities are limited.
5. Women cannot handle high-stress jobs.
6. Teachers have higher expectations of boys than of girls.
7. Women are overlooked for important offices.
8. Men are better problem solvers than women because they are logical.
9. A man is generally the head of the household.
10. Men understand political issues better than women.
11. Parents have higher expectations for their sons than for their daughters.
12. Women cannot control social situations.

13. For the same job, women receive less money than men.
14. Women are generally not elected because they are too emotionally unstable.
15. Teachers pay more attention to boys than to girls.
16. Women are not elected because of sex bias.
17. Women's roles still remain subordinate to men's roles.
18. Men learn faster than women.
19. Parents praise their sons more than their daughters for their accomplishments.
20. Women generally hold lower positions in business.
21. Women are oppressed.
22. Men are more intelligent than women.
23. Most couples prefer boys to girls.
24. From birth girls are treated differently.
25. Women cannot handle the responsibility of political office.
26. Sexual harassment in the workplace is a problem more for women than for men.
27. Women's accomplishments are less valued.
28. Men are more emotionally mature than women.
29. Women are discriminated against both in hiring and promotions.
30. Men are intellectually superior to women.
31. Society confers more unearned privileges on men than on women.
32. Women are often discriminated against.

Factor I. Male Controllability or Male Superiority (Cronbach's $\alpha = .88$)

Factor 1 has 12 statements. The total score ranges from 12 to 60. The higher scores mean the perception of higher level of male controllability or male superiority in handling, understanding, and controlling various situations. These statements include the following:

Men make better business decisions than women (1).
Women cannot handle high-stress jobs (5).

Men understand political issues better than women (10).

Women are generally not elected because they are too emotionally unstable (14).

Men learn faster than women (18).

Men are more intelligent than women (22).

Women cannot handle the responsibility of political office (25).

Men are more emotionally mature than women (28).

Men are intellectually superior to women (30).

Men are better problem solvers than women because they are more logical (8).

Women cannot control social situations (12).

A man is generally the head of the household (9).

Factor 2. Priorities or Preferences for Male Roles (Cronbach α = .82)

This subscale has a total of 10 statements. The total scores range from 10 to 50. The higher scores are indicative of participants' preference for men. They may also exhibit preferences and priorities for male roles.

Educators tend to treat male students more seriously than female students (2).

Teachers have higher expectations of boys than of girls (6).

Parents have higher aspirations for their sons than for their daughters (11).

Teachers pay more attention to boys than to girls (15).

Women are oppressed (21).

Parents praise their sons more than their daughters for their accomplishments (19).

Most couples prefer boys to girls (23).

Women's opportunities are limited (4).

Women's roles still remain subordinate to men's roles (17).

Women's accomplishments are less valued (27).

Factor 3. Biases Against Women or Oppression Against Women (Cronbach α = .72)

This subscale consists of 10 statements. The total scores range from 10 to 50. Higher scores indicate higher level of overt biases and oppressive practices against women.

The number of women holding governmental offices is very small (3).

Women are often overlooked for important offices (7).

Women are often discriminated against (32).

Women are not elected because of sex bias (16).

Women generally hold lower positions in business (20).

From birth, girls are treated differently (24).

Society confers more unearned privileges on men than on women (31).

Women are discriminated against both in hiring and in promotion (29).

Sexual harassment in the workplace is a problem more for women than for men (26).

For the same job, women receive less money (13).

Note. From Sandhu and Bryant (1998).

The Quick Discrimination Index

Ingrid Grieger and Joseph G. Ponterotto (1998)

The Quick Discrimination Index (QDI) is a 30-item, Likert-type, self-report measure of racial and gender attitudes. The instrument itself is titled "Social Attitude Survey" to control for some forms of response bias. Users of the QDI should read development and validity studies on the QDI before use.

Social Attitude Survey

Please respond to all items in the survey. Remember there are no right or wrong answers. The survey is completely anonymous; do not put your name on the survey. Please circle the appropriate number.

1 = *Strongly disagree*   4 = *Agree*
2 = *Disagree*   5 = *Strongly agree*
3 = *Not sure*

1. I do think it is more appropriate for the mother of a newborn baby, rather than the father, to stay with the baby (not work) during the first year.
2. It is as easy for women to succeed in business as it is for men.
3. I really think affirmative action programs on college campuses constitute reverse discrimination.
4. I feel I could develop an intimate relationship with someone from a different race.
5. All Americans should learn to speak two languages.
6. It upsets (or angers) me that a woman has never been president of the United States.
7. Generally speaking, men work harder than women.
8. My friendship network is very racially mixed.
9. I am against affirmative action programs in business.
10. Generally, men seem less concerned with building relationships than women.
11. I would feel OK about my son or daughter dating someone from a different race.
12. It upsets (or angers) me that a racial minority person has never been president of the United States.
13. In the past few years there has been too much attention directed toward multicultural or minority issues in education.
14. I think feminist perspectives should be an integral part of the higher education curriculum.
15. Most of my close friends are from my own racial group.
16. I feel somewhat more secure that a man rather than a woman is currently president of the United States.
17. I think it is (or would be) important for my children to attend schools that are racially mixed.
18. In the past few years there has been too much attention

directed toward multicultural or minority issues in business.

19. Overall, I think racial minorities in America complain too much about racial discrimination.

20. I feel (or would feel) very comfortable having a woman as my primary physician.

21. I think the president of the United States should make a concerted effort to appoint more women and racial minorities to the country's Supreme Court.

22. I think White people's racism toward racial minority groups still constitutes a major problem in America.

23. I think the school system, from elementary school through college, should encourage minority and immigrant children to learn and fully adopt traditional American values.

24. If I were to adopt a child, I would be happy to adopt a child of any race.

25. I think there is as much female physical violence toward men as there is male physical violence toward women.

26. I think the school system, from elementary school through college, should promote traditional American values as well as the values representative of the culturally diverse students in the class.

27. I believe that reading the autobiography of Malcolm X would be of value.

28. I would enjoy living in a neighborhood consisting of a racially diverse population (i.e., Asians, Blacks, Hispanics, Whites).

29. I think it is better if people marry within their own race.

30. Women make too big of a deal out of sexual harassment issues in the workplace.

Scoring Information

There are two methods of scoring the QDI. First, you can simply use the total score, which measures overall sensitivity, awareness, and receptivity to cultural diversity and gender equality. The second scoring procedure involves scoring three separate subscales (factors) of the QDI.

Of the 30 items on the QDI, 15 are worded and scored in a positive direction (high scores indicate high sensitivity to multicultural and gender issues), and 15 are worded and scored in a negative direction (low scores indicate high sensitivity to multicultural and gender issues). Naturally, when the total score responses are tallied, these latter 15 items need to be reverse scored. Reverse scoring simply means that if a respondent circles a 1 they should get 5 points; a 2, 4 points; a 3, 3 points; a 4, 2 points; and a 5, 1 point. The following QDI items need to be reverse scored: 1, 2, 3, 7, 9, 10, 13, 15, 16, 18, 19, 23, 25, 29, and 30. The score range is 30 to 150, with high scores indicating more awareness, sensitivity, and receptivity to racial diversity and gender equality.

If scoring separate subscales (factors), the researcher should not use the total score. As expected, the total score is highly correlated with subscale scores, and to use both would be redundant. When scoring separate subscales, only 23 of the total 30 items are scored. Items in parentheses are reverse-scored.

Factor 1: General (Cognitive) Attitudes Toward Racial Diversity/Multiculturalism

Factor 1 has nine items: (3), (9), (13), (18), (19), 22, (23), 26, 27. The score ranges from 9 to 45.

Factor 2: Affective Attitudes Toward More Personal Contact (Closeness) With Racial Diversity

This subscale contains seven items: 4, 8, 11, (15), 17, 24, (29). The score ranges from 7 to 35.

Factor 3: Attitudes Toward Women's Equity

Factor 3 contains seven items: (1), 6, (7), 14, (16), 20, (30). The score ranges from 7 to 35.

Workplace Perceived
Prejudice Scale

Daya Singh Sandhu and Cheryl B. Aspy (1997)

The Workplace Perceived Prejudice Scale (WPPS) is constructed to measure the prevalence of racism, sexism, and heterosexism in the workplace. The WPPS consists of three Likert-type subscales. Responses range from 1 = *strongly disagree*, 2 = *disagree*, 3 = *not sure*, 4 = *agree*, to 5 = *strongly agree*. Only those statements that pertain to women's equity issues as originally presented in Subscale 2 are presented here. Readers interested in the full scale dealing with racism and heterosexism in addition to sexism in the workplace may consult pages 315–318 in *Counseling for Prejudice Prevention and Reduction* (Sandhu & Aspy, 1997). Each of these subscales with their factors and Cronbach's alpha reliabilities are presented.

Scoring Methods

Two different methods for scoring can be used. A cumulative score on all statements would suggest workplace-perceived prejudice against women. These scores range from 16 to 80. The higher cumulative scores are indicative of higher prejudice against women and lesser degree of equity for women in a workplace. There are three major factors that determine workplace prejudice against women, namely, Women in Authority Positions, Work-Related Gender Bias (Exploitation of Women), and Sexual Attraction.

Subscale 2: Perceived Sexism in the Workplace (Cronbach's α = .81)

Factor 1: Women in Authority Positions (Cronbach's α = .92)

To avoid management problems, it is better that women work separately from men.

Women should not become bosses.

For their own benefit, it is better for women to remain in their traditional professions.

Men are better authority figures than women.

Women overreact about sexual harassment to control men.

Factor 2: Work-Related Gender Bias (Exploitation of Women) (Cronbach's α = .67)

For the same job, women are generally paid less than men.

Women often are given more responsibilities than men when employed in the same job.

The concept of equal pay for equal work does not seem to apply to women in the workplace.

Women have to be more aggressive than men to get ahead in the workplace.

Women are more "tolerated" than respected by men in the workplace.

Factor 3: Sexual Attraction (Cronbach's α = .79)

Physical attractiveness affects job placement and pay.

Sexual attraction is an important issue in the workplace.

Women workers generally face more sexual harassment than men.

Most male employers look at the physical attractiveness of a woman before hiring her for a job.

Male supervisors generally prefer working with and favor women over men.

A male boss has more empathy for female employees than for male employees.

Note. From *Counseling for Prejudice Prevention and Reduction* (pp. 315–318), by D. S. Sandhu and C. B. Aspy, 1997, Alexandria, VA: American Counseling Association. Copyright 1997 by the American Counseling Association. Reprinted with permission.

Situational Attitude Scale for Women (SASW)

William E. Sedlacek (1973)

There are two different forms of this semantic differential scale, Form A and Form B. In each form, a situation is described in a single sentence that is followed by 10 semantic differential scales. Bipolar adjective pairs are used to rate participants' perceptions. The same 10 scenarios are presented in each scale. In Form A, the sex of the participant is not specified in any one of the 10 situations. Form B uses the same situations, but in 9 situations the sex of the participant is specified as a woman. In the remaining situation, the participant is specified as a man. All these situations are written as generally thought of applying to a man. The major purpose of this scale is to assess sexist attitudes toward women in nontraditional sex roles.

Administration

Generally, it takes 15 to 20 minutes to complete each form. The scale is self-administered. Half of the participants complete Form A and the other half complete Form B. The participants are not aware of the difference in these two forms. The scores on these forms are analyzed to find the differences attributed to the sexist attitudes of the participants toward nontraditional sex roles.

Form A

This questionnaire measures how people think and feel about a number of social and personal incidents and situations. It is not a test, so there are no right or wrong answers. Each item or situation is followed by 10 descriptive word scales. Your task is to select, for each descriptive scale, the rating which best describes your feelings toward the item.

Sample item: Going out on a date

Happy   A | B | C | D | E | Sad

Indicate the direction and extent of your feelings (e.g., you might select B) by indicating your choice (B) on your response sheet by blackening in the appropriate space for that word scale.

Sometimes, you may feel as though you had the same item before on the questionnaire. This will not be the case, so do not look back and forth through the items. Do not try to remember how you checked similar items earlier in the questionnaire. Make each item a separate and independent judgement. Respond as honestly as possible without puzzling over individual items. Respond with your first impressions wherever possible.

I. Your best friend earns more money than you do.

1. Relaxed | A | B | C | D | E | Startled
2. Receptive | A | B | C | D | E | Cautious

3. Excited | A | B | C | D | E | Unexcited
4. Glad | A | B | C | D | E | Angered
5. Pleased | A | B | C | D | E | Annoyed
6. Indifferent | A | B | C | D | E | Suspicious
7. Tolerable | A | B | C | D | E | Intolerable
8. Afraid | A | B | C | D | E | Secure
9. Friend | A | B | C | D | E | Enemy
10. Unprotected | A | B | C | D | E | Protected

II. A friend keeps you waiting.

11. Calm | A | B | C | D | E | Nervous
12. Trusting | A | B | C | D | E | Suspicious
13. Afraid | A | B | C | D | E | Safe
14. Friendly | A | B | C | D | E | Unfriendly
15. Tolerant | A | B | C | D | E | Intolerant
16. Bitter | A | B | C | D | E | Pleasant
17. Cooperative | A | B | C | D | E | Uncooperative
18. Accepting | A | B | C | D | E | Belligerent
19. Inferior | A | B | C | D | E | Superior
20. Serious | A | B | C | D | E | Humorous

III. Your best friend gets drunk at your party.

21. Apprehensive | A | B | C | D | E | Confident
22. Nervous | A | B | C | D | E | Calm
23. Angry | A | B | C | D | E | Jovial
24. Unsure | A | B | C | D | E | Sure
25. Slighted | A | B | C | D | E | Understanding
26. Embarrassed | A | B | C | D | E | Not embarrassed
27. Not bothered | A | B | C | D | E | Irritated
28. Aroused | A | B | C | D | E | Passive
29. Disappointed | A | B | C | D | E | Elated
30. Threatened | A | B | C | D | E | Neutral

IV. Your best friend just beat you at tennis.

31. Resentful | A | B | C | D | E | Tolerant
32. Unjustified | A | B | C | D | E | Justified
33. Disgusted | A | B | C | D | E | Pleased
34. Incensed | A | B | C | D | E | Cautious

35. Angry | A | B | C | D | E | Calm
36. Unreasonable | A | B | C | D | E | Reasonable
37. Going too far | A | B | C | D | E | Fair
38. Acceptable | A | B | C | D | E | Objectionable
39. Furious | A | B | C | D | E | Accepting
40. Wrong | A | B | C | D | E | Right

V. You meet the person who will complete your income tax return.

41. Irritated | A | B | C | D | E | Calm
42. Skeptical | A | B | C | D | E | Assured
43. Incredible | A | B | C | D | E | Credible
44. Useful | A | B | C | D | E | Useless
45. Competent | A | B | C | D | E | Incompetent
46. Ridiculous | A | B | C | D | E | Expected
47. Cheated | A | B | C | D | E | Fulfilled
48. Trusting | A | B | C | D | E | Lack of trust
49. Inadequate | A | B | C | D | E | Adequate
50. Humorous | A | B | C | D | E | Serious

VI. You pull into a service station and the attendant looks under the hood.

51. Furious | A | B | C | D | E | Pleased
52. Apprehensive | A | B | C | D | E | Confident
53. Surprised | A | B | C | D | E | Expected
54. Funny | A | B | C | D | E | Not funny
55. Confidence | A | B | C | D | E | Lack of confidence
56. Silly | A | B | C | D | E | Proper
57. Superior | A | B | C | D | E | Inferior
58. Excited | A | B | C | D | E | Not excited
59. Improper | A | B | C | D | E | Proper
60. Feminine | A | B | C | D | E | Masculine

VII. Your best friend makes better grades than you do.

61. Surprised | A | B | C | D | E | Expected
62. Feminine | A | B | C | D | E | Masculine
63. Slow | A | B | C | D | E | Quick
64. Dumb | A | B | C | D | E | Smart

65. Out of place | A | B | C | D | E | In place
66. Oddball | A | B | C | D | E | Normal
67. Humiliated | A | B | C | D | E | Accepting
68. Proper | A | B | C | D | E | Improper
69. Good | A | B | C | D | E | Bad
70. Annoyed | A | B | C | D | E | Pleased

VIII. You go out for a drink with a friend who decides to pick up the check.

71. Embarrassed | A | B | C | D | E | Relaxed
72. Uncomfortable | A | B | C | D | E | Comfortable
73. Unsure | A | B | C | D | E | Confident
74. Unexpected | A | B | C | D | E | Expected
75. Put down | A | B | C | D | E | Not put down
76. Hurt | A | B | C | D | E | Not hurt
77. Annoyed | A | B | C | D | E | Pleased
78. Disappointed | A | B | C | D | E | Satisfied
79. Distasteful | A | B | C | D | E | Tasteful
80. Feminine | A | B | C | D | E | Masculine

IX. Your best friend is accepted to graduate school while you are turned down.

81. Good | A | B | C | D | E | Bad
82. Surprised | A | B | C | D | E | Not surprised
83. Threatened | A | B | C | D | E | Not threatened
84. Unpleasant | A | B | C | D | E | Pleasant
85. Provocative | A | B | C | D | E | Undesirable
86. Disgusted | A | B | C | D | E | Delighted
87. Incompetent | A | B | C | D | E | Competent
88. Problem | A | B | C | D | E | Asset
89. Elated | A | B | C | D | E | Disappointed
90. Comfortable | A | B | C | D | E | Unsettled

X. You do some dishes while a friend watches.

91. Dominated | A | B | C | D | E | Independent
92. Gypped | A | B | C | D | E | Good deal
93. Uncomfortable | A | B | C | D | E | Comfortable
94. Relaxed | A | B | C | D | E | Silly

95.	Nervous	I A I B I C I D I E I	Calm
96.	Disappointed	I A I B I C I D I E I	Elated
97.	Improper	I A I B I C I D I E I	Proper
98.	Humorous	I A I B I C I D I E I	Serious
99.	Out of place	I A I B I C I D I E I	In place
100.	Masculine	I A I B I C I D I E I	Feminine

Form B

The same 10 scenarios are presented in Form B. This time these situations involve a woman. The 10 semantic differential scales remain the same.

I. Your girl friend earns more money than you do.

II. A female friend keeps you waiting.

III. Your girl friend gets drunk at your party.

IV. Your girl friend just beat you at tennis.

V. You meet the woman who will complete your income tax return.

VI. You pull into a service station and the female attendant looks under the hood.

VII. Your girl friend makes better grades than you do.

VIII. You go out for a drink with a girl friend who decides to pick up the check.

IX. Your girl friend is accepted to graduate school while you are turned down.

X. You do some dishes while a girl friend watches.

Sex Role Attitude Scale

Marie W. Osmond and Patricia Y. Martin (1975)

This is a 32-item, 5-point Likert-type scale designed to measure sex role attitudes. Five response categories range from *strongly disagree* (1) to *strongly agree* (5). The scale is self-administered and consists of four general components: (a) familial roles of female and male members, (b) extrafamilial roles of each sex, (c) stereotypes of male–female characteristics and behaviors, and (d) social change as related to sex roles.

Osmond and Martin (1975) examined the reliability of the Sex Role Attitude Scale through a Likert-scaling item analysis. The results indicated that "31 out of 32 items discriminated between the top and bottom quartiles of the sample with associated probabilities of .001 or less" (Osmond & Martin, 1975, p. 746).

Familial Roles

1. Women with children in grammar school should, if at all possible, stay at home rather than work (Grammar School Children).
2. Women with preschool children should not work, if at all possible (Preschool Children).
3. Whoever is the better wage earner, wife or husband, should be the breadwinner (Wage Earner).
4. It is possible for women to satisfy their needs for achievement through their husbands (Achieve Through Husbands).
5. Men should have more freedom to do such things as cook and care for children, if they so desire (Men Free to Cook).
6. A man's self-esteem is severely injured if his wife makes more money than he does (Man's Self-Esteem Hurt).
7. Men should take the same amount of responsibility as women in caring for home and children (Men Re-Home/Children)
8. A husband who is the breadwinner in the family should make all the important decisions (Husband Make Decisions).

Extrafamilial Roles

9. I would feel uncomfortable if my immediate supervisor at work was a woman (Woman Supervisor).
10. To a great extent, women are less able to make a career commitment than men are (Female–Male Commitment).
11. Females should be encouraged to plan for a career, not just a job (Females Plan Career).
12. I would vote for a woman for President of the United States (Women President).
13. Women are less capable of making important decisions than men are (Female–Male: Important Decisions).
14. Men are more capable of assuming leadership than women are (Male–Female: Leadership).

Stereotypes of Male–Female Nature and Behaviors

15. Women generally prefer light conversations over rational discussions (Light Conversation).
16. There is considerable evidence that men, in general, are a "superior species" to women (Male Super-Species).
17. Women really like being dependent on men (Females Like Dependence).
18. Career women generally are neurotic (Career Women Neurotic).
19. Females should go ahead and pamper males — "Tell him how great he is" — because that's a useful way to get what they want (Pamper Men).
20. Men should stop appraising women solely on the basis of appearance and sex appeal (Female Sex Appeal).
21. Either consciously or unconsciously, most women would like to be men (Females Like to be Male).
22. The way men and women behave is more a result of their genetic make-up than of the way they were brought up (Genetic Make-Up).
23. Women are as capable as men of enjoying a full sex life (Female–Male Enjoy Sex).
24. Since men have a natural urge to dominate and lead, women who challenge this actually threaten the welfare of society (Male Dominance Natural).

Social Change as Related to Sex Roles

25. Unlike the race riots, the "battle between the sexes" will never involve violence on any large scale (Battle of Sexes).
26. There should be low-cost, high-quality child-care centers for working women (Child Care Centers).
27. Men need liberation equally as much as women do (Male Liberation).
28. Men's clubs and lodges should be required to admit women (Clubs/Lodges).

29. Women should get equal pay with men for doing the same jobs (Equal Pay).
30. Women should have equal job opportunities with men (Equal Job Opportunities).
31. Women can attain true equality in this country only through a really drastic change in the social structure (Drastic Change).
32. The Equal Rights Amendment related to sex should be ratified as soon as possible (ERA).

Summary Information About Instruments

Instrument	Authors	Contact Person and Address
Gender Equity Perception Scale	Daya Singh Sandhu and Angelia Bryant	Dr. Daya Singh Sandhu Professor and Chair Department of Educational and Counseling Psychology University of Louisville Louisville, KY 40292
Quick Discrimination Index (also known as Social Attitude Survey) Factor 3: Attitudes Toward Women's Equity	Ingrid Grieger and Joseph G. Ponterotto	Dr. Joseph G. Ponterotto Counseling Psychology Program, Room 1008 Graduate School of Education Fordham University at Lincoln Center 113 West 60th St. New York, NY 10023-7478
Workplace Perceived Prejudice Scale Subscale 2: Perceived Sexism In the Workplace Factor 1: Women in Authority Positions Factor 2: Work-Related Gender Bias (Exploitation of Women) Factor 3: Sexual Attraction	Daya Singh Sandhu and Cheryl B. Aspy	Dr. Daya Singh Sandhu Professor and Chair Department of Educational and Counseling Psychology University of Louisville Louisville, KY 40292
The Situational Attitude Scale for Women	William E. Sedlacek	Dr. William E. Sedlacek Professor and Director Counseling Center University of Maryland College Park, MD 20742
Sex Role Attitude Scale	Marie W. Osmond and Patricia Y. Martin	Patricia Y. Martin Department of Sociology Florida State University Tallahassee, FL 32306

References

AAMC Project Committee on Increasing Women's Leadership in Academic Medicine. (1996). Increasing women's leadership in academic medicine. *Academic Medicine, 71*, 801–811.

Aaron, H., Mann, T., & Taylor, T. (1994). *Values and public policy.* Washington, DC: Brookings Institute.

Acker, J. (1989). *Doing comparable worth: Gender, class and pay equity.* Philadelphia: Temple University Press.

Acker, J. (1992). The future of women and work. *Sociological Perspectives, 35*, 53–56.

Adler, J. (1983, June 13). Sally Ride: Ready for liftoff. *Newsweek,* 36–49.

Alexander, J., Berrow, D., Domitrovich, L., Donnelly, M., & McLean, C. (1986). *Women and aging.* New York: Calyx Books.

Allen, R. L. (1995). Stopping sexual harassment: A challenge for community education. In A. F. Hill & E. C. Jordan (Eds.), *Race, gender, and power in America* (pp. 129-141). New York: Oxford University Press.

Allport, G. W. (1954). *The nature of prejudice.* Reading, MA: Addison-Wesley.

Allport, G. W. (1955). *Becoming.* New Haven, CT: Yale University Press.

Alter, J., Gegan, T., Kalb, C., Gwartney, D., & Maher, A. (1998, April 27). It's 4:00 p.m. Do you know where your children are? *Newsweek*, 29-33.

American Alliance for Health, Physical Education, Recreation, and Dance. (1995). *Gender equity through physical education and sport.* Reston, VA: National Association for Girls and Women in Sport.

"American Families" make slow comeback. (1998, May 28). *The Dallas Morning News, 149,* p. 3A.

Amiel, B. (1997, October 6). How gender politics threatens freedom. *Mclean's*, 9.

Angelou, M. (1970). *I know why the caged bird sings.* New York: Random House.

Angelou, M. (1986). *All God's children need traveling shoes.* New York: Random House.

Angelou, M. (1993a). *The complete collected poems of Maya Angelou.* New York: Random House.

Angelou, M. (1993b). *Wouldn't take nothing for my journey now.* New York: Random House.

Anonymous. (1994, March 18). NIH guidelines on the inclusion of women and minorities as subjects in clinical research. *NIH Guide to Grants and Contracts, 23*(11).

Anonymous. (1997, August 9). Breast cancer gets the hard sell [Editorial]. *Lancet, 350*(9075), 377.

Arbuckle, D. (1970). *Counseling: Philosophy, theory and practice* (2nd ed.). Boston: Allyn & Bacon.

Arredondo, P. (1994), Multicultural training: A response. *The Counseling Psychologist, 22,* 308-314.

Arredondo, P., Toporek, R., Brown, S. P., Jones, J., Locke, D. C., Sanchez, J., & Stadler, H. (1996). Operationalization of the multicultural counseling competencies. *Journal of Multicultural Counseling and Development, 24,* 42-78.

Ashbrook, J. B., & Albright, C. R. (1997). *The humanizing brain.* Cleveland, OH: Pilgrim Press.

Aspy, C. (1995). School failures caused by personal goals of teachers and administrators that dwarf social ones. *Education, 15,* 560–567.

Aspy, D. (1986). *This is school.* Amherst, MA: HRD Press.

Aspy, D., Aspy, C., & Roebuck, F. (1984). *The third century in American education.* Amherst, MA: HRD Press.

Aspy, D., & Roebuck, F. (1984). *Kids don't learn from people they don't like.* Amherst, MA: HRD Press.

Aspy, D., & Roebuck, F. (1996). From humane ideas to humane technology and back again many times. In R. N. Cassel (Ed.), *Carl Rogers: Student centered learning* (pp. 50–60). Chula Vista, CA: Project Innovations.

Associated Press. (1998, April 3). Administration backs pay equality. *Edmond Evening Sun,* p. 5A.

Bachman, R., & Saltzman, L. E. (1995). Violence against women: Estimates from the redesigned survey (U.S. Department of Justice, Office of Justice Programs, Bureau of Justice Statistics, NCJ-145325). Washington, DC: Government Printing Office.

Baines, C., Evans, P., & Neysmith, S. (Eds.). (1991). *Women's caring: Feminist perspectives on social welfare.* Toronto, Ontario, Canada: McClelland & Stewart.

Baird, W. (1998, June 10). Parents must watch for "little time bombs." *Edmond Evening Sun,* p. A3.

Barber, B. W. (1995). Struggle, commitment, and determination: An African-American woman's journey to self-development. In P. L. Munhall & V. M. Fitzimons (Eds.), *The emergence of women into the 21st century* (pp. 376–390). New York: NLN Press.

Barna, G. (1994). *Baby busters.* Chicago: Northfield.

Bar-Or, O., Foreyt, J., Bouchard, C., Brownell, K. D., Dietz, W. H., Ravussin, E., Salbe, A. D., Schwenger, S., St. Jeor, S., & Torun, B. (1998). Physical activity, genetic, and nutritional considerations in childhood weight management. *Medicine and Science in Sports and Exercise, 20*(1), 2–10.

Beall, A. E., & Sternberg, R. S. (Eds.). (1993). *The psychology of gender.* New York: Guilford Press.

Beere, C. A. (1979). *Women and women's issues: A handbook of tests and measures.* San Francisco: Jossey-Bass.

Belanger, C., Speizer, F. E., Hennekens, C. H., Rosner, B., Willett, W., & Bain, C. (1980). The nurses' health study: Current findings. *American Journal of Nursing, 80,* 1333.

Bem, S. L. (1989). Genital knowledge and gender constancy in preschool children. *Child Development, 60,* 649–662.

Bennett, W. (1994). *The book of virtues.* New York: Simon & Schuster.

Bensimon, E. M. (1993). A feminist reinterpretation of presidents' definitions of leadership. *Peabody Journal of Education, 68,* 143–156.

Benson, H. (1975). *The relaxation response.* New York: William Morrow.

Benson, H., & Stuart, E. M. (1992). *The wellness book.* New York: Simon & Schuster.

Benson, P. L. (1996, January). *Developmental assets among Minneapolis youth: The urgency of promoting healthy community.* Minneapolis, MN: Search Institute.

Benton, A. L., Hamsher, K., Varney, N. R., & Spreen, O. (1983). *Contributions to neuropsychological assessment.* New York: Oxford University Press.

Berman, R. (Producer), & Frakes, J. (Director). (1996). *Star Trek: First Contact* [Film]. Hollywood, CA: Paramount Pictures.

Blacknall, C. (1984). *Sally Ride: America's first woman in space.* New York: Macmillan.

Bland, C. J., & Schmitz, C. (1986). Characteristics of the successful researcher and implications for faculty development. *Journal of Medical Education, 61*(1), 22–31.

Blankenship, K. M. (1996). Bringing gender and race in: U.S. employment discrimination policy. In E. N. Chow, D. Wilkinson & M. B. Zinn (Eds.), *Race, class, and gender—common bonds, different voices* (pp. 308–330). Thousand Oaks, CA: Sage.

Bloom, A. (1987). *The closing of the American mind.* New York: Simon & Schuster.

Bohan, J. S. (1993). Regarding gender: Essentialism, constructionism, and feminist psychology. *Psychology of Women Quarterly, 17,* 5–21.

Boonin-Vail, D. (1994). *Thomas Hobbes and the science of moral virtue.* New York: Cambridge University Press.

Bork, R. (1996). *Slouching toward Gomorrah.* New York: Regan Books.

Bragg, R. (1998, August 2). Influential NC church considers splitting with Southern Baptists. *The Dallas Morning News,* p. 13A.

Brook, O. G., Anderson, H. R., Bland, J. M., Peacock, J. L., & Stewart, M. C. (1989). Effects on birth weight of smoking, alcohol, caffeine, socioeconomic factors and psychosocial stress. *British Medical Journal, 298*, 795-799.

Brown, D. (1990). Racism and race relations in the university. *Virginia Law Review, 76*, 295.

Bruning, F. (1983, July 25). A ticket to a boring Sally Ride. *Maclean's*, 9.

Burnell, B. S. (1993). *Technological change and women's work experience.* Westport, CT: Bergin & Garvey.

Butler, J. (1990). *Gender trouble: Feminism and the subversion of identity.* New York: Routledge.

Caelleigh, A. S. (1996). Women's search for medical education in the nineteenth century. *Academic Medicine, 71*, 798.

Caine, R. N., & Caine, G. (1997). *Education on the edge of possibility.* Alexandria, VA: Association for Supervision and Curriculum Development.

Camp, C. A. (1997). *Sally Ride: First American woman in space.* Springfield, NJ: Enslow.

Cannon, C. (1996, November/December). Sandra Day O'Connor: The first woman justice on the US Supreme Court. *Working Woman*, 55-57.

Carkhuff, R. R. (1981). *Toward actualizing human potential.* Amherst, MA: HRD Press.

Carkhuff, R. R. (1984). *The exemplar.* Amherst, MA: HRD Press.

Carkhuff, R. R. (1986). *Human processing and human productivity.* Amherst, MA: HRD Press.

Carkhuff, R. R. (1996). *The art of helping.* Amherst, MA: HRD Press.

Carter, S. (1995). *The culture of disbelief.* New York: Basic Books.

Castro, G. (1990). *American feminism: A contemporary history.* New York: New York University Press.

Chafetz, J. S. (1990). *Gender equity: An integrated theory of stability and change.* Newbury Park, CA: Sage.

Chaikin, A. (1996, November/December). Sally Ride: The first American woman in space. *Working Woman*, 43-46.

Chesler, M. A., & Chesney, B. K. (1988). Self-help groups: Empowerment attitudes and behaviors of disabled or chronically ill persons. In H. E. Yuker (Ed.), *Attitudes toward persons and disabilities* (pp. 230-271). New York: Springer.

Chow, E. N., Wilkinson, D., &. Zinn, M. B. (Eds.) (1996). *Race, class, and gender—common bonds, different voices.* Thousand Oaks, CA: Sage.

Christ, C. P. (1980). *Diving deep and surfacing: Women writers on spiritual quests.* Boston: Beacon Press.

Cloud, J. (1998, July 6). Of arms and the boy. *Time, 151,* 58-62.

Cockburn, C. (1985). *Machinery of dominance: Women, men and technical know-how.* London: Pluto Press.

Cohen, J. J. (1996). Preface. *Academic Medicine, 71,* 800.

Cohn, C. (1993). Wars, wimps, and women: Talking gender and thinking war. In M. Cooke & A. Woollacott (Eds.), *Gendering war talk* (pp. 227-246). Princeton, NJ: Princeton University Press.

Colantonio, A. (1988). Lay concepts of health. *Health Values, 12*(5), 3-7.

Collins, P. H. (1989). The social construction of Black feminist thought. *Signs, 14,* 745-773.

Colson, C. (1987). *The inspirational writings of Charles Colson.* New York: Inspirational Press.

Coltrane, S. (1996). *Family man.* New York: Oxford University Press.

Combs, A., Richards, A., & Richards, F. (1988). *Perceptual psychology: A humanistic approach to the study of persons.* New York: University Press of America.

Cosby, C. (1998, July 8). Prejudice permeates American culture [On-line]. Available: http:/www.usatoday.com/news/comment/ncguest.htm.

Crevecoeur, J. H. (1904). *Letters from an American farmer.* New York: Fox Duffield.

Daly, M. (1985). *Beyond God the Father: Toward a philosophy of women's liberation.* Boston: Beacon Press.

de Beauvoir, S. (1953). *The second sex.* New York: Knopf (Original work published 1949).

Delaney, J., Lupton, M. J., & Toth, E. (1977). *The curse: A cultural history of menstruation.* New York: New American Library.

Delworth, U. (1989). Identity in the college years: Issues of gender and ethnicity. *Journal of the National Association of Student Personnel Administrators, 26,* 162-166.

Dempewolff, J. A. (1974). Development and evaluation of a feminism scale. *Psychological Reports, 34,* 651-657.

Desjardins, C. (1989). The meaning of Carol Gilligan's concept of "different voice" for the learning environment. In C. Pearson, D. Shavlik, & J. Touchton (Eds.), *Educating the majority: Women challenging tradition in higher education* (pp. 134-146). New York: MacMillan.

Desjardins, C. (1996, February). Gender based teambuilding: Strengths men and women bring to effective leadership teams. In *Proceedings of the Fifth Annual International Conference of the National Community College Chair Academy* (ERIC Document Reproduction Service No. Ed 394569)

Deuster, P. A. (1996). Exercise in the prevention and treatment of chronic disorders. *Women's Health Issues, 6,* 320-321.

DeVita, C. J., & Pollard, K. M. (1996). Increasing diversity of the U.S. population. *Statistical Bulletin—Metropolitan Insurance Companies, 77*(3), 12-17.

Dewey, J. (1965). *Experience and education.* New York: Collier.

DiOnne, E. (1991). *Why Americans hate politics.* New York: Simon & Schuster.

Dogar, R. (1998, February). Bigger is better. *Working Woman,* 24-25.

D'Souza, D. (1996). *The end of racism.* New York: Free Press.

Duffy, Y. (1981). *All things are possible.* Ann Arbor, MI: Garvin.

Eagley, A. H. (1987). *Sex differences in social behavior: A social-role interpretation.* Hillsdale, NJ: Erlbaum.

Edlin, G., Golanty, E., & Brown, K. M. (1998). *Health and Wellness.* Sudbary, MA: Jones & Bartlett.

Eisner, J. (1998, July 21). Women's issues: 150 years of progress should encourage us to focus. *The Dallas Morning News,* p. 9A.

Erikson, E. (1950). *Childhood and society.* New York: Norton.

Erikson, E. (1963). *Childhood and society* (2nd ed.). New York: Norton.

Erikson, E. (1964). *Insight and responsibility.* New York: Norton.

Erikson, E. (1968). *Identity: Youth and crisis.* New York: Norton.

Espin, O. (1993). Feminist therapy: Not for White women only. *The Counseling Psychologist, 21,* 103-108.

Etaugh, C., & Bowen, E. (1976). Attitudes toward women: Comparison of enrolled and non-enrolled college students. *Psychological Reports, 38,* 229-230.

Ethier, K. A., & Deaux, M. (1994). Negotiating social identity when contexts change: Maintaining identification and responding to threat. *Journal of Personality and Social Psychology, 67,* 243-251.

Etzioni, A. (1993, May/June). Children of the universe. *Utne Reader, 57,* 60.

Evans, S. M., & Nelson, B. J. (1991). Translating wage gains into social change: International lessons from implementing pay equity in Minnesota. In J. Fudge & P. McDermott (Eds.), *Just wages: A feminist assessment of pay equity* (pp. 227-246). Toronto, Ontario, Canada: University of Toronto Press.

Famighetti, R. (1998). *The world almanac and book of facts.* Mahwah, NJ: K-III Reference Corporation.

Fennema, E., Carpenter, T. P., Jacobs, V. R., Franke, M. L., & Levi, L. W. (1998). A longitudinal study of gender differences in young children's mathematical thinking. *Educational Researcher, 27*(5), 6-11.

Ferguson, K. E. (1984). *The feminist case against bureaucracy.* Philadelphia: Temple University Press.

Ferraz, E. M., Gray, R. H., & Cunha, R. M. (1990). Determinants of uterine delivery and intrauterine growth retardation in Northeast Brazil. *International Journal of Epidemiology, 19*, 101-108.

Fine, M., & Asch, A. (1989). *Women with disabilities.* Philadelphia: Temple University Press.

Firoz, F. B. (1995). Eating disorders today. In P. L. Munhall & V. M. Fitzimons (Eds.), *The emergence of women into the 21st century* (pp. 166-177). New York: NLN Press.

Fiske, S. T., Bersoff, D. N., Borgida, E., Deaux, K., & Heilman, M. E. (1991). Social science research on trial: Use of sex stereotyping research in *Price Waterhouse v. Hopkins. American Psychologist, 46*, 1049-1060.

Flax, J. (1990). *Thinking fragments: Psychoanalysis, feminism, and postmodernism in the contemporary West.* Berkeley: University of California Press.

Flax, J. (1992). Beyond equality: Gender justice and difference. In G. Bock & S. James (Eds.), *Beyond equality and difference: Citizenship, feminist politics, and female subjectivity* (pp. 193-210). New York: Routledge.

Fowler, C. A., & Wadsworth, J. S. (1991). Individualism and equality: Critical values in North American culture and the impact on disability. *Journal of Applied Rehabilitation Counseling, 22*(4), 19-23.

Fox, M. V. (1984). *Women astronauts aboard the shuttle.* New York: Julian Messner.

Franke, J. (1995). Women in medicine. *Texas Medicine, 91*(9), 36-39.

Frankl, V. (1973). *Man's search for meaning.* New York: Pocket Books.

Frankl, V. (1975). *The unconscious God.* New York: Simon & Schuster.

Frankl, V. (1990, Fall). Facing the transitoriness of human existence: Aging and the human spirit. *Generations, 14*(4), 7-10.

Freedman, L. S., Simon, R., Foulkes, M. A., Friedman, L., Geller, N. L., Gordon, D. J., & Mowery, R. (1995). Inclusion of women and minorities in clinical trials and the NIH revitalization act of 1993: The perspective of NIH clinical trialists. *Controlled Clinical Trials, 16*, 277-285.

Friedan, B. (1963). *The feminine mystique.* New York: Dell.

Friedan, B. (1993). *The fountain of age.* New York: Simon & Schuster.

Frost, R. (1992). The road not taken. In W. Harmon (Ed.), *The top 500 poems* (p. 900). New York: Columbia University Press.

Fudge, J., & McDermott, P. (1991). *Just wages: A feminist assessment of pay equity.* Toronto, Ontario, Canada: University of Toronto Press.

Gangs, violence rise in schools, study says. (1998, April 13). *The Dallas Morning News,* p. 3A.

Garber, M. (1992). *Vested interests: Cross-dressing and cultural anxiety.* New York: Routledge.

George, M. S., Ketter, T. A., Parekh, P. I., Herscovitch, P., & Post, R. M. (1996). Gender differences in regional cerebral blood flow during transient self-induced sadness or happiness. *Biological Psychiatry, 40*, 859-871.

Gillespie, M. A. (1996, November/December). How the cookie crumbles. *Ms,* 1.

Gilligan, C. (1982). *In a different voice.* Cambridge, MA: Harvard University Press.

Gilligan, C., Lyons, N. P., & Hanmer, T. J. (1990). *Making connections: The relational worlds of adolescent girls at Emma Willard school.* Cambridge, MA: Harvard University Press.

Glazer, N. (1997). *We are all multiculturalists now.* Cambridge, MA: Harvard University Press.

Golden, F. (1983, June 13). Sally's joy ride into the sky. *Time,* 57.

Goldin, C. (1990). *Understanding the gender gap.* New York: Oxford University Press.

Goleman, D. (1995). *Emotional intelligence.* New York: Bantam Books.

Goodlad, J. (1984). *A place called school.* New York: McGraw-Hill.

Gore, S. M. (1995). Inclusion of women and minorities in clinical trials. *Controlled Clinical Trials, 16*, 290-292.

Gray, J. (1992). *Men are from Mars, women are from Venus: A practical guide for improving communication and getting what you want in your relationships.* New York: HarperCollins.

Gray, R. E., & Doan, B. D. (1990). Empowerment and persons with cancer: Politics in cancer medicine. *Journal of Palliative Care, 6*(2), 33–45.

Greco, J. A., & Glusman, J. B. (1998, July 15). Providing effective care for gay and lesbian patients. *Patient Care,* 159–173.

Griffin, A. H., Linder, J., Logan-El, G., & Carkhuff, C. (1987). *Getting away clean.* Amherst, MA: Carkhuff Institute of Human Technology.

Growth of sexual harassment cases. (1998, June 21). *Edmond Evening Sun,* p. 16A.

Grudem, W. (1997, October 27). Do inclusive language bibles distort scripture? Yes. *Christianity Today,* 27–32.

Haas, L. (1992). *Equal parenthood and social policy: A study of parental leave in Sweden.* Albany: State University of New York Press.

Hadnot, I. J. (1998, June 21). Racial boundaries. *The Dallas Morning News,* pp. J1, J10.

Hall, K. (1992). *The Oxford companion to the Supreme Court.* New York: Oxford University Press.

Halmi, K. A. (1998). A 24-year-old woman with anorexia nervosa. *Journal of the American Medical Association, 279,* 1992–1998.

Hanson, J. W., Streissguth, A. P., & Smith, D. W. (1978). The effects of moderate alcohol consumption during pregnancy on fetal growth and morphogenesis. *Journal of Pediatrics, 92,* 457–460.

Hardiman, R. (1982). *White identity development: A process oriented model for describing the racial consciousness of White Americans.* Unpublished doctoral dissertation, University of Massachusetts, Amherst.

Harding, S. (1986). *The science question in feminism.* Ithaca, NY: Cornell University Press.

Harrison, A. E., & Silenzio, W. M. B. (1996). Comprehensive care of lesbian and gay patients and families. *Primary Care, 23,* 31–46.

Haseltine, F. P., & Jacobson, B. G. (1997). *Women's health research: A medical and policy primer.* Washington, DC: Health Press International.

Hassmen, P., & Koivula, N. (1997). Mood, physical working capacity and cognitive performance in the elderly as related to physical activity. *Aging, 9,* 136–142.

Havighurst, R. (1952). *Developmental tasks and education* (2nd ed.). New York: Longmans, Green.

Hawxhurst, D. M., & Morrow, S. L. (1984). *Living our visions: Building feminist community.* Tempe, AZ: Fourth World.

Herman, M. H., & Sedlacek, W. E. (1973). Sexist attitudes among male university students. *Journal of College Student Personnel, 14,* 544-548.

Herrnstein, R., & Murray, C. (1994). *The bell curve.* New York: Free Press.

Hill, A., & Jordan, E. (1995). *Race, gender, and power in America.* New York: Oxford University Press.

Hillyer, B. (1993). *Feminism and disability.* Norman: University of Oklahoma Press.

Himmelfarb, G. (1995). *The de-moralization of society.* New York: Knopf.

Home alone. (1993, May 15). *The Economist,* 74.

Hooks, B. (1981). *Ain't I a woman: Black women and feminism.* Boston: South End Press.

Hornblower, M. (1998, June 1). The boy who loved bombs. *Time, 151,* 42-44.

House, R. M., & Holloway, E. L. (1992). Empowering the counseling professional to work with gay and lesbian issues. In S. H. Dworkin & F. J. Gutierrez (Eds.), *Counseling gay men and lesbians: Journey to the end of the rainbow* (pp. 307-324). Alexandria, VA: American Association of Counseling and Development.

Huntington, S. (1996). *The clash of civilizations and the remaking of world order.* New York: Simon & Schuster.

Hurtado, A. (1989). Relating to privilege: Seduction and rejection in the subordination of White women and women of color. *Signs, 14,* 833-855.

Hurwitz, J., & Hurwitz, S. (1989). *Sally Ride: Shooting for the stars.* New York: Fawcett Columbine.

Infante-Rivard, C., Fernandes, A., Gauthier, R., David, M., & Rivard, G. E. (1993). Fetal loss associated with caffeine intake before and during pregnancy. *Journal of the American Medical Association, 270,* 2940-2943.

Irwin, R. L. (1995). *A circle of empowerment: Women, education, and leadership.* Albany: State University of New York Press.

Ivison, D. J. (1977). The Wechsler Memory Scale: Preliminary findings toward an Australian standardization. *Australian Psychologist, 12,* 303-312.

James, J. (1997, April 6). FSU researchers find investment gender gap. *The Orlando Sentinel*, p. A12.

Jencks, C., Perman, L., & Rainwater, L. (1988). What is a good job?: A new measure of labor-market success. *American Journal of Sociology, 93*, 1322-1357.

Jennings, D. (1998, June 2). Woman to lead Baptist church. *The Dallas Morning News*, pp. 13A, 15A.

Jensen, R. H. (1997, January/February). Bad calls from the bench. *Ms*, 26-28.

Jensvold, M. F., Hamilton, J. A., & Mackey, B. (1994). Including women in clinical trials: How about the women scientists? *Journal of the American Medical Women's Association, 49*, 110-112.

Johnson, H. (1994). *Divided we fall.* New York: Norton.

Jordan, J. (1995). *Civil wars.* New York: Simon & Schuster.

Jordan, J. V., Kaplan, A. G., Miller, J. B., Stiver, I. P., & Surrey, J. L. (1991). *Women's growth in connection: Writings from the Stone Center.* New York: Guilford Press.

Josselson, R. (1996). *Revising herself: The story of women's identity from college to midlife.* New York: Oxford University Press.

Judges from the stone age. (1995, January). *Glamour*, 64.

Kaplan, P. (1993). *The human odyssey: Life-span development.* St. Paul, MN: West.

Katch, R. I., & McArdle, W. D. (1993). *Introduction to nutrition, exercise, and health.* Philadelphia: Lea & Febiger.

Katz, P. A. (1976). *Towards the elimination of racism.* New York: Pergamon Press.

Kelley, K. (1995). *Visions: Maya Angelou* [On-line]. Available: http://bsd.mojones.com/mother_jones/mj95/kelly.html.

Kelly, E. (1995). *Spirituality and religion in counseling and psychotherapy.* Alexandria, VA: American Counseling Association.

Kimball, M. M. (1995). *Feminist visions of gender similarities and differences.* Binghamton, NY: Haworth Press.

Kirby, D., Korpi, M., Barth, R. P., & Cagampang, H. H. (1997). The impact of the postponing sexual involvement curriculum among youths in California. *Family Planning Perspectives, 29*, 100-108.

Kissinger, H. (1994). *Diplomacy.* New York: Simon & Schuster.

Kite, M. E., & Deaux, K. (1987). Gender belief systems: Homosexuality and the implicit inversion theory. *Psychology of Women Quarterly, 11*, 83-96.

Kite, M. E., Deaux, M., & Miele, M. (1991). Stereotypes of young and old: Does age outweigh gender? *Psychology and Aging, 6*, 19-27.

Kleg, M. (1993). *Hate, prejudice and racism.* Albany: State University of New York Press.

Kohn, A. (1997). How not to teach values. *Phi Delta Kappan, 78*, 428-439.

Kopelson, A., Weingrad, H., Harris, T. (Producers), & Schumacher, J. (Director). (1993). *Falling down* [Film]. Burbank, CA: Warner Bros.

Kotkin, J. (1992). *Tribes.* New York: Random House.

Kozol, J. (1991). *Savage inequalities.* New York: HarperCollins.

Kutscher, R. E. (1991). New BLS projections. *Monthly Labor Review, 114*, 3-16.

Labi, N. (1998a, April 6). The hunter and the choirboy. *Time, 151*, 28-37.

Labi, N. (1998b, June 29). The next generation: What do girls want? *Newsweek, 151*, 60-62.

Lauer, R. H. (1986). *Social problems and the quality of life.* Dubuque, IA: Brown.

Lauer, R. H. (1998). *Social problems and the quality of life* (7th ed.). McGraw-Hill.

Lavelle, M. (1998, July 6). The new rules of sexual harassment. *U.S. News & World Report, 125*, 30-31.

Lee, C. C. (1991). Cultural dynamics: Their importance in multicultural counseling. In C. C. Lee & B. L. Richardson (Eds.), *Multicultural issues in counseling: New approaches to diversity* (pp. 11-22). Alexandria, VA: American Association for Counseling and Development.

Lee, C. C., & Walz, G. R. (Eds.). (1998). *Social action: A mandate for counselors.* Alexandria, VA: American Counseling Association.

Lee, J. (1997, June). Fair game. *Women's Sports and Fitness*, 37-40.

Lemon v. Kurtzman, 403 U.S. 602 (1971).

Lewin, K. (1951). *Field theory in social science.* New York: Harper.

Lewin, T. (1998, May 22). More victims and much less sense in the string of shootings at schools. *New York Times*, p. A20.

Lezak, M. D. (1983). *Neuropsychological assessment.* New York: Oxford University Press.

Lickona, T. (1991). *Education for character.* New York: Bantam Books.

Lickona, T. (1993). The return of character education. *Educational Leadership*, 51(30), 6-11.

Lipset, S. (1996). *American exceptionalism.* New York: Norton.

Locke, S., & Colligan, D. (1986). *The healer within.* New York: Dutton.

Lombana, J. H. (1989). Counseling persons with disabilities: Summary and projections. *Journal of Counseling and Development, 68,* 177-179.

Lorber, J. (1993). Why women physicians will never be true equals in the American medical profession. In E. Riska & K. Wegar (Eds.), *Gender, work and medicine: Women and the medical division of labor* (pp. 62-76). London: Sage.

Lorber, J. (1994). *Paradoxes of gender.* New Haven, CT: Yale University Press.

Lott, B. (1990). Dual natures or learned behavior: The challenges to feminist psychology. In R. T. Hare-Mustin & J. Marecek (Eds.), *Making a difference: Psychology and the construction of gender* (pp. 65-101). New Haven, CT: Yale University Press.

Lott, B. (1996). Politics or science? The question of gender sameness/difference. *American Psychologist, 51,* 155-156.

Lucas, J. A. (1992). *Future of the Olympic games.* Champaign, IL: Human Kinetics Books.

Lyness, K. S., & Thompson, D. E. (1997). Above the glass ceiling? A comparison of matched samples of female and male executives. *Journal of Applied Psychology, 82,* 359-375.

MacIntyre, A. (1984). *After virtue.* Notre Dame, IN: Notre Dame University Press.

Mainiero, L. A. (1994). On breaking the glass ceiling: The political seasoning of powerful women executives. *Organizational Dynamics, 22*(4), 5-20.

Mairs, N. (1987). *Plaintext: Deciphering a woman's life.* New York: Harper & Row.

Marcia, J. (1966). Development and validation of ego-identity status. *Journal of Personality and Social Psychology, 3,* 551-558.

Marcia, J. (1980). Identity in adolescence. In J. Adelson (Ed.), *Handbook of adolescent psychology* (pp. 159-187). New York: Wiley.

Markus, M. (1987). Women, success and civil society: Submission to, or subversion of, the achievement principle. In S. Benhaabib & D. Cornell (Eds.), *Feminism as critique: Essays on the politics of gender in late-capitalist societies* (pp. 96-110). Cambridge, MA: Polity Press.

Martin, S. E. (1980). *Breaking and entering: Police women on patrol.* Berkeley: University of California Press.

Maslow, A. (1968). *Toward a psychology of being* (2nd ed.). New York: Van Nostrand.

May, R. (1953). *Man's search for himself.* New York: Dell Books.

May, R. (1967). *Psychology and the human dilemma.* New York: Van Nostrand Reinhold.

Maya Angelou: A short biography (1998). [On-line]. Available: http://www. geocities.com/Athens/1523/mayabio.html.

McCloskey, R. (1994). *The American Supreme Court.* Chicago: University of Chicago Press.

McCormick, T. E. (1990). Counselor–teacher interface: Promoting nonsexist education and career development. *Journal of Multicultural Counseling and Development, 18,* 2–10.

McGee, M. G. (1979). *Human spatial abilities.* New York: Praeger.

McGlone, J. (1977). Sex differences in the cerebral organization of verbal functions in patients with unilateral brain lesions. *Brain, 100,* 775–793.

McWhirter, E. H. (1994). *Counseling for empowerment.* Alexandria, VA: American Counseling Association.

Menard, M. K. (1997). Vitamin and mineral supplement prior to and during pregnancy. *Obstetrics & Gynecology Clinics of North America, 24,* 479–498.

Miller, H. C., Jekel, J. F. (1987). Incidence of low birth infants born to mothers with multiple risk factors. *Yale Journal of Biological Medicine, 60,* 397–404.

Miller, J. B. (1976). *Toward a new psychology of women.* Boston: Beacon Press.

Miller, J. B. (1982). *Women and power.* Wellesley, MA: Stone Center Working Paper Series.

Miller, J. B. (1991). Women and power. In J. V. Jordan, A. G. Kaplan, J. B. Miller, I. P Sriver, & J. L. Surrey (Eds.), *Women's growth connection: Writings from the Stone Center* (pp. 197–205). New York: Guilford Press.

Miller, J. F. (1992). Patient power resources. In J. F. Miller (Ed.), *Coping with chronic illness: Overcoming powerlessness* (2nd ed., pp. 3–18). Philadelphia: Davis.

Miller-Loessi, K. (1992). Toward gender integration in the workplace. *Sociological Perspectives, 35,* 1–15.

Mold, J. W. (1993, October). *Encouraging collaborative teamwork: A goal-oriented approach.* Paper presented at Health Care Teamwork Institute, Queen's College Gerontology Project, Quebec, Ontario, Canada.

Morris-Lipsman, A. (1990). *Notable women.* New York: Scott, Foreman.

Moulton, K. (1998, June 12). Baptists bucking trend among religions. *Edmond Evening Sun, 109,* p. 19.

Myrdal, G. (1944). *An American dilemma: The Negro problem and modern democracy.* New York: Harper.

Naeye, R. L. (1981). Nutritional/nonnutritional interactions that affect the outcome of pregnancy. *American Journal of Clinical Nutrition, 34,* 722-726.

Nelson, L. (1995). Mentoring toward a longed for life. In P. L. Munhall & V. M. Fitzimons (Eds.), *The emergence of women into the 21st century* (pp. 361-375). New York: NLN Press.

NIH Revitalization Act, Subtitle B, Part 1, Section 131-133, June 10, 1993.

Noddings, N. (1984). *Caring: The feminine approach to ethics and moral education.* Berkeley: University of California Press.

Noddings, N. (1998). Perspectives from feminist philosophy. *Educational Researcher, 27*(5), 17-18.

O'Connor, K. (1983). *Sally Ride and the new astronauts: Scientists in space.* New York: Franklin Watts.

Osborne, G. R. (1997, October 27). Do inclusive language bibles distort scripture? No. *Christianity Today,* 33-39.

Osmond, M. W., & Martin, P. Y. (1975). Sex and sexism: A comparison of male and female sex-role attitudes. *Journal of Marriage and the Family, 37,* 744-758.

Paul, E. F. (1989). *Equity and gender: The comparable worth debate.* New Brunswick, NJ: Transaction.

Peck, M. S. (1993). *A world waiting to be born.* New York: Bantam Books.

Pedersen, P. (1994). *A handbook for developing multicultural awareness* (2nd ed.). Alexandria, VA: American Counseling Association.

Pelligrino, E., & Thomasma, D. (1993). *The virtues in medical practice.* New York: Oxford University Press.

Peters, S. (1997). The puzzle of premenstrual syndrome. Putting the pieces together. *Advance for Nurse Practitioners, 5*(10), 41-44.

Pharr, S. (1992). Homophobia as a weapon of sexism. In P. S. Rothenberg (Ed.), *Race, class, and gender in the United States* (2nd ed., pp. 431-440). New York: St. Martin's Press.

Phillips, D. (1989). Future directions and need for child care in the United States. In J. S. Lande, S. Starr, & N. Gunzenhauser (Eds.), *Caring for children* (pp. 78-101). Hillsdale, NJ: Erlbaum.

Pinker, S. (1997). *How the mind works.* New York: Norton.

Pinto, B. M., Marcus, B. H., Clark, M. M. (1996). Promoting physical activity in women: The new challenges. *American Journal of Preventive Medicine, 12*(5), 395–400.

Ponterotto, J. G. & Pedersen, P. B. (1993). *Preventing prejudice: A guide for counselors and educators.* Newbury Park, CA: Sage.

Popenoe, D. (1988). *Disturbing the nest: Family change and decline in modern societies.* New York: Aldine de Gruyter.

Prescott, D. (1957). *The child in the educative process.* New York: McGraw-Hill.

The quiet man. (1985, January). *U.S. News and World Report, 98,* 15.

Rankow, E. J. (1995). Lesbian health issues for the primary care provider. *Journal of Family Practice, 40,* 486–493.

Rankow, E. J., & Tessaro, I. (1998). Cervical cancer risk and papanicolaou screening in a sample of lesbian and bisexual women. *Journal of Family Practice, 47,* 139–143.

Rayburn, W. F., Stanley, J. R., & Garrett, M. E. (1996). Periconceptional folate intake and neural tube defects. *Journal of the American College of Nutrition, 15,* 121–125.

Reber, A. S. (1995). *Dictionary of psychology.* New York: Penguin Books.

Reeve, C. (1998). *Still me.* New York: Random House.

Reskin, B. F., & Roos, P. A. (1990). *Job queues, gender queues: Explaining women's inroads into male occupations.* Philadelphia: Temple University Press.

Resnick, M. D., Bearman, P. S., Blum, R. W., Bauman, K. E., Harris, K. M., Jones, J., Tabor, J., Beuhring, T., Sieving, R. E., Shew, M., Ireland, M., Bearinger, L. H., & Udry, J. R. (1997). Protecting adolescents from harm. *Journal of the American Medical Association, 278,* 823–832.

Rich, A. (1977). *Of women born: Motherhood as experience and as institution.* New York: Norton.

Ride, S. K. (1986). *To space and back.* New York: Lothrup, Lee & Shepard.

Ride, S. K. (1987). *Leadership and America's future in space: A report to the administrator.* Washington, DC: National Aeronautics and Space Administration.

Ride, S. K. (1992). *Voyager: An adventure to the edge of the solar system.* New York: Crown.

Ride, S. K. (1994). *The third planet: Exploring the earth from space.* New York: Crown.

Rittenhouse, C. A. (1991). The emergence of premenstrual syndrome as a social problem. *Social Problems, 38*, 412-425.

Rivers, C. (1991). *More joy than rage: Crossing generations with the new feminism.* Hanover, NH: University Press of New England.

Roberts, C., & Roberts, S. (1998, July 15). Girls' progress brings mixed results. *The Dallas Morning News*, p. 17A.

Roberts, K. T., & Aspy, C. B. (1995). Development of the serenity scale. *Journal of Nursing Measurement, 1*, 145-164.

Robertson, P. (1993). *The turning point.* Dallas, TX: Word.

Roe v. Wade, 41 U.S. 4213 (1973).

Rogers, C. R. (1957). The necessary and sufficient conditions of therapeutic personality change. *Journal of Consulting Psychology, 21*, 95-103.

Rogers, C. R. (1983). *Freedom to learn for the 80s.* Columbus, OH: Merrill.

Rogers, R., & Hammerstein, O., II. (1949). You have to be carefully taught. New York: Williamson Music.

Rosetti, G. (1995). The postlesbian. In P. L. Munhall & V. M. Fitzimons (Eds.), *The emergence of women into the 21st century* (pp. 251-265). New York: NLN Press.

Rossi, A. S. (1995). Commentary. Wanted: Alternative theory and analysis modes. In V. L. Bengston, K. W. Schaie, & L. M. Burton (Eds.), *Adult intergenerational relations* (pp. 264-276). New York: Springer.

Rossner, S. (1998). Childhood obesity and adulthood consequences. *Acta Paediatrica, 87*(1), 1-5.

Rothenberg, P. S. (1992). *Race, class, and gender in the United States* (2nd ed.). New York: St. Martin's Press.

Ruuskanen, J. M., & Ruoppila, I. (1995). Physical activity and psychological well-being among people aged 65 to 84 years. *Age & Ageing, 24*, 292-296.

Ryan, K. (1993). Mining the values in the curriculum. *Educational Leadership, 51*(3), 16-18.

Sadker, M., & Sadker, D. (1985, March). Sexism in the schoolroom of the 80s. *Psychology Today*, 54-57.

Sandel, M. (1996). *Democracy's discontent.* Cambridge, MA: Harvard University Press.

Sandhu, D. S., & Aspy, C. B. (1997). *Counseling for prejudice prevention and reduction.* Alexandria, VA: American Counseling Association.

Sandhu, D. S., & Bryant, A. (1998). *Development of Gender Equity Perception Scale: Preliminary findings.* Manuscript submitted for publication.

Sandhu, D. S., Portes, P. R., & McPhee, S. A. (1996). Assessing cultural adaptation: Psychometric properties of the Cultural Adaptation Pain Scale. *Journal of Multicultural Counseling and Development, 24*(1), 15–25.

Sandra Day O'Connor: Biographical data (1998). [On-line]. Available: http://supct.law.cornell.edu/supct/justices/oconnor.bio.html.

Sarachi, M. (1995). Women: Being and becoming. In P. L. Munhall & V. M. Fitzimons (Eds.), *The emergence of women into the 21st century* (pp. 3–11). New York: NLN Press.

Schenkel, S., & Marcia, J. E. (1972). Attitudes toward premarital intercourse in determining ego identity status in college women. *Journal of Personality, 40,* 472–482.

Schlessinger, A. (1992). *The disuniting of America.* New York: Norton.

The Schomburg Center. (1998). *Maya Angelou* [On-line]. Available: http://www.thomson.com/gale/avs/maya.html.

Schorr, M. (1996, January). Does gender equity promote prosperity, or vice versa? *Working Woman,* 18.

Schwartz, T. (1995). *What really matters.* New York: Bantam Books.

Scott, S. (1986). *Peer pressure reversal.* Amherst, MA: HRD Press.

Scruggs, R., Zipperstein, S., Lyon, R., Gonzalez, V., Cousins, H., & Beverly, R. (1993). *Report to the Deputy Attorney General on the events at Waco, Texas February 28 to April 19, 1993.* Washington, DC: U.S. Department of Justice.

Seachrist, L. (1994, April 15). Disparities detailed in NCI division. *Science, 264,* 340.

Sells, C. W., & Blum, R. W. (1996). Morbidity and mortality among US adolescents: An overview of data and trends. *American Journal of Public Health, 86,* 513–519.

Selye, H. (1956). *The stress of life.* New York: McGraw-Hill.

Shapiro, L. (1998, June 15). Fat, fatter: But who's counting? *Newsweek, 131,* 55.

Sherman, P. J., & Spence, J. T. (1997). A comparison of two cohorts of college students in responses to the Male–Female Relations Questionnaire. *Psychology of Women's Quarterly, 21,* 265–278.

Silvestri, G., & Lukasiewicz, J. (1991). Occupational employment projections. *Monthly Labor Review, 114,* 64–94.

Sizer, T. (1984). *Horace's compromise.* Boston: Houghton Mifflin.

Smilkstein, G. S., & Aspy, C. B. (1995). *Spouse abuse and pregnancy outcome: A prediction study* (Final Report No. MCJ-210600). Washington, DC: Bureau of Maternal and Child Health.

Smilkstein, G. S., Aspy, C. B., & Quiggins, P. A. (1994). Conjugal conflict and violence: A review and theoretical paradigm. *Family Medicine, 26*, 111-116.

Smolla, R. (1995). *A year in the life of the Supreme Court.* Durham, NC: Duke University Press.

Sonnert, G. (1995/1996, Winter). Gender equity in science: Still an elusive goal. *Issues in Science and Technology,* 53-58.

Sotomayor, M. (1994a). Aged Hispanic women: The external circumstances of their lives. In M. Sotomayor (Ed.), *In triple jeopardy— aged Hispanic women: Insights and experiences* (pp. 9-19). Washington, DC: National Hispanic Council on Aging.

Sotomayor, M. (1994b). Foreword. In M. Sotomayor (Ed.), *In triple jeopardy—aged Hispanic women: Insights and experiences* (pp. 1-7). Washington, DC: National Hispanic Council on Aging.

Spencer, D. A. (1988). Public schoolteaching: A suitable job for a woman? In A. Statham, E. M. Miller, & H. O. Mauksch (Eds.), *The worth of women's work* (pp. 233-254). Albany: State University of New York Press.

Steering Committee of the Physicians' Health Study Research Group. (1988). Preliminary report: Findings from the aspirin component of the ongoing physicians' health study. *New England Journal of Medicine, 318*, 262-264.

Stein, S. L., & Weston, L. C. (1976). Attitudes toward women among female college students. *Sex Roles, 2*, 199-202.

Streissguth, A. P., Martin, D. C., Martin, J. C., & Barr, H. M. (1981). The Seattle longitudinal prospective study on alcohol and pregnancy. *Neurobehavioral Toxicology and Teratology, 3*, 223-233.

Strine, M. S. (1992). Understanding how things work: Sexual harassment and academic culture. *Journal of Applied Communication Research, 4*, 391-400.

Stroh, L. K., Brett, H. M., & Reilly, A. H. (1996). Family structure, glass ceiling, and traditional explanations for the differential rate of turnover of female and male managers. *Journal of Vocational Behavior, 49*, 99-118.

Sue, D. W., Arredondo, P., & McDavis, R. J. (1992). Multicultural counseling competencies and standards: A call to the profession. *Journal of Counseling & Development, 70*, 477-481.

Sylwester, R. (1995). *A celebration of neurons.* Alexandria, VA: Association for Supervision and Curriculum Development.

Tajfel, H. (1969). Cognitive aspects of prejudice. *Journal of Social Issues, 25,* 79-97.

Tannen, D. (1994). *Talking from 9 to 5.* New York: William Morrow.

Tavris, C. B. (1991). *Psychological perspectives on human diversity in America.* Washington, DC: American Psychological Association.

Terry, D., & Bruni, F. (1998, May 24). Lethal fantasies of a 15-year-old became a reality. *New York Times,* p. A14.

Thibault, J. M. (1993). *A deepening love affair: The gift of God in later life.* Nashville, TN: Upper Room Books.

Thomas, G., & Roberts, C. (1994). The character of our schooling. *The American School Board Journal, 181*(5), 33-35.

Thurow, L. (1975). *Generating inequality.* New York: Basic Books.

Thurow, L. (1996). *The future of capitalism.* New York: Morrow.

Twain, M. (1897). *Following the equator.* Hartford, CT: American Publishing.

U.S. girls report: Please listen. (1998, June 28). *The Dallas Morning News,* p. 2J.

Walby, S. (1990). *Theorizing patriarchy.* Oxford, England: Basil Blackwell.

Walthall, M. (1998, July 15). U.S. children becoming healthier despite spread of bad habits, study says. *The Dallas Morning News,* pp. 1A, 12A.

Wattenberg, B. (1995). *Values matter most.* Washington, DC: Regnery.

Wechsler, D. (1958). *Measurement and appraisal of adult intelligence.* Baltimore: Williams & Wilkins.

West, C. (1993). *Keeping faith.* New York: Routledge.

West, C. (1994, January 9). The 80s market culture run amok. *Newsweek,* 48-49.

West, C., & Zimmerman, D. (1987). Doing gender. *Gender & Society, 1,* 125-151.

Whyte, J. (1986). *Girls into science and technology: The story of a project.* Boston: Routledge & Kegan Paul.

Wicker, T. (1996). *Tragic failure: Racial integration in America.* New York: William Morrow.

Wilcox, A. (1997). *Self and soul.* New York: Daybreak Books.

William Rehnquist: Biographical data (1998). [On-line] Available: http://supct.law.cornell.edu/supct/justices/.rehnquist.bio.html.

Williams, C. L. (1989). *Gender differences at work: Women and men in nontraditional occupations.* Berkeley: University of California Press.

Williams, S. (1996). *Maya Angelou: A mini-biography* [On-line]. Available: http://members.aol.com/bonvibre/mangelou.html#bio.

Williams, W. M., & Ceci, S. J. (1997). Are Americans becoming more or less alike: Trends in race, class, and ability differences in intelligence. *American Psychologist, 52,* 1226-1235.

Willie, C. V., Kramer, B. M., & Brown, B. S. (1973). *Racism and mental health.* Pittsburgh, PA: University of Pittsburgh Press.

Willis, E. (1992). *No more nice girls: Countercultural essays.* Hanover, NH: University Press of New England.

Wills, G. (1992). *Lincoln at Gettysburg.* New York: Simon & Schuster.

Wilshire, B. (1990). *The moral collapse of the university.* Albany: State University of New York Press.

Wilson, J. (1993). *The moral sense.* New York: Free Press.

Wirth, L. (1945). The problem of minority groups. In R. Linton (Ed.), *The science of man in world crisis* (pp. 347-372). New York: Columbia University Press.

Witkin, G., Tharp, M., Schrof, J. M., Toch, T., & Scattarella, C. (1998, June 1). Again in Springfield, a familiar school scene: Bloody kids, grieving parents, a teen accused of murder. *U.S. News & World Report,* 16-21.

Woititz, J. G. (1983). *Adult children of alcoholics.* Pompano Beach, FL: Health Communications.

Wolf, N. (1992). *The beauty myth.* New York: Anchor.

Wolfe, A. (1998). *One nation after all.* New York: Viking.

Wood, J. T. (1997). *Gendered lives. Communication, gender, and culture* (2nd ed.). Belmont, CA: Wadsworth.

Wood, N. (1993, August 23). Unmarried. . . with children. *Mclean's,* 40.

Woodward, K. (1994, June 13). What is virtue? *Newsweek,* 38.

World Health Organization. (1986). The Ottawa charter for health promotion. *Health Promotion, 1,* iii-v.

Wright, R. (1996, September 6). The false politics of values. *Time,* 42.

Yamato, J. (1992). Something about the subject makes it hard to name. In P. S. Rothenberg (Ed.), *Race, class, and gender in the United States* (pp. 58-66). New York: St. Martin's Press.

Young, I. M. (1990). *Throwing like a girl and other essays in feminist philosophy and social theory.* Bloomington: Indiana University Press.

INDEX